DEREK WILSON is one of the best-known authors of history and biography whose many books, radio features and TV programmes include the international best-seller *Rothschild – A Story of Wealth and Power* and studies of the Astors, Hans Holbein, Francis Drake, Robert Dudley, Earl of Leicester. Of his book *The World Encompassed: Drake's Great Voyage* Professor J. H. Plumb wrote in the *New York Times*: 'Derek Wilson displays excellent judgement not only about his sources but also about the character and actions of Drake himself.' He and his wife live at their homes in Devon and Normandy.

By the same author

East Africa Through a Thousand Years

A Tudor Tapestry

Sail and Steam

The People and the Book

A History of South and Central Africa

White Gold – The Story of African Ivory

The World Encompassed – Drake's Voyage 1577–80

England in the Age of Thomas More

Africa, A Modern History

The Tower 1078–1978

Sweet Robin – Robert Dudley, Earl of Leicester 1533–88

Rothschild – A Story of Wealth & Power

Hans Holbein – Portrait of an Unknown Man

The Astors – Landscape with Millionaires

Dark and Light – The Story of the Guinness Family

The King and the Gentleman – Charles Stuart and Oliver Cromwell 1599–1649

In the Lion's Court – Power, Ambition and Sudden Death in the Reign of Henry VIII

All the King's Women – Love, Sex and Politics in the Life of Charles II

THE
CIRCUMNAVIGATORS

Derek Wilson

CARROLL & GRAF PUBLISHERS
New York

Carroll & Graf Publishers
an imprint of Avalon Publishing Group, Inc.
245 W.17th Street
New York
NY 10011 5300
www.carrollandgraf.com

First published in the UK as *The Circumnavigators*
by Constable, 1989

This revised paperback edition published in the US
by Carroll & Graf, 2003

Reprinted 2004

ISBN 0–7867-1150-7

Printed and bound in the EU

Library of Congress Cataloging-in-Publication Data is available on file.

CONTENTS

ILLUSTRATIONS

Illustrations

Maps

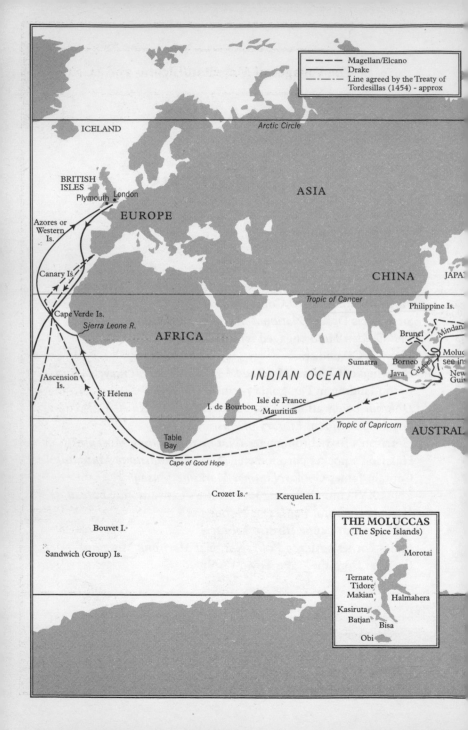

	Magellan/Elcano
	Drake
	Line agreed by the Treaty of Tordesillas (1454) - approx

ICELAND

Arctic Circle

BRITISH ISLES

ASIA

Plymouth London

Azores or Western Is.

EUROPE

Canary Is.

CHINA

JAPA

Tropic of Cancer

Philippine Is.

Cape Verde Is.

Brunei

Mindana

Sierra Leone R.

AFRICA

Moluc see in

Sumatra

Borneo

Celebes

Ascension Is.

INDIAN OCEAN

Java

New Gui

St Helena

Isle de France

I. de Bourbon

Mauritius

Tropic of Capricorn

AUSTRAL

Table Bay

Cape of Good Hope

Crozet Is.

Kerquelen I.

Bouvet I.

THE MOLUCCAS
(The Spice Islands)

Sandwich (Group) Is.

Morotai

Ternate
Tidore
Makian

Halmahera

Kasiruta
Batjan

Bisa

Obi

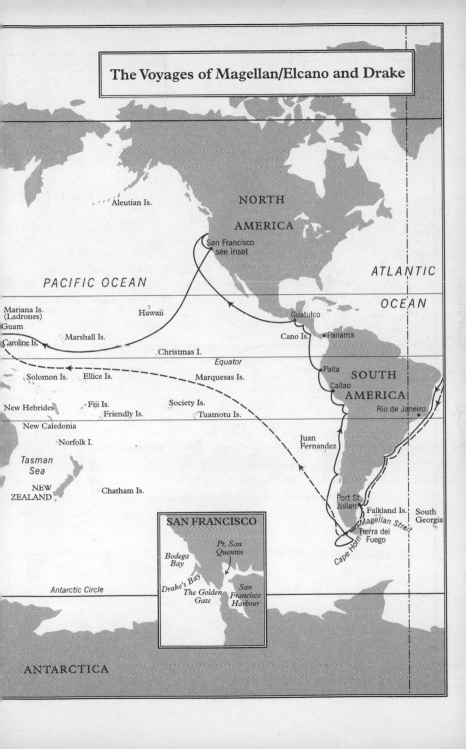

The Voyages of Magellan/Elcano and Drake

NORTH AMERICA

San Francisco
see inset

PACIFIC OCEAN

ATLANTIC OCEAN

Aleutian Is.

Mariana Is.
(Ladrones)
Guam
Caroline Is.

Marshall Is.

Hawaii

Christmas I.

Equator

Guatulco
Cano Is.
Panama

Solomon Is.   Ellice Is.

Marquesas Is.

Paita
Callao

SOUTH
AMERICA

New Hebrides

Fiji Is.

Society Is.

Rio de Janeiro

Friendly Is.

Tuamotu Is.

New Caledonia

Norfolk I.

Juan
Fernandez

Tasman
Sea

NEW
ZEALAND

Chatham Is.

Port St.
Julian

Falkland Is.

South
Georgia

Magellan Strait
Tierra del
Fuego

Cape Horn

SAN FRANCISCO

Pt. San
Quentin

Bodega
Bay

Drake's Bay
The Golden
Gate

San
Francisco
Harbour

Antarctic Circle

ANTARCTICA

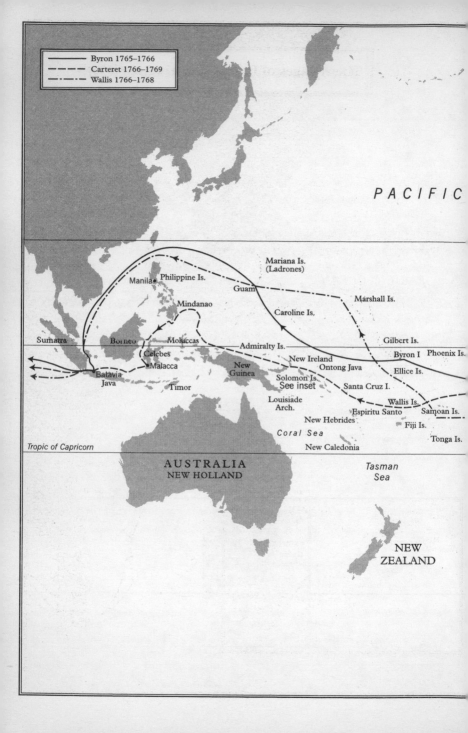

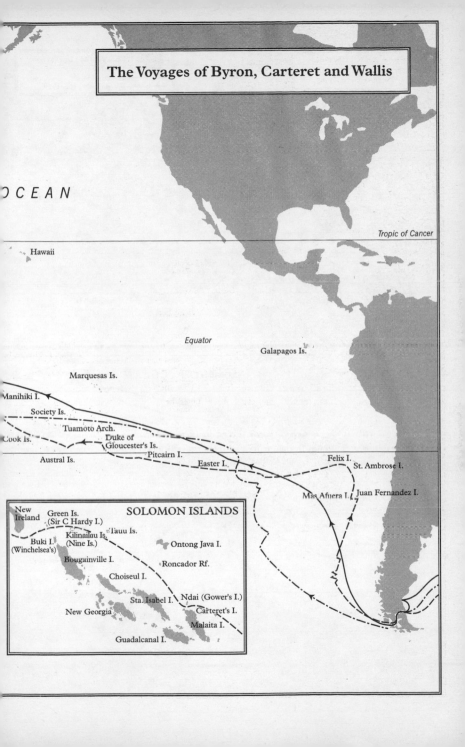

The Voyages of Byron, Carteret and Wallis

OCEAN

Tropic of Cancer

Hawaii

Equator

Galapagos Is.

Marquesas Is.

Manihiki I.

Society Is.

Tuamoto Arch.

Cook Is.

Duke of
Gloucester's Is.

Austral Is.

Pitcairn I.

Easter I.

Felix I.

St. Ambrose I.

Mas Afuera I.

Juan Fernandez I.

New
Ireland

Green Is.
(Sir C Hardy I.)

SOLOMON ISLANDS

Tauu Is.

Buki I.
(Winchelsea's)

Kilinailau Is.
(Nine Is.)

Ontong Java I.

Bougainville I.

Roncador Rf.

Choiseul I.

Sta. Isabel I.

Ndai (Gower's I.)

New Georgia

Carteret's I.

Malaita I.

Guadalcanal I.

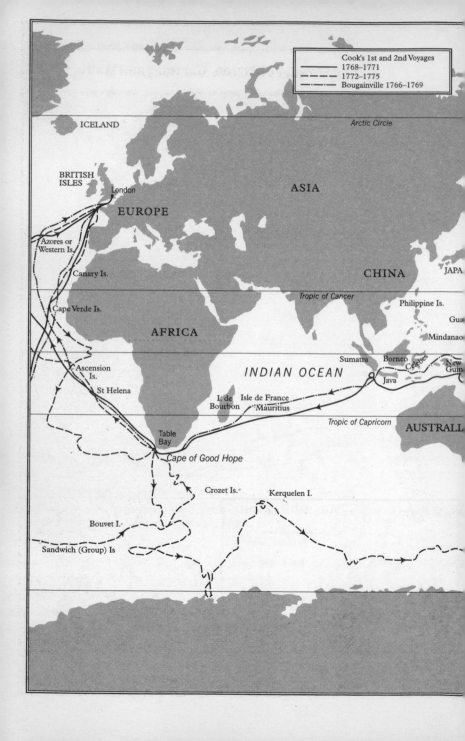

Cook's 1st and 2nd Voyages
——— 1768–1771
– – – 1772–1775
–·–·– Bougainville 1766–1769

ICELAND

Arctic Circle

BRITISH
ISLES

London

EUROPE

ASIA

Azores or
Western Is.

Canary Is.

CHINA

JAPA

Tropic of Cancer

Philippine Is.

Cape Verde Is.

Gua

AFRICA

Mindanao

Sumatra   Borneo

Celebes

New
Guin

INDIAN OCEAN

Ascension
Is.

Java

St Helena

I. de
Bourbon

Isle de France
Mauritius

Table
Bay

Tropic of Capricorn

AUSTRALI

Cape of Good Hope

Crozet Is.

Kerquelen I.

Bouvet I.

Sandwich (Group) Is

The Voyages of Cook and Bougainville

NORTH AMERICA

ATLANTIC OCEAN

PACIFIC OCEAN

Aleutian Is.

Mariana Is. (Ladrones)

Hawaii

Caroline Is.

Marshall Is.

Christmas I.

Equator

Solomon Is.

Ellice Is.

Marquesas Is.

SOUTH AMERICA

New Hebrides

Fiji Is.

Society Is.

Tuamotu Is.

Rio de Janeiro

New Caledonia

Friendly Is.

Norfolk I.

Juan Fernandez

Tasman Sea

Chatham Is.

NEW ZEALAND

Magellan Strait

Cape Horn

Falkland Is.

South Georgia

Antarctic Circle

ANTARCTICA

INTRODUCTION

The mythical tale is told of a medieval Englishman who decided to see the world and, despite the warnings of family and friends, set off westward. After many years of crossing broad seas and encountering strange peoples he landed upon a shore where the natives spoke the English language. Continuing through this country he reached a locality where even his own dialect was used. Then he came upon a village which looked exactly like his own and where the people all knew him. Believing himself bewitched, he fled in terror, retracing his steps and not stopping until he came safe home.

When Sebastian d'Elcano led his little band of seventeen seamen each 'more emaciated than any old worn-out hack horse' through the streets of Seville on 8 September 1522, the wide-eyed citizens who gazed upon the first circumnavigators were people who could not grasp the concept that the earth was a sphere, and that therefore it was theoretically possible to travel around it. Ptolomaic geography was espoused by only a small coterie of radical scholars. It was the expedition begun by Magellan and completed by Elcano that turned their theories into facts. But it also demonstrated that the world's wild oceans and savage lands held a thousand horrors and dangers for sixteenth century mariners and their puny ships. Throughout the rest of the century captains prepared to follow in Elcano's wake were few and far between.

Such were the first, hesitant voyages which began the era of circumnavigation, an era that lasted almost four hundred years and only came to an end in the last years of the nineteenth century. It was a magnificent era, one of the most exciting and formative in the long saga of the human species. During those epic years man fully possessed himself of his own planet. Whether inspired by hope of financial gain, national rivalry, scientific curiosity or the spirit of adventure, generations of travellers set out to 'put a girdle round about the earth'. Some perished in the attempt. Some helped to build up an accurate map of earth's remoter regions. Some emerged from and returned to a homely obscurity. Fortunately, some left a record of their experiences and impressions.

Francis Bacon, usually a wise commentator on the human scene, was mistaken when he wrote, in his essay *Of Travel:*

> It is a strange thing, that in sea voyages, where there is nothing to be seen but sky and sea, men should make diaries; but in land travel, wherein so much is to be observed, for the most part they omit it.

There are several reasons why mariners before and since the sixteenth century wrote accounts of their voyages. There was the need to produce rutters for fellow sailors and to keep logs which might be demanded by owners and financial backers. There were the long days to be filled when a vessel languished becalmed or scudded before the obliging trade winds. And there were strange and terrible experiences to be recorded which would thrill or chill the blood of friends at home. So far from there being 'nothing to be seen but sky and sea', the oceans presented a vivid kaleidoscope of changing moods, and their depths teemed with creatures, curious, beautiful and terrifying. For these and other reasons many of the men who went down to the sea in ships left behind an extensive literature of published works, manuscript journals, letters and log books. It is on such material that this history is largely based.

Captains, ordinary seamen, pirates, merchants, yachtsmen and yachtswomen, these are the principal characters of the long drama of circumnavigation. Their stories are fascinating not only as travellers' tales which tell us of battles with the sea and encounters with strange peoples. Their narratives reveal much more about the voyagers themselves – how they prepared, how they raised the money, how they handled subordinates, how they stood up to crises, how they coped with loneliness. It is always instructive to learn the various ways in which the human spirit reacts when pressed to the limits, for it is a spirit that we all share.

Some readers may question my assertion that the age of circumnavigation has passed. After all, more men and women now travel round the world than ever before: rucksacked youngsters determined to explore their planet before settling to the routine of earning a living; businessmen constantly shuttling between international airports; retired people going to the exciting expense of a world cruise. But this very fact proves my point: circling the globe is no longer the adventure it once was. Just as the 'Dark Continent' has lost its mysterious terrors and can be traversed by a well-maintained Land Rover; just as the South Pole which cost the lives of Scott and his companions is now manned by huts full of men and computerised gadgetry; so distant, 'romantic' locations can today be reached so quickly that the traveller must rest on arrival to recover from jet lag. Human progress has made the world a smaller and safer place. Perhaps it has made it a duller place, too.

Circumnavigation today *can* be made into an adventure but only by a voyager who imposes extra limitations on himself; who tries to accomplish it single-handed, or in the fastest time, or the smallest boat, or by a more taxing route. Going around the world does not, in itself, present the hydra-headed challenge which confronted our ancestors. We can legitimately, therefore, speak of the era of circumnavigation in the past tense.

I am grateful to the following publishers for permission to quote extensively from the works specified: Thorson's Publishing Group Ltd, for J. Ridgway and A. Briggs, *Round the World Non-stop;* Hodder and Stoughton Ltd, for F. Chichester, *Gipsy Moth Circles the World.*

1

PRIMUS

It all began with a death. Not an especially noble death. In fact, when Ferdinand Magellan was brutally felled by a rain of iron-tipped, bamboo spears on 27 April 1521, he suffered a fate he had arrogantly and needlessly brought upon himself. The swarthy, black-bearded Portuguese who had driven his diminishing band of sailors and adventurers through seventeen thousand miles of unimaginable hell, now involved them recklessly in the petty rivalries of two island princes:

> Zzula, lord of the aforesaid island of Mactan . . . begged that on the following night he would send but one boat with some of his men to fight [against his rival, Lapulapu]. The captain general resolved to go there with three boats . . . we set forth, sixty men armed with corselets and helmets . . . and arrived at Mactan three hours before daylight.
>
> When day came we leaped into the water, being forty-nine men, and so went for a distance of two crossbow flights before we could reach the harbour, and the boats could not come farther inshore because of the stones and rocks which were in the water. The other eleven men remained to guard the boats.

Having thus reached land we attacked them. Those people had formed three divisions, of more than one thousand and fifty persons* and immediately they perceived us, they came about us with loud voices and cries, two divisions on our flanks, and one around and before us. When the captain saw this he divided us in two, and thus we began to fight. The hackbutmen [i.e. men armed with primitive handguns] and crossbowmen fired at long range for nearly half an hour but in vain, merely piercing their shields, made of strips of wood unbound, and their arms . . . When those people saw that we fired the hackbuts in vain . . . they fired at us so many arrows and lances of bamboo tipped with iron, and pointed stakes hardened by fire, and stones that we could hardly defend ourselves . . .

But as a good captain and a knight he still stood fast with some others, fighting thus for more than an hour and, as he refused to retire further, an Indian threw a bamboo lance in his face, and the captain immediately killed him with his lance, leaving it in his body. Then, trying to lay hand on his sword, he could draw it out but halfway, because of a wound . . . that he had in his arm. Which seeing, all those people threw themselves on him, and one of them with a large javelin . . . thrust it into his leg, whereby he fell face downward. On this, all at once rushed upon him with lances of iron and of bamboo and . . . they slew our mirror, our light, our comfort and our true guide.[1]

From that moment onwards an attempt at circumnavigation, which had not formed part of Magellan's plans, was inevitable. To accomplish what their dead leader had set out to achieve eighteen months before, a remnant of his followers would have to attempt something he had never contemplated – a long sea

---

*Despite the oddly precise numbering, Pigafetta almost certainly exaggerates. He certainly could not have known the strength of the enemy with such precision. It is, moreover, extremely unlikely that Magellan would, knowingly, have faced odds of 21 to 1.

journey home through enemy-patrolled waters. By an ironical twist of fate the first circuit of the globe which is for ever associated with the name of Ferdinand Magellan would probably never have been attempted if Magellan had survived that skirmish in the Philippines and continued to lead the expedition. He dared not have sailed his tiny, vulnerable fleet westward across the Indian Ocean for, over the last twenty years the Portuguese had made themselves the masters of that ocean, establishing bases around its borders from the Cape to Malacca. And Ferdinand Magellan was a renegade Portuguese, who, after twelve years or more of faithful service to his king, had sold himself to the ruler of Spain and was now seeking to weaken Portugal's hold on the Orient trade. There could be no mercy for such a man if he fell in with ships commanded by any of his erstwhile countrymen.

Ferdinand Magellan was one of those rare men who lived in a remarkable age, and knew it and wanted to be part of it. The tiny village of Sabrosa in the vine-covered hills of Portugal's Douro Littoral claims the explorer as its son. Within that village a plaque on a substantial stone house announces that Ferdinand Magellan was born there 'circa 1480'. The claim has not gone undisputed but, in this case, the geographical accident of a man's birthplace is of no importance. What matters is that Ferdinand's father belonged to the fourth order of Portuguese nobility and that he died while his son and heir was still a minor. Ferdinand thus became a royal ward and, at the age of ten or eleven was taken to Lisbon to be a page in the household of Queen Leonor, consort to John II, the 'perfect prince'.

King John, who earned his nickname by being shrewd, intelligent and forceful, showed remarkable similarities to his English contemporary and ally, Henry VII. It was John who finally broke the power of the feudal nobility, established the authority of the crown and gave royal power a sound financial base. He took a keen interest in overseas trade and the expansion of empire and was frequently to be found in the *casa da*

mina, the office and warehouse complex on the ground floor of
the palace. From its waterfront windows he could watch the
ships coming to their moorings in the Tagus to offload their
cargoes of gold, slaves and ivory, brought from his African
dominions. The palace, like many other buildings in the
Alfama, Lisbon's ancient quarter, did not survive the 1755
earthquake but it takes little imagination to picture an impres-
sionable boy standing at one of its arched casements and
observing as excitedly as his sovereign the comings and goings
in the harbour and determining that one day he too would sail
to the lands of the East, rich in spices, precious metals, silk,
monkeys and multi-coloured parrots.

For over half a century Portugal had been trying to break the
Muslim stranglehold on the Orient trade. She had fought fruit-
less battles with the Levantine Moors. She had sent ill-fated
expeditions to search for Prester John, the African Christian
king of legend. She had, more profitably, probed the western
seaboard of the southern continent, building forts and trading
posts from which to plunder the land of the black men. Then,
in 1488, some three years before young Magellan came to
Lisbon, the streets of the capital buzzed with the news that
Captain Diaz had found Africa's southernmost tip and sailed
past it into another ocean. The seaway to the East was open.

John II wasted no time in exploiting this new discovery. He
sent Pedro da Covilha overland to Asia to spy out the strengths
and weaknesses of the Arab and Persian merchant princes who
controlled Indian Ocean trade. He sent his captains on secret
voyages into the southern Atlantic to learn more about the
prevailing winds and currents. At the same time he cleared the
diplomatic ground with Spain. In 1492–3 Christopher
Colombus had set off westwards in an attempt to reach those
very golden lands that King John's captains were seeking and
returned, as he claimed, triumphant and successful. Originally
he had offered his services to the 'perfect prince' and John had
considered his scheme. But the royal advisers asserted (rightly,
as we now know) that Columbus vastly underestimated the

distance from Iberia to Cathay by the western route. So the Genoese captain offered his services to the Spanish crown, an example not lost on young Magellan.

The immediate result was a hotting up of the race to establish commercial links with the Orient. To forestall this rivalry leading to colonial warfare between two Christian princes, Rodrigo Borgia who as Alexander VI had dragged the papacy to its lowest level of corruption, calmly divided the world in two. His line was drawn a hundred leagues west of the Cape Verde Islands. He allotted all new found land west of it to Spain and instructed John's captains to confine their activities to the east. The Portuguese king immediately protested that the demarcation would interfere with navigation on the Orient route, for Portuguese ships now stood well out into the Atlantic after leaving the Cape Yerde Islands to avoid the south-east trade winds. In 1494 the concerned parties met at Tordesillas in north-west Spain and agreed on a compromise: Alexander's line was moved a further 270 leagues to the west. This treaty, which set the pattern of European 'armchair colonisation' for centuries to come, proved remarkably effective as far as Atlantic exploration was concerned. But what would happen when Portuguese and Spanish conquistadores, expanding their legitimate spheres of influence, met at the backside of the world? With their imperfect grasp of terrestrial measurement they could not accurately continue the line of Tordesillas through eastern lands and seas. The result was a free-for-all.

All that lay in the future in 1495 when John II died, to be succeeded by Manuel 'the Fortunate'. The new king completed John's plans for a major expedition to the Indian Ocean and, in the summer of 1497, Vasco da Gama sailed out of the Tagus with four prime ships. He returned twenty-six months later with half his fleet and less than a third of his crew but what a voyage he had accomplished! Soon all Europe was excited by his discoveries – gold mines in East Africa, 'Christian' princes in India, markets brimming with gems and spices. Manuel himself, writing to Rome, announced his intention of wresting control of the Orient trade from the Muslims and awarded himself a title appropriate to his grand design: 'Lord of Guinea and of the conquest of the navigation and commerce of Ethiopia, Arabia, Persia and India'.[2]

Da Gama, Diaz and the other brave captains of their generation were Magellan's boyhood heroes. He watched their ships entering and leaving port, saw them received at court with all the pomp and honour due to men who have given faithful and spectacular service, heard them tell their tales of strange lands and peoples. He followed closely the plans being made to exploit da Gama's discoveries. And when, in 1505, Captain Francisco d'Almeida was sent with a fleet of twenty armed ships to batter Arab trading posts into submission, Ferdinand Magellan was among the young adventurers who served in his expedition.

From the young soldier's point of view the events of the next seven years must have been thrilling and satisfying beyond measure. Almeida, and his successor, Alfonso de Albuquerques, fell upon the Arab and Indian coast towns with unbridled brutality. Mozambique and Sofala were captured. Kilwa was burned. Mombasa was destroyed. Off Diu a hastily-assembled Gujerati-Egyptian fleet was shattered. The vital entrepôt of Goa was seized and soon supplanted Calicut as the pivotal point of Indian Ocean trade. By 1511 irresistible Portuguese power had reached distant Malacca. Magellan was present at many of the major battles of this *blitzkrieg*. He familiarised himself with the eastern seas and became an expert navigator. During these campaigns Magellan sailed as far east as Malacca, and may have travelled on to the tiny, all-important Spice Islands (the Moluccas) of Ternate and Tidore.*

When Magellan returned home in 1512 he had a better understanding than most men living of eastern seas and islands and of the Arab, Indian, Indonesian and Chinese mercantile fleets that were now forced to share with those of Portugal the

*There is no direct evidence that he reached the Moluccas in his service of the Portuguese king.[3]

luxury trade of the Orient. Though he spent the next few years in Europe and North Africa, he could not escape the spell the East had cast upon him. From friends such as Francisco Serrao he received first-hand accounts of the destruction of a Javanese war fleet in 1513 which laid the Spice Islands open to direct Portuguese trade. He received news of the people and the Muslim courts of those islands. Other friends helped him to compile maps and charts of the maze of islands lying between Malaysia and New Guinea.*

And that is how Magellan fell in with Rui Faleiro, who would prove to be his evil genius. Faleiro was an astrologer. He was a mathematician. And he was mad. Specifically, he believed, with all the passion of the megalomaniac, that he had cracked the major problem facing all Renaissance cosmo-graphers: the calculation of longitude. Equipped with his navigational aids,† Faleiro insisted, explorers could now con-fidently venture across unknown seas and lay bare their secrets. One of his 'discoveries' was that no great distance lay between newly-discovered America and the Spice Islands. A corollary of this 'fact' was that, if the demarcation line of Tordesillas was drawn around the globe, the Moluccas would be found to lie well and truly within the Spanish hemisphere. In all this Faleiro was wrong. For Magellan the error would prove fatal.

The young soldier spent most of the years 1513–1515 fighting in Morocco. In a skirmish before the walls of Azamor he received a leg wound which left him with a permanent limp. By now Magellan had developed into a tough, proud, ruthless campaigner in his mid-thirties; the kind of man who makes loyal friends and implacable enemies. In Africa he ran into trouble. Someone accused him of trading with the enemy.

*The first European sighting of New Guinea was that of the Portuguese Antonio d'Abreu in 1512.
†Later (1535), Faleiro's ideas were published in the *Tractado del Espheray del arte del marear: con el regemieto de las alturas: coalguas reglas nueuemete ascritas muy necessartas.*

Magellan tried in vain to clear his name and when King
Manuel, after Magellan's years of loyal service, refused him
promotion, he felt the slight very deeply. In 1517, he shook the
native dust of Portugal from his feet and travelled to Seville to
sell his sword to Charles I of Spain. But he had more than
valour to offer. Rui Faleiro went with him and together they
had devised a scheme to make good Spain's claim to the Spice
Islands and establish a regular trade route – a westerly trade
route.

They planned their campaign carefully. They had already
made contact with another Portuguese *émigré* who was highly
placed in the department dealing with voyages to the Spanish
Indies. Arrived in Seville, Magellan cemented this relationship
by marrying Señor Barbosa's daughter. He then sought and
won the patronage of one of Charles's closest advisers, the
Bishop of Burgos. With this influential support the two men
were ready to travel on to the court at Valladolid to present
their case to the king. Charles must have been impressed by the
theoretical arguments of Faleiro and the practical experience of
Magellan. Although he was preoccupied with his candidature
for the throne of the Holy Roman Empire (he was elected
emperor as Charles V in 1519), he gave the newcomers five
ships for the projected voyage, and invested them with the
Order of Santiago.

Information about the New World was flooding into the
royal court of Spain and, by 1519, a special body, the Council
of the Indies, had emerged to deal with all matters concerning
the exploration and exploitation of the overseas empire (the
Bishop of Burgos chaired this council). Charles's ministers now
knew that the Americas formed a major land barrier between
Europe and Asia. His *conquistadores* were steadily extending
their control over parts of the continent. His captains were
seeking a way round it. His more adventurous subjects had
already established settlements on both Atlantic and Pacific
coasts. The scheme set forth by Magellan and Faleiro fitted in
perfectly with this programme of expansion, a programme

given urgency by Portugal's stunning success in the East. Information about the projected voyage was not slow in reaching Lisbon, and Manuel, furious at the activities of the two 'traitors', sent agents to Spain to sabotage the undertaking.

The months spent in preparation were particularly anxious ones for Magellan. In addition to the usual problems of raising reliable crewmen, and hard bargaining with ship-chandlers and victuallers, who always tried to sell inferior merchandise at inflated prices, he had to be on his guard against the Portuguese, who hated him, and the Spaniards, who did not fully trust him. Then there was the matter of Rui Faleiro. The astrologer had been appointed joint captain-general of the expedition but was quite unfit for command, as even Magellan could now see. Magellan must also have had some concern for his family. For the first time in his life he would be departing on a long and dangerous journey, leaving behind a wife and child. Over and above all this was the anxiety about money.

The basic realities of life have changed little in five and a half centuries. Talk to any modern pioneer venturer and he will tell you that the toughest part of any expedition is getting it off the ground. One reason why circumnavigators, polar explorers, Himalayan climbers and their like are a race apart is that they possess, not only total dedication and bottomless self-confidence, but the thick skin acquired from selling themselves to potential backers. Whether it is kings and courtiers or bankers and international corporations who must be approached, the business of raising cash is never easy. That was as true for Francis Chichester in 1966 as it was in 1518 for Ferdinand Magellan:

> ... to raise the money we were still short of I had to approach all the suppliers, and ask if they would contribute in return for advertisement. Most firms refused, but some rallied round ... All these business dealings not only caused me immense worry but also prevented me from carrying out the offshore sailing and the much-needed sailing drill which I had planned. As a

result it was not till I was on the ocean that I discovered *Gipsy Moth IV*'s three major vices, which spoiled my plan for the project and nearly wrecked the voyage.[4]

Eventually, the great international banking house of Fugger came to Magellan's aid, prepared to back his highly speculative venture in the hope that the immediate profits of the voyage and the long-term income derived from trade with the Spice Islands would handsomely repay their investment. Gradually, the leader's other problems were sorted out. Faleiro decided to stay at home because his horoscope revealed that if he embarked on the voyage he would not survive it. Perhaps he was not as crazy as he appeared. Because few Spanish seamen would submit to his leadership, Magellan had to scour the waterfront to assemble a motley crew of 265 soldiers, sailors and gentleman adventurers – Portuguese, Italian, Dutch, French, Greek, Spanish and one English gunner. His vessels were: the flagship *Trinidad* (110 tons), the *San Antonio* (120 tons), the *Concepcion* (90 tons), the *Victoria* (85 tons), and the *Santiago*. None of these ships was new or sufficiently robust to cope with the worst conditions it might encounter. The largest had an overall length of less than eighty feet (about the size of a modern luxury pleasure yacht), into which were crammed stores, trade goods and a crew of fifty men.

It must have been with enormous relief that Magellan boarded the *Trinidad* off Sanlucar de Barrameda on 20 September 1519 and gave orders for the fleet to weigh anchor. His task was to find a channel connecting the Atlantic with the 'South Sea'. Ever since 1513 when Vasco Nufiez de Balboa had:

> . . . stared at the Pacific – and all his men
> Looked at each other with a wild surmise –
> Silent upon a peak in Darien*

*Keats's *On First Looking into Chapman's Homer*. Keats seems to have mistakenly believed that Cortes was the first conquistador to cross the Isthmus of Panama, according to this poem.

it had been generally assumed that a fairly narrow strip of land separated the two oceans. Several captains had already patrolled the coasts of South and Central America looking for the breach which they felt must be there. Magellan's was by far the best equipped such expedition. Having found and penetrated the strait, his task was to make the short crossing of the South Sea and establish a trading post on the Moluccas. He carried 20,000 hawk-bells, rolls of velvet, 2,000 pounds of mercury, as well as mirrors and articles of brass in order to do business with the merchant princes of the islands. And what then? No document exists detailing Magellan's plans for the homeward leg of the journey but there is no reason to suppose that he intended anything other than to return along his outward route. Failing that, his first contingency plan must have been to make for a safe haven on the coast of Panama. (One of the surviving ships attempted this, as we shall see.) To risk his cargo, his ships and his life by trespassing in the waters consigned to the Portuguese, who would probably by then have been waiting for him, would have been very foolhardy.

Six days sailing brought the fleet to the Spanish Canary Islands where Magellan completed the provisioning of his ships. Leaving Tenerife on 3 October the captain general set his course southwards along the coast of Africa, making use of winds and currents by now well known to Portuguese navigators. Then, presumably trying for the SE trade winds to carry him across the Atlantic narrows to Brazil, he hit the Doldrums. For two weeks his ships wallowed on oily seas and his men endured the morale-sapping humidity which caused even the lightest task to bring them out in a sweat. On a small, claustrophobic, sailing craft being becalmed is worse than being storm-tossed. As a twentieth century yachtsman observed, there is little to do but lie around listlessly and brood:

> We appear to be well and truly in the doldrums. It's oppressively hot and we're hardly moving. I went on deck before breakfast to try and dry off the sweat before getting hot

again, eating breakfast . . . By supper time the great heat was slightly less. I'm thankful I suggested that John and I would wash up each evening after supper. The galley is a hell hole during daytime . . . An oppressive night. I lay bathed in sweat in the saloon, trying hard to slow my pulse rate. Between the hour from four to five we covered one-tenth of a mile. 'Will we ever get out of these doldrums?' I heard muttered in the thick darkness.[5]

For Magellan's crews it was even worse, crammed as they were by night into whatever sleeping places they could find on deck and having little to do by day but gather in small groups and grumble about their leaders. Nor was it only the men who were disaffected. The Spanish captains of Magellan's ships were not happy serving under a foreigner. They already carried mutiny in their hearts.

It would be hard to exaggerate the difficulties of command on these early, pioneering voyages. The dangers and discomforts experienced by sailors were bad enough without the added fear of the unknown into which their superiors were leading them. Small wonder that ships were usually manned by the desperate and the reckless. Magellan's crews included a large proportion of criminals and men who had gone to sea to escape creditors. At the other end of the social scale were the gentleman adventurers who hoped to make their fortunes in private trading and colonial exploitation of newly-discovered lands. Such men, like the ships' captains, expected to be consulted on all major decisions. But voyages of exploration cannot be run by committees, and several circumnavigation attempts came to grief because of a failure to grasp this basic fact (Fenton's expedition and Cavendish's second round-the-world bid, to name but two; see below, pp. 47ff). There has to be someone in command, someone with a clear vision, someone capable of sufficient enthusiasm, determination and, if necessary, ruthlessness to drive men beyond the known limits of their endurance. Magellan was such a man. He would prove it at Port St Julian.

His ships broke out of the Doldrums at last and made landfall on the coast of Brazil on 29 November. This territory,
added to the discoverers' charts in 1501, was a no man's land.
Although claimed by Portugal, it remained unsettled and
unexplored. On 13 December the little fleet anchored in the
wide bay of Rio de Janeiro and the next two weeks were
devoted to essential repairs and taking on fresh water. This was
the last accurately located place on Magellan's maps. When he
led his ships out of the harbour after Christmas, he was heading
into the unknown.

The fleet sailed steadily south-west by south before the
prevailing winds, turning into every wide bay that might be the
entrance to a channel. On Easter Saturday (31 March) 1520 it
came to anchor in Port St Julian, far to the South in latitude
49° 20′. It was, and still is, a desolate spot where there is but
sparse vegetation to break the monotonous grey of sea, sky and
rocks. But it was sheltered and, with the southern winter
drawing on rapidly, the captain general decided to wait here
until the spring. Not so his senior officers. They had resolved
on a showdown. They had tolerated long enough this arrogant
Portuguese with his insane quest for a mythical passage to the
South Sea. On Easter morning the captains of the *Concepcion*,
San Antonio and *Victoria*, representing perhaps a majority of
the officers, delivered a petition demanding that in future
Magellan should consult with them before setting course. They
also made it clear that they and their men were unwilling to sail
farther along that hostile coast in search of a strait which other
sailors had sought in vain.

It was one of those moments when fortunes and reputations
are made or lost. Magellan was outmanned, outgunned and, it
seemed, outmanoeuvred. Yet he responded with firmness. He
rejected the petition, sent the petitioners back to their ships and
took stock of the situation. That night, when the mutineers
made their move, he was ready for them. Under cover of darkness, a boatload of armed men from the *Concepcion* boarded
the *San Antonio* and overpowered the loyal members of the

crew. But almost simultaneously Magellan sent men to capture the *Victoria*. Her captain, Luis de Mendoza, was killed and his body hanged from a yardarm. The *San Antonio*'s anchor cables were cut and she tried to slip away in the darkness. A burst of gunfire from the flagship put a swift end to that manoeuvre. The *Concepcion* surrendered without a struggle and long before dawn Magellan had re-established control of his fleet.

Now was the time for reprisals and these created an even greater test for the captain general's leadership. He had to make examples, to demonstrate the power of 'cord and knife' bestowed upon him as commander, and to break once and for all the back of incipient rebellion. Yet he dared not indulge in draconian punishment. Disease and shipboard accidents took a steady toll of life without Magellan further depleting his crews with a spate of executions. His solution was to use capital punishinent sparingly but dramatically. As a first step he took the already dead body of Mendoza, had it quartered and the portions displayed prominently on the ships of the fleet. Next he ordered Gaspar de Quesada, captain of the *Concepcion*, to suffer the indignity of being publicly beheaded by one of his own servants. Two other ringleaders, he announced, would be consigned to the lingering death of being marooned on the coast of Patagonia, when the ships weighed anchor. Magellan sentenced a further forty mutineers to death. It was only a gesture and within days he commuted the penalty: the offenders were clapped in irons and condemned to hard labour for the remainder of the five month stay in St Julian's Bay.

Magellan did not win the hearts of his men nor had he put an end to disaffection. There would be further crises of command but the captain general had, for the time being, gained the grudging obedience of his crews. The handful of sailors who survived the voyage brought back conflicting opinions of their tough little commander and historians have been divided ever since in their assessment of Magellan's devious and mercurial character.

Before leaving the depressing haven of St Julian the fleet

suffered another setback. The *Santiago* was shipwrecked while reconnoitring the coast to the south. Only after a group of men had made an appalling four month journey across the snow-covered terrain to bring Magellan news of the disaster could the crew be rescued.

On 24 August, when the worst of the winter was past, the four remaining vessels resumed their voyage. Day after day the lookouts scanned the coastline for the entrance to a strait that their leader insisted, seemingly against all the evidence, was there. Not until 21 October, St Ursula's day, was a significant cape of grey-brown cliffs observed with a channel beyond. Magellan marked it on the chart and gave it the name 'Cape Virgins' (St Ursula was supposed to have been martyred along with eleven thousand maidenly companions). He took his ships into the channel and seems to have been favoured with unusually calm weather. Thousands of sailing vessels later found great difficulty beating into the strait against the contra-currents set up by ocean swell and the tidal race around the cape, often made worse by offshore gales:

I had only a moment to douse sail and lash all solid when it struck like a shot from a cannon, and for the first half hour it was something to be remembered by way of a gale. For thirty hours it kept on blowing hard. The sloop could carry no more than a three-reefed mainsail and forestaysail; with these she held on stoutly and was not blown out of the strait.[6]

Magellan set two ships to explore the channel and after five days they returned with the triumphant news that the waterway broadened out and continued unchecked to westward. For the Portuguese commander this was the high point of the voyage. As the *Concepcion* and the *San Antonio* sailed back into view, cannon blazing and flags flying, he knew that he was vindicated.

But if Magellan was delighted that the new route to the

Indies lay open, others were not. The seaway before them was bordered by desolate lands. Along the shore rows of corpses could be seen impaled on poles. Beyond them the night sky was lit by the glow of a thousand fires (hence the name Magellan gave this place – Tierra del Fuego). Who could tell what horrors might lurk further within the strait? Fear played on jealousies and rivalries. At the first opportunity the captain of the *San Antonio* was overpowered and the largest ship in the fleet slipped past its companions and set course for Spain.

Despite this setback, Magellan pressed on, probing inlets and channels in search of the real strait. His men endured cold, storms and hunger as they threaded their way past snow-topped peaks and scrub-covered rock along the 334-mile waterway which, for all they knew, had no outlet:

> On 27 November [Magellan] came out into the South Sea, blessing God, who had been pleased to permit him to find what he so much desired, being the first that ever went that way, which will perpetuate his memory for ever.[7]

The passage of the straits had been entirely due to Magellan's determination and fierce discipline. It was an achievement that changed the course of history. Thus, probably no place on earth is more fittingly named than the Straits of Magellan.

Hardships passed were as nothing compared with what now lay ahead. Magellan's fleet travelled over nine thousand miles in three months and eight days without making a landfall. Thanks to chance and the SE trade winds the voyagers missed Easter Island, Pitcairn, the Society Islands, the Marquesas, the Carolines, the Gilbert Islands and the thousand and one other atolls and volcanic ridges thrust up from the floor of the Pacific.

It was a nightmare crossing. Men died from scurvy, malnutrition and sheer exhaustion. And they were the lucky ones. Their shipmates, driven by the primal urge to survive, forced stagnant water, sawdust and boiled-up bits of leather into their aching stomachs. And all for a purpose which rapidly lost the last vestiges of credibility. For, the further Magellan's ships sailed towards the taunting emptiness of the horizon the more pointless the exercise became.* The only fact established beyond doubt by the crews' appalling ordeal was that the European geographers' calculations about the width of the Pacific were wildly inaccurate. The gap between 'farthest East' and 'farthest West' was vast. Moreover, it seemed to consist of nothing but empty ocean. What all this proved beyond doubt to Magellan's dwindling band of mariners was that there was no practicable, alternative route to the Orient. The great 'South Sea' was a barrier to commerce; not a highway. It is hard to conceive the emotions which must have been unleashed on 6 March 1521 when the cry 'Land ahead' rang from the *Concepcion's* masthead. It can only be compared with the last-minute reprieve received by a prisoner in the condemned cell.

The long-awaited landfall was the island of Guam, the southernmost tip of the Mariana Ridge. Today a plaque marks the spot where Magellan stepped ashore. It is a valuable tourist attraction but the Micronesians do not remember their first European visitor with affection. They tell how he dubbed their ancestors 'thieves', murdered several of them and set fire to one of their villages before proceeding on his way. Mistakes are inevitable when different cultures meet for the first time. Magellan's men were ravenous, desperate and fearful of strangers. The local people were curious and acquisitive. Iron they prized above all things – for weapons and fishing spears. Out they came in their canoes to welcome the strangers, who watched them anxiously. But the small, brown-skinned men brought coconuts and fruit. They seemed friendly and when they came aboard and saw iron spikes, sail needles and steel knives they were very excited. They began to help themselves – in exchange for the food. More canoes arrived, with more offerings and more demands for metal in exchange. Magellan

---

*In fact islands were sighted twice – Pukapuka on 24 January and, probably, the Carolines on 4 February – but wind and tide prevented Magellan finding anchorage and he was obliged to leave these havens astern.

was afraid of his men being outnumbered and overpowered on their own decks. He ordered the natives off. Next day he sent shore parties to fetch water and hunt for meat. No sooner had the sailors left the beach than a group of young men made off with one of the boats. That was the point at which Magellan's brittle patience snapped. Conditioned by months of conflict with argumentative captains and surly crews to regard tolerance as weakness, he reacted swiftly and brutally. He ordered a group of islanders aboard the *Trinidad* to be shot down by crossbowmen. Then he gathered a force and went in search of his missing boat. Finding it, he punished the culprits with death, then fired their village. It was a savage act, even for that brutal age. It reveals a man whose judgement had been affected by the ordeal of command in impossible circumstances; a man at the end of his tether.

Six weeks later the captain general's inflexibility, magnified now to the point of paranoia, cost him his life. He saw himself as one of the great *conquistadores*. When his convoy reached the Philippines, he planted the Castilian flag at Massava, on Easter day (31 March) and claimed the islands for Spain. But Magellan was not another Cortes or Pizarro with an army at his back and time a-plenty to impose his will on an alien people. He led a raggle-taggle band of men, far from being in first class fighting trim, whose dreams were not of colonial adventure but of getting safe home. Perhaps he believed that the God who had brought him safely through such appalling hardships had a great work for him to accomplish; that nothing and no one could stand against him and the fulfilment of his destiny. Recklessly and heeding no advice, he set about imposing his will by force upon the islanders. For their part, the local rulers regarded the strange white men with their massive, fire-belching 'canoes' and their impregnable steel tunics as warriors sent by the gods to help them in their own local warfare. Eagerly the lords of Cebu and Mactan made alliance with Magellan, accepting a Spanish overlordship they had no intention of honouring and a baptism they did not understand.

Then they enlisted his aid against the troublesome Lapulapu, a rebellious prince of Mactan. Magellan agreed to attack Lapulapu's stronghold, brushing aside the united protest of all his officers. On 27 April he led a frontal assault through the shallow water of a wide bay out of range of any covering fire from his ships. In the brief battle Magellan, eight Europeans and four islanders were cut down. A subsequent appeal for the return of their bodies was rejected.

This was not the end of the voyagers' misfortunes. The two captains who now took over the leadership of the expedition succeeded in alienating their ally, the King of Cebu. At a royal banquet they and twenty-five of their men were murdered. The survivors lost no time in escaping. But once at sea they had to face another problem. None of their ships was in good shape after more than two years of open warfare with the sea and the fifth column attacks of teredo worms below the waterline. But the *Concepcion* was quite unfit for further service. She was stripped and burned and her crew transferred to the remaining two vessels.

The next six months was a period of aimless wandering among the confusion of islands that make up the Sundas and Indonesia. The captains had no charts and no clear objective. More than one commander was voted into and, later, out of office. Indecision and divided counsels threatened to complete the disintegration of the expedition. The mariners' route was decided more than anything else by the reception they experienced at their ports of call. After their previous experiences they were on their guard and were quick to weigh anchor at the slightest suspicion of hostility. But at Palawan the local ruler welcomed them warmly and made a blood pact to signify his friendship. The weary travellers found his land a veritable paradise. It was, in the words of Antonio Pigafetta, an Italian gentleman adventurer, who wrote an account of the voyage:

> a large island, where grow rice, ginger, swine, goats, poultry, figs half a cubit long and as thick as the arm [bananas],

which are good, and some others much smaller, which are better than all the others. There are also coconuts, sweet potato, sugarcanes, roots like turnips, and rice cooked under the fire in bamboos or wood, which lasts longer than that cooked in pots. We could well call that land the Land of Promise, because before finding it we suffered very great hunger, so that many times we were ready perforce to abandon our ships and go ashore that we might not starve to death.[8]

Amidst such plenty and fêted by the smiling, naked islanders, many of the voyagers must have felt, like Tennyson's Lotos Eaters:

Surely, surely, slumber is more sweet than toil, the shore
Than labour in the deep mid-ocean, wind and wave and oar;
O rest ye, brother mariners, we will not wander more.

Yet there could be no tarrying. They sailed on to Brunei and a welcome that set their eyes wide with its magnificence and generosity. This ancient sultanate, Islamised in the previous century, was at the height of its prosperity and power. By conquest and commerce Sultan Bulkiah and his predecessors had extended their influence over most of Borneo and many islands of Indonesia, Malaysia and the Philippines. The travellers had heard of Bulkiah's legendary wealth but they were quite unprepared for the reality. Royal barges ornamented with gold came out to meet them, bearing gifts. Their envoys were conveyed on richly caparisoned elephants to the chief ministers' residence, where they feasted off plates of gold and fine porcelain. When the captains were summoned to the sultan's palace they found themselves surrounded by a gaudy display of luxury such as any European monarch might envy. The great audience hall was hung with silk and decorated with ornaments of precious metal set with gems. Bulkiah, himself, could only be glimpsed in an adjoining room screened by a scarlet curtain and the visitors' messages had to be conveyed through a hierarchy of intermediaries. For the first time the Europcans were in the presence of a 'savage' ruler who rivalled their own king in power and magnificence. They admired the splendour and appreciated the sumptuous repast set before them but, when the time came to present their own tawdry gifts to this monarch, they could only feel embarrassed.

Yet, once again, they had to make a hasty departure. The only aspect of western technology that impressed Bulkiah was shipbuilding. He tried to lure the Europeans into a trap so that he could seize the *Victoria* and the *Trinidad*. But the travellers were, by now, extremely cautious and they made good their escape. For several weeks they wandered among the islands behaving more like pirates than envoys of His Most Catholic Majesty. They took what they wanted by force, including pilots to guide them through the reefs and channels and detained prominent men as hostages to ensure the good behaviour of their subjects. At last, they reached the Spice Islands, the commercial goal of the whole enterprise. The ruler of Tidore received them enthusiastically, probably because he saw Spain as a counterbalance to the powerful Portuguese whose visits were becoming increasingly frequent. The two ships were very soon loaded with cargoes of cloves, bought very cheaply. For the first time captains and mariners could allow themselves to indulge the dream of returning home wealthy men, standing high in royal favour. They had made a trade treaty between their king and one of the rulers of the rich Moluccas. They could reasonably look forward to a rapturous reception in Spain.

If they could reach Spain. This was now the problem that tormented their minds. There were two possible ways back to their own land, and both were dangerous. Eastward lay the horrors of the empty Pacific that they had already experienced. Westward lay an established trade route to Europe but one dominated by their Portuguese enemies. They decided on the Indian Ocean route but, when the time for departure came, the

Trinidad was found to be taking in water. So there was a last minute change of plan. It was decided that, rather than lose the favourable trade winds, the *Victoria* should sail immediately. The *Trinidad* would be properly repaired and then essay the Pacific crossing to the Spanish settlement at Panama, whence crew and cargo could travel over land to the Atlantic coast and return to Spain in one of the regular convoys.

Thus, on 21 December, the *Victoria,* with a crew of forty-four Europeans and thirteen Indonesians, sailed out of the anchorage, their sixty heavy-hearted comrades accompanying them as long as possible in Moluccan canoes and eventually waving their farewells as the tiny craft fell far astern. Not until 6 April 1522 did the *Trinidad* weigh anchor, under the command of Gonzalo Gomez de Espinosa. After three months, during which all the horrors of the outward voyage had repeated themselves and thirty-five men had died of scurvy, malnutrition and fever, she was forced to turn back. She reached the Moluccas again in November only to discover a large Portuguese fleet dominating the islands. Espinosa surrendered with his twenty-two surviving crewmen. They were eventually sent back to Spain but only four of them arrived in 1525 to become the second group of men to circumnavigate the globe.

Meanwhile the *Victoria* was scarcely faring better. Her captain was now Juan Sebastian d'Elcano, a Basque mariner promoted by the vicissitudes of the voyage from relative obscurity to ship's captain. He was different in character from Magellan and faced fewer difficulties but he showed that, like his dead leader, he too could be firm and single-minded in the pursuit of an objective. His task was simply to get his ship and his men home and to avoid a clash with the Portuguese. Thus, he steered a south-westerly course across the Indian Ocean to avoid the Portuguese bases along the coasts of India and Africa and the sea lanes between them. This meant another long journey through empty, uncharted seas which was almost as arduous as the trek across the Pacific. The *Victoria* left Timor on 11 February, sailed in a wide arc as far as 42° S and did not round the Cape of Good Hope till 19 May. During those three months their only landfall was on uninhabited Amsterdam Island. Hunger and scurvy were again the worst problems the crew had to face. Inevitably, the men came close to mutiny and insisted on making for Mozambique, a Portuguese colony on the African coast. Elcano refused to buy immediate relief at the cost of the success of the expedition. But when they neared the Cape and ran into unremitting westerly gales, the captain must have doubted whether he had made the right decision. For seven weeks the *Victoria* battled against contrary winds, fighting hard for every league of ocean. Her foremast was carried away. She was leaking badly. Constant handling of sails and manning of pumps called for superhuman endurance from her emaciated crew. One by one they died and their bodies were committed to the deep by comrades who wondered whether they would be next. The *Victoria* at last entered the Atlantic and set a northerly course with half the complement which had left the Spice Islands.

Now Elcano could not avoid the unwelcome reality that the ship must put in at some harbour where the men could rest and find fresh food. That meant facing the unknown dangers of African tribesmen, if they made a landfall on the mainland, or the all-too-easily-guessed reaction of a zealous Portuguese governor, if they stopped at the Cape Verde Islands. After discussing the matter with the senior mariners Elcano opted for the devil he knew. On 10 July the *Victoria* anchored off Santiago in the Cape Verde Islands. Elcano sent a boat ashore having rehearsed with the sailors the story they were to tell. They were to represent the *Victoria* as the damaged laggard of a convoy from the Americas, which had parted with its companions and taken so long to cross the Atlantic that its victuals were exhausted. The ruse worked – at first. Twice the skiff returned laden with sacks of rice. But on its third visit to the town someone became suspicious. The sailors in the boat were arrested and a message sent to Elcano demanding the surrender of his ship. The captain had no alternative but to cut and run, leaving thirteen invaluable crewmen behind.

The leaking, undermanned vessel wallowed northwards along the African coast. Every league nearer home was bought with more death, more water shipped, more men collapsing with fatigue and sickness at their posts. It seemed that success would be denied just as it was becoming a possibility. The men urged Elcano to jettison some of the cargo to lighten the ship. He refused, and for a compelling reason: the spices on board the *Victoria* were valuable enough to pay the costs of the expedition and yield a handsome profit. The powerful courtiers and merchants who had backed Magellan would not look kindly on a captain who had deliberately wasted their investment. And it would avail Elcano nothing to insist that he had done so to save his ship and his men. So for two more months the *Victoria* pursued her uncertain course back to Spain.

On 8 September she came slowly to her berth in Seville. The first task of Elcano and his men was to give thanks to God for their deliverance and to pray for their dead companions. Barefoot, haggard, most of them clad in tatters, they marched up from the harbour, carrying lighted candles, to the church of Santa Maria de la Victoria. One observer said that each one looked 'more emaciated than any old worn-out hack horse'. There were eighteen of them. Another seventeen later returned from prison in the Moluccas and the Cape Verde Islands. Three million years earlier, human beings had appeared on this planet. Now the planet had been symbolically claimed by their descendants.

In Seville and in their home towns and villages the returning mariners were received as heroes. Like astronauts in our own generation, they were men who had endured the unspeakable and seen the unimaginable, men with strange tales to tell to their wide-eyed neighbours. Elcano himself was summoned to the royal court at Valladolid, to be honoured by the king – but only after he had satisfied an official enquiry that the appalling loss of ships and men was not the result of bad leadership. In fact, neither the politicians nor the businessmen who had backed the expedition had cause for complaint. Spain had staked her claim to colonisation and trade in the Orient and the cargo brought back by the little *Victoria* more than made up for the losses of the other vessels. The fifty tons of cloves, cinnamon, mace, nutmegs and sandalwood were worth, ounce for ounce, more than gold in a Europe where the rich paid handsomely to acquire flavourings for insipid or over-salted food.

Risk of capital is always better rewarded than risk of life and limb. Elcano's recompense was modest. He was granted a royal pension of five hundred ducats a year (which, in fact, was never paid during his lifetime) and the right to a coat of arms. Appropriately, the shield was surmounted by a crest, incorporated in which was a terrestrial globe and the legend *Primus Circumdedisti Me.*

And Ferdinand Magellan? He was forgotten. Neither in Portugal nor Spain was there any interest in a man who had sailed *half-way* round the world.

2

A PELICAN IN HER PIETY

In whose half of the world did the Spice Islands lie? That was the question which remained to be resolved after the Magellan-Elcano voyage. Portugal and Spain now both had treaties proclaiming their overlordship. Each nation claimed that the Moluccas were situated on its side of the boundary line established by the Treaty of Tordesillas. In March 1524 a commission of lawyers, mariners and geographers met to resolve the matter. Juan Sebastian d'Elcano was among those presenting the Spanish case. After several sessions the commission broke up in disagreement and the free-for-all continued.

Within weeks the ministers at Valladolid had resolved on a new expedition to retrace Magellan's outward voyage, re-establish contact with the friendly princes of the East Indies, and reaffirm the treaty claims already made. A fleet of seven ships was fitted out and manned with 450 officers and men. Elcano was appointed second-in-command. Was it a testament to national ambition, or human avarice and folly, to ignore the immense cost in life and material of the first circumnavigation? Whatever the motivation, the voyage was a disaster. It was almost an exact re-run of Magellan's expedition. Savage storms off Patagonia and through the Straits reduced the convoy to four vessels before it embarked on the Pacific crossing. Within days these had scattered, leaving individual captains to make their own decisions whether to go on or back. The flagship maintained its course across the empty ocean with men dying daily of fever, scurvy and malnutrition. On 30 July 1526 Elcano assumed command on the demise of the captain general. Five days later he, too, was dead. Leadership was destined to change hands three more times before Fernando de la Torre (who began the voyage as a mere man-at-arms) brought eight survivors back to Spain in 1536.

That was the last attempt at a voyage of circumnavigation for half a century. This was not so much because men were frightened by the prospect. The human species has a remarkable resilience and European sailors continued to brave wide oceans in ships scarcely equal to the task. Nor was it because rulers were less inspired by greed or national rivalry. Spain and Portugal continued to compete for the Orient trade. The reason that no captains left Lisbon or Seville bent on a circuit of the globe was that neither of the leading maritime nations needed to go to such lengths. Portugal's eastward route to India and the Spice Islands was well established. As for Spain, once she had secured control of the central American isthmus, she had no need to hazard men and ships in the storms and icy waters far to the south.

It was Spain who took the initiative of exploring the Pacific from her bases on the American seaboard. The principal objective was to find a way of getting from Mexico to the Moluccas *and back again*. Thanks to the work of the pioneers, it was now quite possible to reach the Spice Islands across the South Sea but, in both of Elcano's expeditions, some captains had tried to sail home eastwards from the Orient – and failed. In tackling this problem some Spanish mariners became involuntary circumnavigators. For example, in 1542 Ruy López de Villalobos set out from Mexico and reached Mindanao. It was he who named this group of islands the Philippines, after the heir to the Spanish throne (the future Philip II). Twice Villalobos tried to sail home to Central America. Twice his ships were driven back by contrary winds, by which time they were unfit for further service. If he was to get his men safe home there was only one course of action left open to him: he surrendered to the Portuguese at Tidore. Villalobos and some of his colleagues died in captivity. The survivors were eventually sent home on a returning Portuguese ship.

The puzzle was not solved until 1565 Miguel López de Legazpi, sent out as first governor of the Philippines, despatched an expedition back to Mexico with Andrés de Urdaneta as pilot. Urdaneta was then an Augustinian friar in his fifties but forty years before he had travelled as Elcano's page on the ill-fated voyage which resulted in the death of the first circumnavigator. Ever since then he had been a student of ocean winds and currents. Now he put his knowledge to good use. Taking advantage of the SW monsoons and the Japan current, he guided his ship, the *San Pablo*, into the zone of the summer westerlies. In four months he crossed the ocean from Cebu to Acapulco and brought the East within reach of Spain's waving commercial tentacles. His successors never succeeded in wresting control of the spice trade from the Portuguese but they did establish through the Philippines a mercantile system which was just as profitable. It involved the exchange of Peruvian silver, for which there was a great demand in China, for silk and porcelain; which commanded high prices in Spain and the colonies.

By the last decades of the sixteenth century Spain was operating a truly phenomenal transoceanic commerce based on the export of bullion from the Pacific ports of Peru and Mexico (New Spain). Tens of millions of pesos left Callao and Acapulco annually; some bound for Manila; the rest sent home to Seville via the isthmus. Nor was the Spanish quest for new sources of precious metal abandoned. The Incas had a legend about gold coming from 'islands in the west'. Several expeditions were sent out in search of this new Eldorado. In 1568 Alvaro de Mendafia claimed to have located it. He called his newly discovered islands the Solomons, after the legendary wealthy king. Twenty-seven years later he returned to found a colony. It was a lamentable failure. No mines of gold or silver were discovered and the local people, not without cause, became hostile. Then the Solomons were 'lost'. For almost two centuries no mariner, with the exception of another Spaniard, de Quiros, was able to locate them. Steadily these elusive islands grew into a legend. Mariners' tales told of a land abounding in precious metals hidden somewhere in the vast expanse of the Great South Sea.

But the majority of adventurous and avaricious seamen looked, not to the mythical Solomons for rich pickings, but to the loaded argosies plying the Atlantic and Pacific along Spain's dangerously exposed and over-extended trade routes. Which brings us to the brave, rumbustious and not wholly admirable Francis Drake:

> He is low in stature, thick set and very robust. He has a fine countenance, is ruddy of complexion and has a fair beard . . . In one leg he has the ball of an arquebus that was shot at him in the Indies. He is a great mariner, the son and relative of seamen, and particularly of John Hawkins in whose company he was for a long time . . . Francis Drake read the psalms and preached . . . He also carried with him, from his country, a negro, named Diego, who spoke Spanish and English, and whom he had taken prisoner from a frigate in the North Sea [i.e. the Atlantic], near Nombre de Dios, about seven or eight years previously.[1]

Thus was Francis Drake described by a Portuguese fellow mariner who sailed with him. He might also have added that Drake was fearless, ruthless and fierce in his hatred of Spain and Catholicism. In an age when religious apathy and tolera-tion were virtually unheard of, this Devonshire seaman was aggressively Protestant. He was the son of a tenant farmer-turned-clergyman who had suffered at the hands of Catholic persecutors during the reign of 'Bloody' Mary. Young Francis was only seven when his family were harried from their home on the slopes of Dartmoor. During his teenage years and his early twenties he had opportunities to witness what can happen when religious fanaticism and political power go hand-in-hand. These were the years during which relations between Philip II's Spain and Elizabeth I's England were steadily deteriorating. Philip's most sacred ambition was to restore the stubborn queen and her subjects to papal allegiance. Naturally, the leaders of the island race were determined to resist such pressures. But it was not only in matters religious that rivalry between the two nations manifested itself. England was experiencing a period of unprecedented maritime expansion. Her merchants and captains wanted access to overseas ports and markets and mounted a determined challenge to the Spanish and Portuguese monopolists.

While England and Spain drifted into a state of undeclared war, the politicians on both sides, as politicians always do, protested their peaceful intentions. Diplomatic niceties were observed and there was a genuine reluctance, in London and Madrid, to become involved in the expense of open hostility. The seamen of both nations lacked both the sophistry and the stomach for such detachment. They were in the front line of the conflict, risking life and livelihood. Spanish colonists and shipowners suffered raids on their American settlements and piratical attacks on their homeward- bound convoys. English captains and supercargoes were afflicted with constant harassment by Spanish officials. Their vessels and goods were confiscated. A still worse fate awaited those who were arrested, for they might be handed over to the Holy Inquisition as heretics. In 1572, Morgan Gilbert, a former shipmate of Francis Drake, received two hundred lashes in an Inquisition dungeon and was sentenced to twenty years on the galleys. Others were tortured, imprisoned, even burned. Tennyson was not exaggerating when he described in *The Revenge* how Captain Richard Grenville delayed at the Azores to convey his sick men back aboard, despite the imminent arrival of a Spanish fleet. The poet goes on to express the feelings of the scurvy and fever-ridden crewmen:

> And they blessed him in their pain, that they were not left to Spain,
> To the thumbscrew and the stake for the glory of the Lord.

Drake knew many men who had suffered at the hands of the Spaniards and, in 1568, he experienced at first hand the perfidy and brutality of Philip's agents. He was sailing with his relative, John Hawkins, when the fleet, badly storm-battered, was forced to put in at the Caribbean island of San Juan de Ulua. While Hawkins's men and ships were recuperating, a Spanish fleet arrived. The English admiral negotiated for permission to stay in port until his vessels were ready for sea and then to depart peacefully. The Spanish officials pretended friendship to lure the 'heretics' into a sense of false security, then massacred all the English sailors ashore and opened fire on their ships. Hawkins eventually escaped, to return home with two of the six ships and fifty of the four hundred men he had led out of port months before. That fearful day remained forever vivid in Francis Drake's memory. Hatred of Spain and desire for revenge were, thenceforth, his overmastering passions.

By 1577 he had perfected in his own mind a scheme that would strike a terrible blow at Spain and pour rich booty into the coffers of his avaricious queen. He would do what no other privateer-captain had ever attempted: he would lead an expedition through the Straits of Magellan and fall upon the unguarded and unsuspecting Spanish settlements along the Pacific seaboard. Having loaded his ships with loot, he would either return the way he had come or sail on along the American coast until he discovered the 'Straits of Anian', the north-west passage which, geographers insisted, lay to the north of the continent. The plan was presented to the queen and backed heavily by Drake's friends at court. Elizabeth hesitated. For months she would neither forbid the enterprise nor sanction an expedition which would be highly provocative to her brother monarch in the Escorial.

It was late July before she gave her consent to a venture officially described as a commercial operation bound for Alexandria. But Drake could not start out even then. He had to waste precious weeks in London sorting out the business end of the enterprise, drawing up contracts with backers who included merchants, courtiers and the queen, herself. Then it was post-haste to Plymouth to oversee personally the provisioning of ships and mustering of crews. By the time he was ready to sail the period of equinoctial gales had arrived, and that meant further delays. It was 15 November before Drake weighed anchor in the *Pelican* and led his little fleet out into the Sound. A fortnight later they were all back again, battered into harbour by Channel storms. Not until 13 December was Drake's convoy of tiny ships able to escape the land and begin its historic voyage.

Tiny they certainly were. The *Pelican* (100 tons) was about a hundred feet overall and twenty in the beam. Her consort, the *Elizabeth,* was a mere eighty tons. There was a store ship or canter named the *Swan* and a fifteen ton bark, *Christopher,* which was the fleet's messenger, used for contact between the vessels, scouting out anchorages, searching for missing members of the convoy, etc. Last and least was the tiny merchantman *Marigold* which would prove unequal to the task and was probably only included because she was provided by the queen's favourite, Sir Christopher Hatton. With this puny flotilla and a hundred and sixty-four men, Francis Drake set out to do battle, not only with the might of Spain, but also with the world's most awesome expanses of ocean.

He followed the now-established track of vessels bound for the Americas. Coasting the western seaboard of Saharan Africa, he called at the Cape Verde Islands for revictualling.

There he had the first of many strokes of good fortune. Or perhaps one should not call it fortune. Drake was one of those bold, aggressive commanders who grabbed the slenderest of opportunities and turned every half chance into a triumph. Off the harbour of Praia he fell in with two Brazil-bound carracks. He captured one of them and went aboard to examine his prize. He found the Portuguese vessel laden with a variety of supplies for the colonists: wine, woollen cloth, velvet, swords – all valuable commodities to mariners facing a long voyage. The *Mary*, herself, was a well-found ship of 100 tons and a welcome addition to Drake's fleet. But, most important of all, she was carrying a highly-experienced pilot, Nun a da Silva, a man who had made many voyages to the Americas, was very familiar with Atlantic winds and currents and conversant with stellar navigation in the southern hemisphere. Drake had no hesitation in kidnapping the little Portuguese, though he released all his comrades. With a prize crew aboard the *Mary,* the convoy sailed south-westward and the admiral took every opportunity of spending time with da Silva, comparing charts and rutters. He treated his captive well. Da Silva ate at Drake's table, enjoyed the best accommodation available and, in general, had everything he wanted – except his freedom.

The convoy wallowed through the Doldrums. For hours on end the sweating and idle mariners had nothing to do but grumble, quarrel and wish they were ashore. It was that sultry atmosphere that nurtured those rivalries and discontents that were to burgeon into the worst crisis of the voyage. The problem was the gentlemen and, in particular, their ringleader, Thomas Doughty. In the sixteenth century it was the custom for adventurous young men of wealth and influence to acquire berths on long-distance voyages. It was an opportunity to see the world, to dabble in trade and to enhance their reputations. Unfortunately, the presence of such idle coxcombs rarely did anything to enhance the smooth-running of the vessels to which they were assigned. On this expedition, as on many others, the relationship of the gentlemen to the officers was ambiguous.

Doughty and his friends had a financial stake in the venture and powerful contacts at court. They were soon giving themselves airs and Drake, to some extent, acquiesced in their affectation. He was a snob and had the self-made man's exaggerated respect for wealth and privilege. The gentlemen added a tone of culture and refinement to the enterprise which Drake found almost irresistible.

No captain had ever sailed the seven seas in quite the style that Drake affected. He regarded himself as more of an ambassador than a mariner. In his cabin he was served on silver plate. His personal entourage included a drummer and a trumpeter to herald his arrival and a group of musicians to play to him at mealtimes.

Thomas Doughty was all that a part of Drake aspired to be and was not – highly educated, poised, politically astute, able to converse easily with philosophers and princes. He had served in the Irish wars and was an intimate of Sir Christopher Hatton and others close to the queen. This cultivated gentleman was, without doubt, a young man on his way to the top. He was also an intriguer. He thrilled to be party to secrets and enjoyed the power that clandestine knowledge gave him over the lives of others. He had embarked on this enterprise with one trump card up his sleeve: he was the secret agent of Lord Burghley, Elizabeth's first minister. Burghley, a cautious and astute statesman, had been opposed to the venture from the start and had officially been kept in the dark as to its true objectives. He envisaged the notorious Drake stirring up all manner of diplomatic hornets' nests. He, therefore, needed someone on the expedition to keep him privately informed of all that happened. Thomas Doughty was that person and he relished the power he believed that it gave him over Drake.

Doughty had been made captain of the *Mary* and the ship soon became the fleet's focus of discontent. As incidents, insults and rumours increased Drake did nothing but when Doughty and his cronies beat up John Brewer, whom Drake had sent to the *Mary* with a message, the admiral could no longer ignore the challenge to his authority. He stripped Doughty of his command and had him conveyed aboard the little store ship, *Swan*. This action may have postponed the inevitable show-down; it did not prevent it.

The ships reached Brazil, revictualled and turned south. The weather grew colder. The biting *pampero* shrieked down from the Andes, churning up violent storms and scattering the fleet. Men fell ill with dysentery and fever. The crews grew fearful. Drake had still not told them where they were headed. It was obvious now, that this was no trip to Alexandria, nor even a raid upon the Spanish Main and that their leader was taking them into more dangerous and more distant waters. Doughty and his friends played on these anxieties. Untold horrors lay ahead and the prospects for safe return were remote if Drake was not challenged, they urged. Drake could see the whole enterprise falling apart if he did not act. He tried to defuse the situation by making Doughty an object of ridicule. He had him tied to the *Pelican's* mainmast for a couple of days where he was the butt of jeers and crude jokes. All this achieved was the heightening of personal rivalry. The proud gentleman could not, now, back down. It was Drake or Doughty.

And so they came to doleful St Julian's Bay. The desolate spot which had decided the fate of Magellan's expedition was to perform the same service for Drake's. The admiral convened a drumhead court on the beach. What followed was not a trial in which the interests of justice were served. Drake merely used legal forms for his own ends. He had evidence brought of all the prisoner's misdemeanours, then harangued the 'jury' into demanding Doughty's death. The unfortunate gentleman challenged the admiral's authority to impose a capital sentence. He was probably right to do so. Although Drake frequently boasted of the commission he held from the queen, he never produced it or permitted anyone else to scrutinise it. Now, he blustered away the challenge, for there could be no turning back. Death there must be if he were to regain that position of unquestioned authority which alone could force his men to go where no Englishmen, and very few men of any race, had ever been.

The drama – one might more accurately say the 'theatricality' – of Doughty's last hours strikes modern readers as bizarre, but it was the kind of show the Tudor age expected. On the morning of 2 July, the condemned man made his confession to the expedition's chaplain. Then he and his judge knelt side by side to receive Holy Communion together on the deck of the *Pelican*. This was followed by a civilised dinner in the great cabin during which Drake and Doughty conversed cheerfully and the prisoner even toasted the success of the voyage. This concluded, the entire company was rowed across to a small island in the bay and formed up in a square around the block. Drake and Doughty were landed and walked for a while along the shore, deep in conversation. At last, they returned and embraced. Doughty knelt and prayed aloud for the queen, the admiral and the company. Then, turning to the executioner, he spoke his last words: 'Strike clean and with care, for I have a short neck'. The sword flashed once. 'Lo, this is the end of traitors!' Drake shouted. It remained only for the body to receive a decent burial. Drake marked the island on his chart and named it 'The Island of True Justice and Judgement'. That was too much of a mouthful for his men. They called it, 'The Island of Blood'.

The voyagers had to stay another six weeks in St Julian's Bay, waiting for the worst of the winter weather to pass. Those were uncomfortable, demoralising days and Drake had to stage other dramatic demonstrations of authority in order to stamp his will on the enterprise and quench the last, smoking embers of mutiny. It was during this period that Drake renamed his ship the *Golden Hind*, in honour of Sir Christopher Hatton, whose coat of arms bore 'a hind trippant or'. It was a prudent gesture, for the man he had recently executed (some would say 'murdered') was a member of Hatton's household.

The fleet, reduced to three ships, because the *Swan* and the *Christopher* had been scuttled, and the *Mary* broken up for parts at St Julian's Bay, set sail on 17 August. Six days later they lay at anchor within the Straits of Magellan. They had an easy passage and emerged, on 6 September, into what Magellan had called *Mar Pacifico*. But for these first Englishmen the ocean failed to live up to its name. They ran straight into a north-westerly gale, which almost put an abrupt and tragic end to the voyage:

> The day being come the sight of sun and land was taken from us so that there followed as it were a palpable darkness by the space of 56 days without the sight of sun, moon or star as . . . we thus . . . continued without hope at the pleasure of God in the violent force of the wind's intolerable working of the wrathful seas and the grisely beholding (sometimes) of the cragged rocks and fearful height, and monstrous mountains being to us a lee shore where into we were continually drawn by the winds and carried by the mountain-like billows of the sea . . . If at any time we had a little opportunity to seek some harbour for refuge to come to anchor and rest till God in mercy might . . . give us more safe sailing at the seas, such was the malice of the mountains that they seemed to agree together in one consent and join their forces together to work our overthrow and to consume us, so that every mountain sent down upon us their several intolerable winds with that horror that they made the bottom of the seas to be dry land where we anchored, sending us headlong upon the tops of mounting and swelling waves of the seas over the rocks, the sight whereof at our going in was as fearful as death.[2]

On the morning of 30 September the little *Marigold* foundered. On the decks of the other vessels the cries of men threshing around in the icy seas were clearly heard by comrades helpless to render any assistance.

At last there came a lull in the storm. The two ships clawed their way north-westward and found what appeared to be a safe anchorage in a cove to the north of Cape Pilar. But within hours an offshore wind beat down with such ferocity that anchor cables parted and the exhausted mariners had to put to sea once more. This time the *Golden Hind* and the *Elizabeth* were separated. The flagship was driven far to the south-east before the wind abated. Drake found himself in 57° near a cluster of islands to which he gave the name 'Elizabethides'. In fact, he had discovered, without realising it, the southernmost point of the American continent. Later generations of sailors would know it as Cape Horn.

It was 7 November by the time the *Golden Hind* regained the western end of the straits and there was no sign of her sister ship. In fact this was because the *Elizabeth* was by now well on her way back through the channel. Captain John Wynter and his men had had their bellyful of Francis Drake's perilous mystery tour. The sailing master probably spoke for all when he declared that 'Mr Drake hired him for Alexandria, but if he had known that this had been the Alexandria, he would have been hanged in England rather than have come in this voyage'.[3] The *Elizabeth* reached Ilfracombe on 2 September 1579.

Meanwhile, Drake settled to the main purpose of his voyage: doing as much damage as possible to and extracting as much plunder as possible from the ill-protected nerve centre of Spain's commercial empire. With one small ship and his storm-and-disease-depleted crew (the complement was now down to about eighty), this man the Spaniards called *El Draco,* the Dragon, spread havoc and confusion along the entire seaboard. Merchant captains at anchor and citizens about their lawful occasions on the quayside were stunned by the wholly unprece-dented vision of an enemy ship coming into harbour with cannons blazing. At several 'ports of call' the Englishmen were able to help themselves to coin, food, ship's supplies, trade goods and charts – all valuable to mariners far from home in strange waters. From various prisoners, whom he took a pride in treating well and entertaining royally, Drake also gathered information. The most intriguing news concerned a mouth-watering potential prize. The *Nuestra Señora de la Concepcion* had recently sailed from Callao, the port of Lima, headed for Panama with a major consignment of silver.

Drake went in pursuit. Two weeks later (1 March 1579), he caught up with the galleon off Cape San Francisco, just above the line. She was, as he had already discovered, well armed. So, instead of brazening it out with her, Drake resorted to cunning. He disguised the *Golden Hind* as a sluggish merchantman. This was done by the simple expedient of hoisting a Spanish flag, running out several water-filled wine jars on a stern line and then hoisting full sail. It was an old pirate trick, intended to disarm an enemy by making it seem that there could not possibly be anything to fear from a craft which could make such poor speed through the water. The stratagem worked admirably. The *Nuestra Señora* altered course and came within hailing distance. Only at the last moment did armed men suddenly appear above the *Golden Hind's* deck rail. One of her cannon exploded into life and the *Nuestra Señora's* mizzen mast fell over the stern in a tangle of rigging. While the Spaniard's deck was still a confusion of cries, shouted orders and running feet, Drake's pinnace slipped round to her far side with a boarding party. It was all over in a few minutes without a shot fired from the Spanish ship which was coarsely nick-named by her sailors *Cacafuego* (*Shitfire*).

With the Spanish crew transferred aboard the *Golden Hind* as his 'guests', Drake examined his haul at leisure. As the inventory was checked off, he and his men knew that all the dangers and suffering they had endured had been worthwhile. Thirteen hundred bars of silver (26 tons) were ferried across to the English ship. There were fourteen chests of coin. In addition, a search of the cabins yielded a large quantity of plate and jewellery. None of the wide-eyed Englishmen had ever seen such treasure, worth perhaps £40,000,000 in modern value.

The voyage was 'made'. That fact lifted a great weight of anxiety from Drake's mind. Until the capture of this stunning prize he was fearful about his reception in England. Enemies would be waiting. There would be accusations to be faced –

murder, piracy, needless risk of ships and men. Elizabeth and Burghley would not hesitate to throw him to the wolves if the political situation required it. But now he had an insurance against persecution. No one, not the queen, nor her council, and certainly not his powerful backers would quibble over legal or diplomatic niceties if he brought home such a vast profit.

Reaching home was now Drake's sole objective. But how? To return the way he had come was out of the question. Spanish warships were already in pursuit and merchant captains and garrison commanders would be on the lookout for the English corsairs. That left two possibilities; the mythical Straits of Anian and the known but nightmarish western route. Neither was much more attractive than running the gauntlet of the angry Spaniards.

Drake's first move was to stand out to sea to avoid his pursuers. Then he headed north-westwards, intending to pick up the coast of North America and follow it in search of the passage which would, if the geographers were right, bring him back to the Atlantic. The *Golden Hind* reached a high Pacific latitude and may have been on a parallel with modern Vancouver before wind and weather forced her to turn back. It was cold. There were frequent fogs and fierce north-westerly gales blew intermittently. By the time the heavily-laden ship had been at sea for fifty days she was leaking badly and food supplies were dangerously low. Drake turned eastwards, urgently seeking an anchorage. Eventually, he found a haven on the coast in a latitude variously recorded in early documents as between 38°N and 48°N.

For over a century scholars have argued about the exact location of this landfall which, because of subsequent events, took on a special significance in the history of the USA. While Drake beached his ship to carry out the necessary repairs, he also patiently established friendly relations with the shy Indians who lived in that place. On 26 June 1579 a remarkable ceremony occurred. The chief came down to the white men's camp attended by hundreds of his people, dancing, chanting and

bearing gifts. The ruler made a speech and then presented
Drake with a feathered head-dress, necklaces and other adornments. Unable to understand what was meant by these rituals,
the visitors put their own interpretation on them:

> . . . the king and divers others made several orations, or
> rather, indeed, if we had understood them, supplications,
> that he would take the province and kingdom into his hand,
> and become their king and patron; making signs that they
> would resign unto him their right and title in the whole land;
> which that they might make us indeed believe that it was
> their true meaning and intent, the king himself, with all the
> rest, with one consent and with great reverence, joyfully
> singing a song, set the crown upon his head, enriched his
> neck with all their chains, and offering unto him many other
> things, honoured him by the name of *Hyóh*. Adding there-
> unto (as it might seem) a song and dance of triumph; because
> they were not only visited of the gods (for so they still judged
> us to be), but the great and chief God was now become their
> God, their king and patron, and themselves were become the
> only happy and blessed people in the world.
> These things being so freely offered, our general thought
> not meet to reject or refuse the same, . . .
> Wherefore, in the name and to the use of her most excel-
> lent majesty, he took the sceptre, crown, and dignity of the
> said country into his hand . . .[4]

Before leaving the locality, Drake set up a brass plate claiming
the territory in the name of his queen and naming it Nova
Albion. This first English colonisation occurred five years
before a similar claim was made to land on the east coast and
seven years before the establishment of the ill-fated Roanoke
settlement in what is now North Carolina. It is a pity, therefore,
that no documentary or archaeological evidence has yet
appeared enabling us to fix 'Drake's Bay' beyond dispute.
The Englishmen stayed in this pleasant land until 23 July, by

which time Drake had abandoned any thought of the north-ward route home. All that he had learned from captured charts and interrogated prisoners indicated to him that this was a good time of year to attempt a Pacific crossing. With Spaniards to the south and storms to the north, this was the only option left open to him. He was committed. He would have to attempt the third circumnavigation of the world and he would have to try to become the first captain to complete such a circum-navigation.

This meant, first of all, facing an ocean completely unknown to English navigators, then confronting Orient seas patrolled by Spanish and Portuguese men of war. For the first of those tasks he was singularly ill-equipped. There can be little doubt that Drake's Spanish charts underestimated the width of the Pacific. Philip's subjects had been regularly sailing the Manila route for little more than a decade and, although many earlier miscon-ceptions had been cleared up, the lack of any accurate means of measuring longitude left considerable scope for cartographers' optimism. Drake had probably discovered that the galleons from Acapulco could make the crossing in under three months. Beyond that he knew nothing. He would be proceeding, as mariners called it, 'by guess and by God'.

In fact, the *Golden Hind* enjoyed a trouble-free crossing. Sixty-six days with the trade winds at her back brought her to the Caroline Islands where she was soon surrounded by Polynesian canoes whose occupants brandished fruit, fish and coconuts, suggesting that they wanted to trade. Drake had read of Magellan's experiences in these waters and was wary. As soon as there was any sign of trouble, he fired off a culverin to frighten the importunate natives and, when that failed to disperse them, he had his arquebusiers shoot directly at the boats, killing about twenty men. Drake had not come all this way to be stopped now by a bunch of 'thieving savages'.

On 21 October the voyagers reached Mindanao, took on fresh food and water and then sailed south in search of the Spice Islands. Drake hoped to crown his achievements by establishing an English presence in the Orient trade. Yet, only after wandering chartless for days among the reefs and islands did he come to Ternate. Sultan Baab received the newcomers in princely splendour:

> The king at last coming from the castle, with 8 or 10 more grave senators following him, had a very rich canopy (adorned in the midst with embossings of gold) borne over him, and was guarded with 12 lances, the points turned downward. Our men (accompanied with *Moro* the king's brother) arose to meet him, and he very graciously did welcome and entertain them. He was for person of low voice, temperate in speech, in kingly demeanour, and a Moor by nation. His attire was after the fashion of the rest of his country, but far more sumptuous, as his condition and state required: From the waist to the ground was all cloth of gold, and that very rich: his legs bare, but on his feet a pair of shoes of goat skin, dyed red. In the attire of his head, were finely wreathed in diverse rings of plated gold, of an inch or an inch and a half in breadth, which made a fair and princely show, somewhat resembling a crown in form. About his neck he had a chain of perfect gold, the links very great and one fold double. On his left hand was a diamond, an emerald, a ruby, and a turkey [turquoise], 4 very fair and perfect jewels. On his right hand, in one ring, a big and perfect turkey and in another ring many diamonds of a smaller size, very artificially set and couched together.
>
> As thus he sat in his chair of state, at his right side there stood a page with a very costly fan (richly embroidered and beset with sapphires) breathing and gathering the air to refresh the king, the place being very hot, both by reason of the sun, and the assembly of so great a multitude.[5]

Baab was delighted to welcome the Englishmen and trade with them. To him they represented one more piece on the gaming board of oriental politics. He had become adept at playing off the Spaniards and Portuguese against each other and against his rival, the Sultan of Tidore. Now here was the representative of a third European monarch who claimed that his queen was anxious to establish regular commercial relations and was an enemy both of Spain and Portugal.

The *Golden Hind*'s crew crammed a consignment of cloves into what little space remained in her hold. It nearly proved her undoing. On 9 January, while threading her way through the coral outcrops south of Celebes, she ran onto a reef and stuck fast. Drake's first move was to lighten ship. Overboard went eight cannon, valuable casks of fresh food and the newly-acquired cloves. It made no difference. Next, Drake tried to find a purchase point for one of the spare anchors, hoping to take a cable end round the windlass and haul the ship into deep water. This stratagem, also, failed. There seemed nothing to be done but to resign themselves to the mercy of God. Drake called upon the chaplain, Francis Fletcher, to say prayers and preach a morale-boosting sermon. Unfortunately for him, the parson exceeded his brief. Calling upon every member of the crew to repent his sins and get right with God, Fletcher drew special attention to the part they had all played in the condemnation of Thomas Doughty. Soon afterwards a sudden change of wind carried the *Golden Hind* clear of the reef.

They were safe and under way again. But Drake was furious. His just dealings in the Doughty affair had been challenged – and in the name of God. How could he deal with his recalcitrant chaplain? The bizarre answer he came up with indicates just how sensitive Drake was about the events in St Julian's Bay. He called the ship's company together and solemnly excommunicated Francis Fletcher from the Christian Church. He confined the poor man to the foredeck and forced him to carry a placard stating that he was 'Ye Falsest Knave That Liveth'.

The *Golden Hind* reached Java safely and here Drake and his men were again royally received by one of the Muslim rulers. But the visitors had to make a hurried and unceremonious departure when a Portuguese convoy was reported approaching the island. Fortunately there had been time to careen the ship once more. The strains imposed on the erstwhile *Pelican* throughout her long odyssey were beginning to tell. Once again, her commander had to point her bowsprit at the empty ocean. Like Elcano, Drake was obliged to give a wide berth to the Portuguese shipping lane from Malacca, via Goa, Mombasa and Mozambique to the Cape. So he had to set a direct course for the southern tip of Africa. Being denied ports of call was a severe hardship. The eighty-four days of comparatively easy sailing across the Indian Ocean stretched to the utmost the supply of water and victuals and forced the crew to dig once more into their reserves of strength and stamina. It was a weak and listless company of men that sailed into the Atlantic on 18 June 1580. They were reduced to fifty-nine in number and several more would have died of thirst had it not been for the spare canvas rigged to catch every drop of rainwater from passing squalls. Another month would go by before they could make a landfall (on the coast of Sierra Leone) to refill their casks. Then, for the first time in over two years, they were back in familiar waters, navigating by familiar stars and plotting their course on familiar, well-worn charts.

In mid-September they entered the Channel and the excited travellers were soon pointing out well-known landmarks to each other and longing to get ashore. But when, on the 26th, they came to rest in Plymouth Sound and some of Drake's friends came aboard, they advised him to wear away and anchor by St Nicholas Island while secret messages were despatched to the court. The political situation, they said, was very sensitive. Complaints about Drake's activities had been pouring in. So, for another month the crew had to wait while their captain was summoned to London to be privately interrogated by the queen. Only then did they know whether they were to be welcomed back as heroes or clapped in irons.

It was, of course, the money that clinched the matter. All the backers of the enterprise received a 4,700 per cent return on their investment. Elizabeth's own share amounted to £160,000 plus the glittering presents that Drake strewed at her feet. The proceeds of this one venture were almost enough to cover government expenditure for a whole year, something the nation's hard-pressed treasury could not ignore. The Spanish ambassador might rant and threaten and demand that Drake be punished; it was out of the question for the queen and council to disown him. Nor would the people have stood for it. Drake was a public hero. His exploits were being turned into ballads and talked about in every alehouse in the kingdom.

It needed only a romantic and patriotic gesture to set the seal on this remarkable enterprise. That was provided on 4 April 1581. The *Golden Hind* had been brought to Greenwich and completely refurbished by an army of painters and carpenters. There, while crowds cheered and musicians played, Elizabeth I went aboard the ship that had circled the globe and there Francis Drake kneeled before his sovereign to receive a knighthood.

3

THE TRIUMPH OF DESIRE

Drake never followed up the commercial contacts he had made in the Spice Islands and, although his great voyage had inspired many young adventurers, none of them immediately set out to emulate the exploit. One reason for this was, undoubtedly, the growing hostility with Spain which provided action enough in the northern Atlantic for captains seeking booty and the clash of arms. England could ill afford to send some of her best ships and men across thousands of miles of ocean while the conflict with Philip II threatened to erupt into open warfare.

Another reason for the lack of interest in circumnavigation was the failure of the Fenton expedition. In 1581 Edward Fenton, a soldier of fortune, was appointed by a commercial consortium headed by the Earl of Leicester to command a fleet to the Orient. The backers had two objectives: they wanted to cement profitable relations with the Sultan of Ternate and they wanted to discover the North-West Passage which would open for England a virtually private route to the wealth of the East. The known but hazardous southerly route was expressly forbidden in Fenton's instructions: 'You shall goe on your course by Cape de Bona Speranca, not passing by the Streight of Magellan, either going or returning'.[1] The hard-headed money men had no interest in circumnavigation for its own sake. Nor, to judge from his subsequent actions, had Fenton.

He was a man wholly unfitted to such an undertaking. Scarcely had his four ships set sail in May 1582 when he was arguing with his officers, and it soon became clear to them that he had no intention of obeying his instructions. He spoke wildly of seizing the tiny island of St Helena and proclaiming himself its king. When his captains refused to support him in such madness he turned back to plunder Portuguese settlements in the Cape Verde Islands and along the West African coast. He bartered one of his ships for provisions and lost another through shipwreck in the Plate estuary. After that he had no alternative but to return, ignominiously, to England.

It is difficult to assess the character of a man like Edward Fenton across the divide of four centuries but the attempt is instructive because it makes clear the immense strain long sailing voyages put upon any mariners unequal to the task. Edward was one of those unhappy men overshadowed by a brilliant younger brother. Geoffrey was a fine scholar who attracted the patronage of several leading courtiers, and was accepted among the literary *cognoscenti* of the day. He settled in Paris and, before the age of thirty, had won fame as an author and translator. Edward could not bear the thought of settling to the dull life of a Nottinghamshire landowner on the estate inherited from his father, while his brother covered himself in glory. He sold his patrimony and went off to serve as a soldier in Ireland. Apart from a brief interlude when he accompanied Frobisher on his third voyage in search of the North-West Passage, Fenton remained in the troublesome province for fourteen years. He returned home in September 1580. It is probably no coincidence that Geoffrey had arrived in Ireland four months earlier and had already begun to make a mark there (within a year he was appointed secretary to the lord deputy).

Edward went to the royal court, desperately seeking some

new adventure to enhance his reputation. More than one project was discussed before the ill-fated 1582 expedition was planned. When Fenton eventually put to sea it was as an inexperienced sailor leading captains who knew the Atlantic far better than he did. He was no mariner, nor was he a very accomplished commander. Above all, his heart was not in the venture; he saw it largely as a vehicle for enhancing his reputation and escaping from his own mediocrity. Thus, the absurd talk of becoming 'King of St Helena' and the subsequent frenzied attacks on Portuguese and Spanish ships and settlements. It is easy, even for seasoned sailors, when at sea and under stress, to lose touch with reality:

> I became convinced that I wasn't really wanted at home – that it wouldn't matter to anyone if I never got home and at the same time I wanted to get to England and have done with the voyage as soon as possible . . . I began to weave for myself a completely new life, independent from and quite different to anything that I had experienced before. It would be a fine thing to start life all over again . . . a new pattern of living, a clean sweep away from everything that had gone before. I would go off into some wilderness in pursuit of ideas – break away from the humdrum for ever.[2]

Forced to return home in disgrace, Fenton made a crazed attack on his lieutenant, William Hawkins, in a desperate attempt to silence him. Thereafter, he was probably fortunate to be allowed to live out his life in relative obscurity. But to the end of his days (he died in 1603) he had to suffer the slow torture of observing his brother's continued success in Ireland. Geoffrey, knighted in 1589, added a distinguished political reputation to the one he had already established as a man of letters and died in 1609 a wealthy and honoured royal servant.

But if Edward Fenton's is a sad story, that of Thomas Cavendish plumbs tragic depths of Sophoclean profundity. Cavendish deserves better than the history-book footnotes where his name usually appears. For he was the first *true* circumnavigator. That is to say, he was the first captain to set out with the declared objective of sailing around the world and to accomplish that objective.

Cavendish was a well-educated, twenty-year-old gentleman, newly established at the queen's court on that exciting day in September 1580 when Drake returned triumphantly from his round-the-world voyage and he was captivated by the great mariner's exploits. It was not long before he had conceived the audacious plan of repeating those exploits. The task was formidable, as the stories of the returning seamen must have made clear. Drake had accomplished it against all the odds and Drake was an experienced master mariner who had first gone to sea before Cavendish was born. The young courtier had little to support his own pretensions apart from his enthusiasm, the information and advice he picked up in conversation with deep-sea captains in London alehouses, and a substantial income from his Suffolk estates. It was the last of these that brought him his first chance of maritime adventure. In 1584 Sir Walter Raleigh was eagerly seeking support for a colonising voyage to North America. Cavendish mortgaged some of his lands to provide and equip a fifty ton barque and he captained her himself. He spent the summer of 1585 crossing and recrossing the Atlantic in a fleet under the command of Sir Richard Grenville. Although he fell out with the admiral, the reality of an ocean voyage did nothing to dispel his romantic notions of battling with the elements and seeing strange lands. As soon as he returned he set about raising money, ships and crews for his great voyage.

On 21 July 1586 Thomas Cavendish sailed out of Plymouth in his new vessel, the *Desire* (120–140 tons), aptly named by one whose yearning for adventure was so great. Two smaller ships, the *Content* and the *Hugh Gallant*, made up his squadron. It may have been the queen's intention when she gave permission for the voyage that the young commander should join forces with the Earl of Cumberland currently fitting out a similar fleet. But Cavendish wisely avoided the problems of shared leadership by getting away a full month before George Clifford's flotilla. It was as well; the earl's ships reached Brazil ill-provisioned and too late in the season and were forced to turn back. Cavendish's expedition undoubtedly benefited from single leadership and clarity of purpose. There was the customary gaggle of gentlemen adventurers (one of whom left an account of the voyage) but they seem to have offered no challenge to Cavendish's authority.

The first objective was to reach the straits of Magellan in the middle of the southern summer with ships and men in a fit state to attempt the passage. In this Cavendish was successful. He made a landfall at Sierra Leone, then crossed the Atlantic, reaching Brazil on 1 November. He spent three weeks resting his men and revictualling his ships. He even took time to build a 10 ton pinnace to hold extra stores. Working down the Patagonian coast, he sailed into and named Port Desire. Here his men took advantage of the large seal and penguin colonies to eat plenty of fresh meat and to lay in enough for several days ahead. The fleet sailed on and reached the entrance to the straits on 6 January. The timing could scarcely have been better and for two weeks they proceeded westwards with favourable winds. Half-way through they came upon a deserted Spanish settlement which had been intended as a lock and chain upon the backdoor of Philip II's empire. The fate of the colonists upon that wild and barren coast must have been terrible. Cavendish named the place Port Famine because of 'the noisome stench and vile savour wherewith it was infected through the contagion of the Spaniards' pined and dead carcases'.[3] However, he endured the smell long enough to help himself to twelve abandoned cannon.

The voyagers were almost through the narrows when they ran into 'most vile and filthie fowle weather'[4] which obliged them to spend three and a half weeks skulking in what shelter they could find and hazarding the 'best cables and anchors that we had for to hold, which, if they had failed we had been in

danger to have been cast away, or at least famished'.[5] Food
supplies were already low and one account states 'we fed
almost altogether on mussels and limpets and birds or such as
we could get on shore, seeking for them every day as the fowls
of the air do'.[6] At last, on 24 February, they passed Cape Pilar
and Cavendish became the first commander to lead a convoy
intact into the Pacific.

The soft underbelly of Spain's American empire now lay
exposed, and he was intent on inflicting severe wounds upon it *en
passant*. In the event, he indulged in an orgy of destruction
surpassing even that perpetrated by Drake. One reason for this
was that the enemy was now in a better state of preparedness than
it had been eight years before. As the English fleet proceeded
northwards, alarm signals went before it, carried by sea and land.
Coastal towns looked to their defences and occasionally the
colonists went onto the offensive. When Cavendish sent a party
ashore for fresh water south of Valparaiso two hundred horsemen
appeared over the dunes. In the ensuing skirmish twelve
Englishmen were slain and several others were taken prisoner.

In April 1587 the fleet entered the tropic zone and Cavendish
put into Arica where he took four merchant ships and held
them to ransom, demanding the return of his captured men. But
the Spanish authorities were under strict instructions not to
give way to terrorism. Thus when the English sailed away
without their colleagues they left four prime merchant vessels at
the bottom of the harbour. Those were the first of more than a
dozen ships and three towns that Cavendish burned along that
coast, having first plundered them of anything of value. Among
the assorted merchandise that fell into his hands there was very
little in the way of treasure, but food, wine, navigational instruments and charts were almost as welcome to men with
thousands of miles sailing still ahead. Cavendish was particularly pleased to capture a Greek pilot, Jorge Carandino, who
knew the local waters, and to replace the leaky *Hugh Gallant*
with another vessel renamed the *George*.

The fleet had been careened and refitted on the coast of

Mexico when Cavendish received news of a great ship on her way back from the Philippines richly laden with oriental merchandise. He sailed to southern California and there patrolled impatiently back and forth waiting for the argosy. She was sighted, at last, on 4 November and, after some fierce hand-to-hand fighting she surrendered. The 700-ton *Santa Ana* was a formidable opponent. But for the fact that her cannon were stowed below decks because no enemy was anticipated on that coast Cavendish's challenge might have had a very different outcome.

This great ship 'was one of the richest vessels that ever sailed on the seas; and was able to have made many hundreds wealthy if we had had means to have brought it home'.[7] The *Santa Ana* yielded 22,000 gold pesos and 600 tons of silk, pearls, satin, civet and other goods. She was not as rich a prize as the *Cacafuego* but her capture had 'made' Cavendish's voyage even though he could ship only a fraction of the merchandise. Cavendish spent two weeks sorting through the cargo. Fifty tons of it was transferred to his own vessels. The rest was burned with the ship. The commander's problem was a manpower shortage. We have no details but it is clear that scurvy, ship's fever and battle had all taken their toll. The *George* had already been scuttled because there were not enough sailors to man her. Cavendish had enough crewmen for two ships and, since the mariners had to be fed, victuals accounted for much of the space in the holds. It must have been galling to watch the richly-laden *Santa Ana* slip beneath the waters of San Lucas Bay in a cloud of steam and smoke, but Cavendish and his men were in good heart as they set sail for Cathay on 19 November.

With the aid of a Spanish pilot, Alonso of Valladolid, removed from the *Santa Ana,* and favoured by wind and weather, Cavendish made the crossing to Guam in forty-five days. This was about three weeks shorter than Drake's time for an almost identical voyage. The sailing went well but Cavendish had other anxieties. Soon after leaving the American coast the *Content* was lost to view. Nothing more was ever heard of her. The most likely explanation is that her captain turned the vessel round and tried to return home the way he had come and that the *Content* was either lost at sea or fell foul of the Spaniards. After the capture of the *Santa Ana* there had been argument among the men over the spoil. Cavendish had given in to their demands for an immediate share-out. This was his first real sign of weakness as a leader and it was certainly a tactical blunder. With their purses already well lined, the sailors had no incentive to face the largely-unknown dangers of the wide, empty Pacific. Small wonder, then, if the *Content*'s captain, either willingly or under pressure from his crew, took what he believed to be the easier route home.

Cavendish, holding to his purpose, now came to what he regarded as the most important part of the voyage: gathering information about the Orient trade. The *Desire* reached the Philippines on 14 January 1588 and anchored off Samór whose people proved friendly and informative about the Spaniards. Cavendish was scarcely circumspect in his dealings with the enemy. He toured the islands, carefully noting details of strategic interest. His men had occasional brushes with the Spaniards. And he even sent messages of defiance to the authorities. Yet, when the pilot, Alonso, was detected smuggling a message to the Spanish governor, Cavendish promptly had him hanged from a yardarm. The English swaggered around with such braggadocio that the outraged Bishop of the Philippines complained to his royal master:

> The grief that afflicts me is not because the barbarian infidel has robbed us of the ship *Santa Ana* . . . but because an English youth of about twenty-two years, with a wretched little vessel of about a hundred tons and forty or fifty companions, should dare to come to my own place of residence, defy us, and boast of the damage he had wrought . . . He went from our midst laughing, without anyone molesting or troubling him.[8]

Among Cavendish's boasts was the promise that he would return to wrest control of the Orient trade from the Portuguese and Spanish. This he was clearly resolved to do. Having mastered the southerly route himself, he believed that other English mariners could and would employ their superior ships and seamanship to establish regular contact with these profitable markets. There was no need to wait for the discovery of a north-west passage; Cathay and the Spice Islands lay open via two clearly-established routes.

Having almost no cargo space available, Cavendish could not take commercial advantage of his position. He, therefore, bypassed the Moluccas, sailing between those islands and the Celebes, entered the Indian Ocean via the Straits of Lombok and coasted along the southern shore of Java. All the time he was adding information to his charts and rutters and compiling a dossier on enemy depots and fortifications. The bland description of the route in surviving documents should not blind us to Cavendish's real achievements as a navigator. Malaysia and Indonesia present any sailor with a formidable maze of islands and shoals, in which countless ships have come to grief. The *Golden Hind's* voyage very nearly ended in these waters. Yet, the *Desire* made a leisurely and safe three month cruise through the region. Cavendish's success was certainly partly due to good weather. But more important was his use of local knowledge. He made a point of establishing good relations with the rulers and people of the islands. He gave impressive gifts of cannon and other items of booty to the Muslim princes. In return he received fresh produce, information on reefs and channels, and native pilots to guide his ship to safety.

He left Java on 16 March, having careened the *Desire* and seen her well-fitted and provisioned for the homeward voyage. He took the southerly route across the Indian Ocean and a month and a day brought his men in sight of the Cape of Good Hope. The *Desire* reached St Helena on 8 June and rested there for twelve days before embarking on the final leg of the voyage.

She entered the English Channel on 3 September and immediately ran into a storm which shredded her sun-bleached canvas. On the ninth of the month the little ship limped into Plymouth with her weary crew, who only now discovered that their success was the gilt on the gingerbread of a providential English escape from Philip II's invincible Armada.

Thomas Cavendish savoured his triumph to the full. He immediately set to work smartening up the *Desire* and, while ballads and broadsheets proclaimed his exploits throughout the length and breadth of England, he sailed his refurbished flagship round to Greenwich to show her off to the queen. When Elizabeth and her court came down to the quayside they were confronted by a dazzling spectacle: the *Desire* was dressed overall, her flags and pennants gleaming with rich colour and cloth of gold; her sails of blue damask; her crew resplendent in silks and gold ornaments. Cavendish dined her majesty in a great cabin hung with silks and served her from rich plate captured from the Spaniards. The young captain showered his sovereign with fine gifts in addition to the share of the profits which she legitimately claimed. It was all very impressive and the queen was impressed.

She was right to be and Cavendish was right to enjoy his moment of glory. But all this costly, swaggering splendour was not just self-indulgent glorification. Cavendish was already planning his next voyage, to be virtually a repeat of his first circumnavigation. He wanted backing from the court and the City. He wanted to demonstrate that sailing freely round the world was not a rare exploit but could become a habit for English mariners. To achieve all this he needed publicity.

PR and advertising techniques may have been honed to menacing perfection in our century but they are not new.

Shortly after this Richard Morris-Adams arrived from London with Monica Dixon and Simon Weaver from Barwell Sports Management, a public relations firm representing Debenhams, the department store giant. The four of us met on the yacht at the mooring under the wood.

I took them on a quick tour of the boat; then while examining the Blake's marine toilet installation adjoining my cabin, Simon made a suggestion.

'What would you think about naming the yacht *Debenhams,* John?'

I looked down at the toilet, and tried to imagine how twenty-five thousand used one-pound notes would look piled up in it.

'It has a certain romantic ring to it,' I grinned, and the deal was struck. The bank manager thought it was a good idea too.[9]

Even in the sixteenth century adventurers had to draw themselves to the attention of people who mattered. Such behaviour is often unpopular with lesser spirits who frown upon immodest display. Cavendish was certainly misunderstood by some of his contemporaries who accused him of running through the profits of his voyage and being compelled to organise another to recoup his wasted fortune: 'although his great wealth was thought to have sufficed him for his whole life, yet he saw the end thereof within very short time'.[10] But Cavendish was not a wastrel. If he had been, his end would have been little more than poetic justice – the fall that comes after folly and pride. He was a passionate visionary, a restless adventurer who could never again be content to return to his Suffolk acres or even to the court of Gloriana.

He was, moreover, goaded onwards by the rivalry of other captains. During the years immediately after 1588 several voyages to the East Indies (as India and the lands and islands beyond now came to be called) via the Straits of Magellan or the Cape of Good Hope were planned. Many never got beyond the drawing board and those expeditions that did put to sea were frustrated by bad weather or poor leadership. Nor was England the only nation interested in wresting long-distance trade from the hands of Spanish and Portuguese captains. Dutch mariners, enthusiastically backed by their government, were catching up fast in the study and practice of navigation. It was, therefore, only a matter of time before someone began to reap rich rewards from the Orient trade. Cavendish, now in the prime of life, was not prepared to yield to others the primacy in a commerce he had pioneered.

In the years 1589–91 he spent money freely but not on self-indulgent luxury. Most of his funds went on ships. He completely refitted the *Desire* and he bought other vessels for his projected voyage. Some of these were sent on privateering ventures, to earn their keep while preparations were completed for the next expedition. Those preparations dragged on month after month, eating up capital and repaying it only with frustration. One ship was lost in the Thames Estuary. Another proved unsuitable and had to be replaced. There were the usual wrangles with chandlers. Ships' suppliers were notorious for trying to palm off their customers with inferior gear and stale food. They knew all the tricks of the trade, such as rotten cordage refurbished to look new, barrels half-filled with mouldy flour, then topped up with fresh and the substitution of inferior merchandise for items bought and paid for. Amidst the bustle of crowded quaysides and warehouses it was easy to swindle ships' captains who had a hundred and one other problems on their minds. By the time deceptions were discovered the victims were hundreds of ocean leagues away, perhaps never to return. Over the centuries dishonest chandlers were probably responsible for as many maritime disasters as storms, shoals and poor navigation. So Cavendish and his agents needed extreme vigilance if the expedition was to be properly supplied. In the event they were not careful enough.

Another problem was finding reliable crews. Only a very rare breed of mariner was prepared to brave the dangers of a long voyage with a less than fifty per cent chance of returning. It was well-known on the waterfronts that although the sailors who had come home on the *Desire* had profited handsomely from the voyage they had numbered but forty out of an original complement of a hundred and twenty-three. Seasoned mariners preferred short, privateering voyages offering less risk and more profit. Even to man such ventures as those captains often had to resort to royal warrants of impressment or take aboard a proportion of unskilled volunteers drawn from the ranks of the criminal and the desperate. Too many of Cavendish's crewmen were unreliable, faint-hearted and potentially mutinous. Some deserted at Plymouth. Others made trouble later.

But the major weakness of the new venture was divided leadership. Cavendish found himself running rapidly through his own resources and it was probably for this reason and against his better judgement that he now involved others in the enterprise. After the success of his first venture there were many young gallants eager to join his next. These gentleman adventurers could provide money, men and influential contacts. Cavendish, irrevocably committed to the voyage, had little choice but to admit some of these applicants to his company and his counsels.

Worst of all, as things turned out, he had to take John Davis into partnership. Davis, one of the truly great navigators of the age, was some ten years older than Cavendish, had accomplished three remarkable Arctic voyages in search of a northwest passage and had essayed expeditions to the East Indies by both easterly and westerly routes. He was highly respected in maritime circles and had excellent connections at court. In theory he and Cavendish had much to gain from each other and much to give to a joint venture. But they were both individualists, accustomed to sole command and their coming together was to have fatal results. In retrospect, Davis claimed that he had teamed up with Cavendish out of regard for the younger man and against the advice of his friends. We do not know Cavendish's version of how the partnership came into being. The arrangement was that the two men should keep company until the coast of California was reached; thereafter Cavendish should complete the circumnavigation, while Davis sailed north in search of the Straits of Anian, the supposed entrance to the North-West Passage.

On 26 August 1591 Cavendish led out of Plymouth a more impressive fleet than the one he had commanded five years before. His flagship, the *Galleon Leicester* was a prime ship of 400 tons. The gallant *Desire* sailed again, under the command of John Davis. The *Roebuck* was a 240-ton privateer. Davis provided a ship of comparable size called the *Daintie*. The storeship was a vessel known as the *Black Pinnace*. Aboard were 350 sailors and soldiers. It was an impressive panoply.

But it failed. And the failure literally broke Thomas Cavendish's heart.

The main events can be quickly outlined. Because of the aggravating problems over equipping and manning the fleet, Cavendish had set out too late. Twenty-seven days becalmed in the Doldrums caused more disastrous delay. It was then that the men discovered that much of the casked food was inedible. They suffered the pangs of hunger and they blamed the leader for their plight. When, at last, the Englishmen reached Brazil they had to spend valuable weeks recuperating, foraging and raiding settlements for fresh food. Not until 24 January did they set out on the long southward haul towards the Straits. Now they ran into savage storms. Several hands were lost. The *Daintie* turned for home. The flagship was parted from the three remaining vessels. Her boats were lost so that it was impossible to send men ashore for food or water. Only on 18 March was the fleet reunited at Port Desire. From this point we can witness the rapid deterioration of Cavendish's character as conditions worsened and the expedition fell apart.

He transferred his flag to his old ship, the *Desire,* because he regarded the men of the *Galleon Leicester* as 'the most abject minded and mutinous company that ever was carried out of England'.[11] The sensible course would now have been to winter at Port Desire but Cavendish insisted on sailing for the Straits immediately. If Davis and the other experienced mariners protested, as surely they must have done, the commander over-rode them. His independence of judgement was rapidly turning to a paranoiac suspicion of anyone who opposed him. His firm leadership was deteriorating into a combination of fanatical raving, bullying and threats. The success of the expedition had now become an obsession. Anything that challenged that success was deliberate, personal persecution from the hand of either man or God.

We know all this because of a remarkable document in Cavendish's own hand written towards the end of the voyage. It is a tragic attempt at self-vindication and blame-shifting. Nothing illustrates as clearly as the following extracts the strains that a long sailing voyage could put upon a man's mind.

The ships battled through the Straits of Magellan against contrary winds for four weeks:

> At length being forced by the extremity of storms and the narrowness of the strait, being not able to turn to windward any longer, we got into a harbour where we rode from the 18th day of April till the 10th of May, in all which time we never had other than most furious contrary winds, and after that the month of May was come in nothing but such flights of snow and extremity of frosts, as in all the time of my life I never saw none to be compared with them. This extremity caused the weak men in my ship only to decay, for, in 7 or 8 days in this extremity there died 40 men and sickened 70; so that there was not 50 men that were able to stand upon the hatches.'[12]

Everyone now looked to the commander for an initiative. Cavendish called the company together and declared his intention of abandoning his present course and crossing the southern Atlantic to make for China by way of the Cape of Good Hope:

> These persuasions, with many others which I used, seemed to content them for the present but they were no sooner gone

from me but forthwith all manner of discontents were aired amongst themselves and to go that way they plainly and resolutely determined never to give their willing consents.[13]

Instead, the men suggested a return to Brazil for revictualling and refitting, so that they could make another attempt on the westerly route when the weather improved. Cavendish gave way with great reluctance and, apparently, despite the advice of Davis, who, with his sights fixed on his own personal quest, wanted to winter at Port Desire or Port St Julian.

Cavendish returned to the *Galleon Leicester* and, presumably to impress the troublesome crew with his ruthless determination to let nothing hamper his plans, he immediately had eight of the sickest men rowed ashore, where they were left to die. The result of this on the morale of their comrades can easily be imagined.

Out of the Straits, the ships battled northwards through storms and high seas. They kept well together, despite the conditions, until 21 May. At first light on that day the lookout on the flagship reported that the *Desire* and the *Black Pinnace* had been lost to sight. Cavendish was convinced that this was deliberate treachery by Davis, whom he castigated as:

. . . that villain that hath been the death of me and the decay of the whole action whose only treachery in running from me hath been an utter ruin of all . . . his intention was ever to run away. This is God's will that I should put him in trust that should be the end of my life, and the decay of the whole action: For had not these two small ships parted from us we could not have miscarried on the coast of Brazil, for the only decay of us was that we could not get into their barred harbours. What became of these small ships I am not able to judge, but sure it is most like they went back again for Port Desire, a place of relief for two so small ships, for they might lie on ground there without danger and being so few men they might relieve themselves with seals and birds and so take a good time of year and pass the straits. The men in these small ships were all lusty and in health, wherefore the likelier to hold out. The short of all is this: Davis his only intent was utterly to overthrow me, which he hath well performed . . .[14]

Davis later denied the charge of desertion. He claimed that it was the flagship which altered course during the night and that he had spent several weeks searching for his leader. But Cavendish's surmise was certainly correct: the two lost ships *did* put into Port Desire and they *did* subsequently make three attempts to sail through the Straits. The temptation for Davis must have been considerable. By slipping into a shallow harbour where the *Galleon Leicester* could not follow he might rid himself of a commander who was no longer making rational decisions. We shall never know the truth. What is clear is that Cavendish made no attempt to find his errant vessels, but sailed resolutely on for Brazil.

Events rapidly moved from bad to worse. Raiding along the Brazilian coast brought some provisions but Cavendish lost several men. The *Roebuck* was severely mauled by storms. The crews, now totally demoralised, were anxious to return home while their ships were still intact. Their leader treated them with contempt. He secretly resolved to transfer men, food and gear from the *Roebuck* to his own ship, burn the consort and then sail once more for the Straits. It was a desperate stratagem and the men, to whom Cavendish must by now have become transparent, would have none of it:

> they forthwith openly began to murmur and mutiny, affirming plainly that . . . they would go home.[15]

Cavendish called the company together and bludgeoned them with his tongue. They should not, he ranted, give way to cowardice and:

> go about to undertake any base or disordered course but

> . . . cheerfully go forward to attempt either to make them-
> selves famous in resolutely dying, or in living to performe
> that which [would] be to their perpetual reputations.[16]

This 'death or glory' speech did not impress Cavendish's
exhausted men:

> . . . forthwith they all with one consent affirmed plainly they
> would never go that way again, and that they would all
> rather stay ashore in that desert island than in such case to
> go for the straits.[17]

At that Cavendish lost his temper:

> . . . one of the chiefest of their faction most proudly and stub-
> bornly uttered these words to my face in presence of all the
> rest, which I, seeing took this bold companion by the bosom
> and with my own hands put a rope about his neck meaning
> resolutely to strangle him, for weapon about me I had
> none.[18]

It is not surprising that the *Roebuck's* crew took the first
opportunity to desert.

Cavendish was now obsessed with thoughts of failure and
death. He told his men on one occasion that if they refused to
sail for the Straits, 'I was determined that ship and all should
sink in the seas together.'[19] From this point he ceased to exercise any effective leadership. The mariners ignored his rantings.
The ship steered a zig-zag course across the Atlantic, missed a
projected landfall on St Helena, and then made for England.
Cavendish, utterly broken, spent most of the time in his cabin,
composing a vindication of his actions, writing his will and
contemplating suicide:

> . . . amongst such hellhounds my spirit was clean spent,
> wishing myself upon any desert place in the world, there to

die, rather than thus basely to return home again, which course I had put in execution, had I found an island which the charts make to be in 8 degrees to the southwards of the line, I swear to you I sought it well with diligence, meaning, if I had found it, to have there ended my unfortunate life.[20]

Did he, eventually, commit suicide or did he die simply of a lack of desire to remain alive? We shall never know. Somewhere out in the Atlantic his body was consigned to the ocean that had, in the end, defeated him.

4

THE FIRST TRAVELOGUE

The world, or rather the European conception of it, was changing. By 1600, geographers had a roughly accurate knowledge of the principal landmasses of Asia, Africa and the Americas, although the Pacific and any islands and continents it might contain were still mysteries, and existing charts underestimated the ocean's width. Merchants appreciated the commercial potential of India, China and the Spice Islands and were ready to believe that as yet undiscovered lands might abound in mineral and vegetable wealth. Thus, despite the appalling experiences recorded by long-distance mariners, there was plenty of incentive for ocean voyages to the Orient, using either the eastern or western route.

Political changes also added a spur to voyages of exploration. In the year that Drake returned triumphantly from his circumnavigation, the crowns of Spain and Portugal were united. The overseas interests of these once-rival nations were thus merged into the first truly worldwide empire. With the wealth of both East and West flowing into Philip II's coffers, he seemed secure and invincible. But this was an illusion. The administrative strains placed upon his government by ruling far-flung colonies as well as the Habsburg dominions in Europe were intolerable. Also, the very extent of his power and the fact that it was used to reinforce and propagate an inflexible Catholicism obliged other nations to challenge the monumental authority of Spain. Predominantly it was the Dutch and the English who sallied forth as champions of Protestantism and it was these nations which also took over as leaders of maritime enterprise for the next two hundred years. In 1588 Philip's attempt to cower England with his great Armada was frustrated. The following year saw Spain's final failure to crush the Dutch Republic, which had been wrested from the northern part of the Spanish Netherlands. The conflict continued for a further twenty years but the territory ruled by the States General maintained its independence and even carried the war to the enemy. More than that; there flourished for a few decades in the United Provinces a civilisation rivalled for brilliance only by that of Renaissance Italy. Antwerp became the commercial centre of Europe and its rich burghers patronised artistic geniuses such as Rubens, Van Dyck and Rembrandt. This atmosphere of excited liberty allowed outstanding statesmen and scientists to develop their ideas. It encouraged merchants to conceive and execute bold trading ventures. It was this tiny land, thrust into an aggressive nationhood, which now rapidly developed a breed of truly remarkable seafarers.

In the command of the sea and in the conduct of the war on the water resides the entire prosperity of the country.[1]

Thus was the strategic position analysed by the Dutch authorities in 1596. Soon they were despatching from their harbours mercantile fleets to challenge the Habsburg monopoly of the Orient trade. Rivalry in the East took on a new professionalism with the formation of mercantile companies. On 31 December 1600 Elizabeth of England granted a charter to 'the governor and company of merchants trading into the East Indies'. The United Provinces were not slow to follow suit; the

United Dutch East India Company was founded in 1602. France, Scotland, Spain, Denmark, Sweden and Austria soon emulated the pioneers. Nor were merchant vessels the only ships leaving Dutch ports. Privateers sailed forth armed with letters of marque to harass Spanish shipping – and explorers began probing new routes to the markets of the East. Between 1598 and 1623 no fewer than five circumnavigation voyages were launched from Dutch ports; as many as had sailed in the whole seventy-nine years which had elapsed since Magellan's embarkation.

Two expeditions set out in 1598. That of Sebold Van Weert failed and it was that of Oliver Van Noort which gained the accolade as the first Dutch circumnavigation. In July he left Rotterdam with four ships, the *Maurice, Concord, Hope* and *Henry Frederike*. Like earlier captains, Van Noort aimed to establish a firm commercial base for trade with the Moluccas. Although he did get home again with a cargo of cloves it was only after experiencing the same difficulties which had beset his predecessors. A year after setting out the convoy was still in the Atlantic, having been delayed by bad weather and a clash with the Portuguese. Inevitably, men and ships were beginning to feel the strain. Several of the crew had already died of fever and scurvy before Van Noort made a landfall on the southern coast of Brazil. The vegetation was sparse but what there was the sailors made good use of:

. . . we found little but herbs and two trees of sour plums, which cured the sick in fifteen days .

The Dutch were the first to make a serious study of scurvy* and its possible remedies, although it was a Spanish monk, Antonio de la Ascension who wrote the first clear description of the disease and its symptoms, in 1602:

*The name entered the language via the Danish *scorbuck* from the Old Icelandic *skyrbjügr*, meaning 'ulcerated sores'.

The first symptom they notice is a pain in the whole body which makes it so sensitive to touch . . . After this, all the body, especially from the waist down, becomes covered with purple spots larger than great mustard seeds. Then from this bad humour some strips or bands come behind the knee joints, two fingers and more wide like wales [weals] . . . These become as hard as stones, and the legs and the thighs become so straight and stiff with them that they cannot be extended or drawn up a degree more than the state in which they were when attacked . . . The sensitiveness of the bodies of these sick people is so great that . . . the best aid which can be rendered them is not even to touch the bedclothes . . . the upper and lower gums of the mouth in the inside of the mouth and outside the teeth, become swollen to such a size that neither the teeth nor the molars can be brought together. The teeth become so loose and without support that they move while moving the head . . . With this they cannot eat anything but food in liquid form or drinks, . . . they come to be so weakened in this condition that their natural vigour fails them, and they die all of a sudden, while talking.[2]

Recommended 'cures' ranged from dilute sulphuric acid and mercury to giving up smoking. But the Dutch East India captains were great believers in the efficacy of fresh fruit and vegetables. Thanks to their reports, the Company ordered gardens to be established by their factors at regular ports of call. They even experimented with miniature kitchen gardens aboard their ships but wind and wave soon put an end to such horticultural ambitions. However, the comparative success of the Dutch in warding off the worst ravages of scurvy seems to have made little impact on the policies of other maritime nations and no systematic medical research was done until the mid-eighteenth century. Thus it was almost two hundred years before it was realised that the anti-scorbutic element was most plentifully supplied by citrus fruits and certain vegetables such as onions and sauerkraut.

It was 4 November 1599 before the ships reached Cape Virgins and then the currents and violent, changeable winds prevented them entering the straits for three weeks. On his way through to the South Sea Van Noort met the remnants of Van Weert's expedition, limping home, having failed to battle their way through the straits against contrary winds. Van Noort pressed on but it took him ten weeks to reach the Pacific. Privation, the sight of their homeward bound countrymen, the loss of thirty-five of their number in a skirmish with some Patagonians, the monotonous burials of the victims of disease, and the forlorn spectacle of that barren coast had a devastating effect on morale. During the passage, the vice admiral tried to persuade Van Noort to turn back. When argument failed, he put himself at the head of all the malcontents and tried to force his superior's hand. He paid a terrible price for his unsuccessful mutiny; he was marooned on that desolate shore. Van Noort had that strain of brutality that both Drake and Magellan had possessed and which was essential to success on these early voyages.

By February 1600, when he began to work his way up the South American coast, he had already lost one of his ships and half his men. In May he picked up the trade winds and crossed the Pacific. He touched at the Marianas and the Philippines and, six months later, reached Ternate. But his difficulties were far from over. He eventually reached Amsterdam on 26 August 1601 with one ship and a very depleted company.

Thirteen years passed before the next serious attempt was made. It was planned as a privateering-cum-commercial venture in the style of Drake and Cavendish. George Spielbergen, a German in the pay of the Dutch government, left the Texel on 8 August 1614 with six ships. Two had been lost by the time he reached Patagonia but he successfully negotiated the straits and spent several months raiding along the coast of Peru and Mexico before he braved the Pacific crossing. Although he reached home on 1 July 1617 with only two vessels the profits from looting and a cargo of spices more than made up for his losses.

But the most important of these early Dutch voyages was the one which began ten months after Spielbergen's. Ironically it was an attempt by Dutchmen to escape restrictions imposed, not by Spaniards or Portuguese, but by other Dutchmen. Having broken the Hispano-Portuguese stranglehold on the Orient trade, the East India Company became just as jealously monopolistic as the merchants they had displaced. They proclaimed that the passage of Magellan's Straits and the Cape of Good Hope was open only to members of the company. Thus, when the enterprising, independent merchant Isaac Lemaire of Antwerp wanted to set forth on an Orient venture he had to think in terms of finding another route to the rich eastern markets. To lead the expedition he chose an experienced sailor who had made three voyages to the Indies, William Cornelius Schouten Van Hoorn. Together the two men organised a carefully planned venture. Isaac's son, Jacob Lemaire, travelled as supercargo with Schouten in the 360-ton *Eendracht* and Schouten's brother John commanded the support vessel *Hoore* (110 tons).

They left the Texel on 14 June 1615 and touched at the Cape Verde Islands and the coast of Sierra Leone. Interestingly, Schouten took on board 750 ripe lemons there, which he had dried and added to the regular diet of his eighty-seven crew members, as long as they lasted. In this way he avoided scurvy almost completely throughout most of the voyage. One wonders why this lesson was lost on contemporary mariners and why captains experimented over many decades with a variety of foodstuffs such as decoctions of malt and meat extracts, most of which were not as efficacious as the simple lemon. Schouten made straight for Port Desire and there put his ships in order for the next crucial stage of the voyage. For the plan was to find a way into the South Sea, *around* Tierra del Fuego. Drake had been blown far to the south and found open sea. It was possible, therefore, that South America was not joined onto some southern continent. But even if that were the case, could men and ships survive the storms, fogs and bitter cold of that ice-strewn stretch of water? Certainly, the vessels would have to be in the best possible trim before attempting this ascent to the high south latitude. But even the most care-fully-laid plans can come unstuck. While the ships were being careened at Port Desire a few moments' carelessness almost ruined the entire expedition. Some sailors, burning accretions from the *Hoore's* bottom, accidentally set fire to the ship. Despite the efforts of the entire company she was soon ablaze from stem to stern. Fortunately, most of her stores had been unloaded but her loss was, nevertheless, a severe blow.

The *Eendracht* was under way again early in January 1616 and, on the 24th in 55°50′S the lookout sighted what appeared to be a channel between Tierra del Fuego and another landmass which Schouten presumed to be the Antarctic continent (in reality it is a large island). Schouten sailed through and named the passage Lemaire (modern spelling Le Maire) Strait. The land to the south he called Staten Land, after the States General. He continued south-west in fair weather until 29 January, a historic day. For it was on that Monday that the *Eendracht* encountered 'a high, hilly land, covered over with snow, ending with a sharp point, which we called Cape Hoorn'.[3] What the Dutchmen had sighted was the Elizabethides discovered by Drake but fog prevented them discerning that they were islands. Thus Cape Hoorn was named after Schouten's home town and marked on the chart as the southern point of Tierra del Fuego. Later generations would change the spelling to 'Horn' and assume that that title derived from the appearance of the granite pinnacle – *sic transit gloria mundi*. Onward the *Eendracht* sailed, through open, easy seas, until, on 12 February, Schouten calculated that he could steer a northerly course. It was one of the most important moments in the history of circumnavigation. From then onwards the significance of Magellan's discovery would gradually dwindle. Passage through the straits could be slow and difficult. Doubling the Horn could be hazardous but, if undertaken at the right time of year, it was faster. More and more bold captains and stout ships would attempt it. Schouten realised, at least in part, how valuable his discovery was. No wonder he and his men celebrated with cheers and an extra ration of wine.

The expedition continued to be well favoured. The *Eendracht* made a good crossing of the Pacific and took on a rich cargo of spices in the Moluccas. Schouten lost only three men during the whole voyage. All went well until he reached the East India Company's factory at Bantam on the coast of Java. There, the governor, Jan Pieterzoon Coen, was outraged at the appearance of 'interlopers'. He refused to believe the 'cock and bull' story of a new route to the East, confiscated the *Eendracht* and her cargo, and sent Schouten and his men back to Europe under escort. They arrived on 7 July 1617 and became the fastest men to have circled the globe. It was not the kind of homecoming Isaac Lemaire had hoped for. It faced him with a long, but ultimately successful, legal battle for the restitution of his ship and cargo. Also Schouten brought him the sad news that among the voyage's few fatalities was his son, who had died at Mauritius.

Of the captains who followed Schouten round the Horn in the next few years the most notable was the unfortunate James l'Hermite. In 1623 he led a fleet of eleven ships bent on nothing less than the conquest of Peru. By the time he had reached the Pacific his convoy was already greatly depleted. He had to content himself with raiding Spanish coastal settlements and then making for home via the Dutch factories in the East Indies. Scurvy took a heavy toll of his crew and l'Hermite, himself, died off Java. Only one ship straggled back to the Texel in July 1626.

Now that two clear pathways had been found linking the Atlantic and the Pacific, the number of the mariners who made the round-the-world journey increased. Many of these ventures have left no records. Even if this were not so, it would be tedious to narrate every voyage. What is fascinating from this point onwards is to see what kind of men risked their lives in such a hazardous enterprise and what motivated them to do so.

Some were merchants. Some were explorers. Some were pirates. Some were adventurers. And a few do not fit neatly into any of those categories.

William Dampier was one of those colourful, enterprising characters who defy any attempt to put them into neat pigeon-holes: a naval officer who was also a buccaneer; a scientific observer with more than a hint of the charlatan about him; a man of action whose deeds fell far short of the heroic; a fine navigator but a poor captain; a companion of rogues, who enjoyed the patronage of courtiers and philosophers; and an enthralling raconteur whose writing we read with absorbed fascination, while at the same time wondering just how much we should believe. Dampier was certainly the first man to sail round the world three times and, in so doing, to undergo a variety of amazingly bizarre adventures. One of those voyages he recorded in what has become one of the classics of maritime writing and one which inspired men as diverse as Defoe, Anson, Cook and R. L. Stevenson. For all these reasons William Dampier emerges as one of the most endearing characters in the history of circumnavigation.

'I had very early inclinations to see the world.' So Dampier wrote in one of his books, which are the only, sketchy, sources of information about his early life. He was born near Yeovil in Somerset in 1652 of farming stock. By the time he was sixteen he had lost both parents, and his guardians, with the boy's willing consent, apprenticed him to a Weymouth shipowner. He was obviously a restless young man, for he soon gave up his apprenticeship and signed on aboard an East-Indiaman and, when she returned to port, he transferred to a naval man-of-war. Within the space of five years he had travelled to the chill waters of Newfoundland, the steamy heat of Java, and taken part in two naval engagements against the Dutch. Such sudden changes of direction were to mark the whole course of his life.

As abruptly as he had taken up a maritime vocation he left it. His next job was that of an assistant plantation manager in Jamaica. That was abandoned in favour of life aboard a

Caribbean coastal trader and from this he graduated to being a lumberjack at Campeche on the coast of Yucatan. This rough-and- ready way of life appealed to a strong young man and was also very lucrative. So much so that, after three years, he was able to return to England with sufficient capital to set himself up as a merchant trading to the West Indies. It is easy to imagine William, fashionably dressed and bewigged, his purse well-lined, swaggering his way into London society and turning the heads of the young ladies with exciting stories of his adventures. At any rate, he seems to have impressed a certain Judith, kinswoman of the Duchess of Grafton, for they were soon married. A runaway romance? A shotgun wedding? We do not know, for Judith remains a shadowy figure, one of the many instant patterns which came and went in the kaleidoscope that made up Dampier's life. It is probably very significant that within six months he was on his way back to Campeche.

He never got there. Disembarking in Jamaica, he devoted several months to trading and then joined a party of buccaneers. The decision is not as odd as it might, at first, seem. On Jamaica the buccaneers lived like lords – at least, they did so until unscrupulous publicans and bordello-keepers had extracted from them the profits of their latest voyage. In Port Royal, the 'sin city' of the Caribbean, there was more money per head of population than in London. Dampier saw for himself the excitement that seized the town when the cannon at Fort Charles announced the entry of a pirate ship to the harbour, the seamen spending gold as if from bottomless purses, the self-styled heroes telling tales of brave exploits to an audience of admiring catchpennies, the eccentric captains sitting on the harbour wall with barrels of rum from which draughts were offered gratis to passers-by. He saw for himself that living legend, Sir Henry Morgan, the pirate king who but eight years before had marched an army of desperadoes across the Isthmus of Darien, looted and burned Panama, been clapped in irons and sent to London, only to return with the king's commission as Lieutenant-Governor of Jamaica. Under a

lenient administration, piracy, directed largely against the
Spanish colonies, thrived. For, whatever the official policies in
London and Madrid, it was generally accepted that there was
'no peace beyond the line' (i.e. the treaty of Tordesillas
demarcation line). To a twenty-seven-year-old, eager for new
experiences, the buccaneering life seemed to offer freedom,
travel, excitement and wealth. Dampier tells us that he only
joined a band of these seaborne brigands after the crew of a
ship he was travelling in defected en *bloc*. That may or may not
be true. What *is* clear is that he scarcely gave a thought to his
wife, his domestic responsibilities or the small Dorset estate he
was in the process of buying. All were abandoned for the
opportunity of seeing new lands and being a member of the
'brotherhood'.

Years later, when he was writing the account of his wanderings, he offered no justification for a decision many would
regard as reckless and immature, beyond that simple statement
that he had 'inclinations to see the world'. Doubtless, that inner
compulsion was, for him, its own justification. He was an
obsessive voyager and a fascinated observer, and life aboard a
pirate ship offered the only opportunity for relative freedom to
travel to unknown shores. Such an overriding compulsion is far
from unique, even to-day:

> I travelled in much the same way that other people stayed
> still – it was the way of life that suited me. As for purpose
> and goals in life, I didn't have any. Purpose sounded too
> single-minded for me, too restricted by fixed ideas. I
> preferred to be flexible. Also I rejected the concept of goals
> and ambitions; they implied success or failure. I wasn't inter-
> ested in measuring myself against others or competing with
> them.[4]

Three years of the unruly democracy of the brotherhood took
him, under various leaders, on marauding raids along the
Atlantic and Pacific seaboards of Central and South America.

By the summer of 1683 he had fetched up in Virginia. Here he learned that a Creole captain by the name of Cook was projecting a privateering voyage to the South Sea and hastened to sign on with him. Cook recruited seventy men and, Dampier assures us, they all swore to keep 'some particular rules, especially of temperance and sobriety, by reason of the length of our intended voyage'.[5]

The first stop was the Cape Verde Islands, where the ship was beached for scrubbing down. The leisurely stay gave Dampier time to explore – and to write an account of what he saw. It was his keen eye and vivid powers of description that set the young traveller apart from all circumnavigators before him. He was passionately interested in what he saw and he kept a record, not just for the benefit of other mariners, but for all those who loved to hear stories of distant lands. Perhaps he resolved from the first to publish his journal as soon as he reached home again. Certainly he guarded it as his most treasured possession and when, later, he lost everything else through being wrecked or cast adrift, he always kept his precious pages with him, tightly wrapped in sailcloth. Everything of interest went into his narrative – geographical features, observations about wind and current, anthropological details and curiosities of natural history – such as the strange wading birds of the island of Sal, which congregate so closely that from a distance they look like a red brick wall:

I saw a few flamingo which is a sort of large fowl, much like a heron in shape, but bigger, and of a reddish colour. They delight to keep together in great companies, and feed in mud or ponds, or in such places where there is not much water . . . They build their nests in shallow ponds, where there is much mud, which they scrape together, making little hillocks, like small islands, appearing out of the water a foot and half high from the bottom. They make the foundation of these hillocks broad, bringing them up tapering to the top, where they leave a small hollow pit to lay their eggs in; and when they either lay their eggs or hatch them, they stand all the while, not on the hillock, but close by it with their legs on the ground and in the water, resting themselves against the hillock, and covering the hollow nests upon it with their rumps: for their legs are very long; and building thus, as they do, upon the ground, they could neither draw their legs conveniently into their nests, nor sit down upon them otherwise than by resting their whole bodies there, to the prejudice of their eggs or their young, were it not for this admirable contrivance, which they have by natural instinct. They never lay more than two eggs, and seldom fewer. The young ones cannot fly till they are almost full grown; but will run prodigiously fast; yet we have taken many of them. The flesh of both young and old is lean and black, yet very good meat, tasting neither fishy, nor any way unsavoury. Their tongues are large, having a large knob of fat at the root, which is an excellent bit: A dish of Flamingo's tongues being fit for a Prince's table.[6]

In such passages – and they are many – Dampier, the companion of cut-throats and roisterers, resembles nothing so much as a kind of globetrotting version of Gilbert White, the self-effacing parson of Selborne. He has both the fascinated involvement and the scientific detachment of the true naturalist. Seventeenth-century professional sailors were not the most reflective of men. They were coarsened by rough conditions and could do little more than live for the moment a life which might be quickly cut short by accident or disease. And buccaneers, we must assume, were among the hardest and least sensitive of all seafarers. What, one wonders, did Cook's crew make of this young member of the company who spent most of his off-duty hours scribbling, who seldom joined in their drunken sprees ashore (more than once in his journal Dampier expressed stern disapproval of intoxication) and who could become very excited at the sight of a shoal of red lobsters 'no bigger than the top of man's little finger'.[7]

In the Cape Verde Islands the pirates seized a fine Danish, 36-gun ship and in her they put to sea early in the New Year (1684). They were immediately caught in the Doldrums. Occasional thunderstorms would arise but afterwards 'the wind would shuffle around to the southward again and fall flat calm'.[8] At length the humid equatorial spell was broken and Cook set course for Magellan's Strait. But the violence of the prevailing westerlies prevented him wearing into the channel. He stood to the south with the wind on his starboard beam and quarter carrying him far from the land. For a week the ship was driven on and on into the region of bitter cold. She was in 60°S before a shift in wind direction allowed a long tack to the north-west. Then, on St Valentine's Day, the full fury of the Horn's weather fell upon her. Seventeen non-stop days of rain-soaked tempests, veering between SW and WSW, lashed her back towards the land. All this time Cook and his men had no sight of sun, moon or stars and therefore no means of fixing their longitude. Daily they expected to catch a fleeting glimpse through the spray of some too-near craggy foreland or to distinguish the ominous crash of breakers from the cacophony of wind and wave. But when the weather cleared and astronomical calculations were again possible they found that they were in the South Sea. It had been an appalling passage, especially as some of the men were too ill with scurvy to work. The only positive aspect of the experience was that twenty-three barrels of rain water had been collected.

Cook made directly for an island well known to all the buccaneers who preyed on the Pacific seaboard; a place of deep harbours, timbered hillsides and abundant sweet water; a place where they were impervious to Spanish attack because '50 men in [the anchorage] may be able to keep off 1000'.[9] This was Juan Fernandez, some three hundred miles off the coast. Its first Spanish discoverer, who had conferred his own name upon it, had tried unsuccessfully to colonise the island. All he had achieved was to make Juan Fernandez even more attractive to the enemies of his country by introducing goats, which had multiplied and flourished. Dampier had been before to this pleasant, lonely Eden destined to win itself a place in history and literature. He now expatiated lovingly upon its virtues. Its grass was 'kindly, thick and flourishing'. Its trees afforded 'large and good timber for building but none fit for masts'. The cabbage trees had 'a good head and very sweet'. Meat was to be had in abundance from goats, seals and sea lions and the fish were so plentiful 'that two men in an hour's time will take with hook and line as many as will serve 100 men'.[10]

A fortnight's rest was enough to make the crew impatient to be away up the coast in search of prizes. They were soon in luck; a convoy of three ill-armed merchant vessels fell into their clutches. But the cargo proved something of a disappointment – flour and quince marmalade! A consignment of 800,000 pieces of eight the ships were to have carried was removed at the last moment when the rumour went around that pirates were in the vicinity. Cook put prize crews aboard the merchantmen and made for the Galapagos Islands. Such uninhabited, secluded places as Galapagos, Cocos and Juan Fernandez were the natural temporary habitats of buccaneers and have become the very stuff of pirate legend. Few of them were ever 'treasure islands', where maritime thieves concealed vast fortunes of stolen gold and jewels for no very good reason. But they did serve as invaluable, secure havens where captains 'on the account' could stop for watering, revictualling and careening and where they could establish depots of surplus items that might prove useful later. So, at the Galapagos Islands Cook unloaded most of the stolen flour to act as a reserve supply if needed.

What interested Dampier about the Galapagos, as we might imagine, was the giant turtles. He devoted four pages to describing these creatures and comparing them with species he had seen in the West Indies. The great, ponderous beasts fascinated Dampier and he carefully noted many facts about them.

It is reported of these creatures that they are nine days engendering, and in the water, the male on the female's back. It is observable, that the males, while engendering, do not easily forsake their female. For I have gone and taken hold of the male, when engendering, and a very bad striker may strike them then, for the male is not shy at all. But the female, seeing a boat when they rise to blow, would make her escape, but that the male grasps her with his two fore fins and holds her fast. When they are thus coupled, it is best to strike the female first, then you are sure of the male also.[11]

It has to be said that many of Dampier's observations about turtles are concerned with culinary practicalities. These animals and their eggs were great delicacies for mariners. It is, therefore, not at all surprising that several species have become extinct since Dampier's day.

The pirates continued northwards looking for victims. In July, off the coast of Mexico, Captain Cook died. He had been ill some time, presumably of ship's fever, although Dampier gives no details. His body was carried ashore for burial and his place was taken by the quartermaster, Edward Davis, 'by consent of all the company, for it was his place by succession'. The buccaneer bands had no rules but they did have their own constitutional practices, which usually amounted to a combination of tyranny and democracy. A captain held sway by the force of his personality and by sheer brutality. If he died or failed to command majority support, his crew often split into factions, and either a successor was elected or they divided into two bands. The pirate companies were in a constant state of fragmentation and coalescence which, not infrequently, degenerated into open warfare. In this case Edward Davis had general approval but it was not long before he and his followers joined forces with another group led by Captain Swan of the *Cygnet,* out of London.

Swan seems to have been the more intelligent and resourceful of the two leaders, even though he was a reluctant pirate. He was a merchant captain who had been forced by a mutinous crew to go 'on the account' and was, so Dampier assures us, eager to find an opportunity of abandoning the criminal life. After ten months of mixed fortunes, Davis and Swan parted company again. The former remained on the South American coast, but the stocky captain of the *Cygnet* wanted to cross the Pacific. To his men he held out the lure of rich pickings from the Spanish Manila trade. It seems, however, that his real concern was to escape from pirate-infested waters, get rid of his troublemakers, resume legitimate trade and return to England as soon as possible. Dampier decided to transfer his allegiance not, he assures us, 'from any dislike to my old captain', but from a desire to see new lands. From the *Cygnet's* quarterdeck he watched his old companions sail out of the harbour while Swan fired a fifteen-gun salute in their honour.

The crew of the *Cygnet* were far from unanimous in their desire to set course across the empty Pacific, and the captain had resort to trickery to gain their agreement. He had two sets of charts: Spanish ones which showed the distance from Acapulco to Guam as between 2,300 and 2,400 leagues; and English ones which computed the same distance as less than 2,000 leagues. In fact, even the Spanish charts underestimated the distance by more than 200 leagues (about 600 miles). Swan assured his men that the English calculations were the true ones. Drake, he told them, had made the crossing in fifty days (in fact, Drake took sixty-six days) and that was over a century before, in a much inferior ship. There was, therefore, no doubt that the *Cygnet* and her consort, a tiny barque commanded by Captain Teat, could complete the voyage in forty days or less. Swan won his followers over but it was not without some misgivings that they agreed to go on short rations and set sail on 31 March 1686.

They had good winds and weather and most days were able to make well over a hundred miles (their best daily run was 216 miles, their worst 64). To the nervous Captain Swan this excellent progress was a two-edged sword: it kept the men's spirits up but it also made them discontented with their daily ration of eight spoonfuls of boiled maize. Since the crossing would soon be complete, they insisted, there was no need for such economy. On the twentieth day Swan reluctantly agreed to increase the dole to ten spoonfuls. After a month at sea, the sailors began to scour the horizon with growing anxiety. After thirty-nine days they had, by the rough computation of log and line, reached the latitude of the Ladrones (the Marianas), according to the English charts, but there was no sign of land. Food was running short and they had not been able to catch any fish to supplement their miserable maize diet. A few days more and the crew were plotting mutiny and cannibalism. When their victuals ran out they resolved to kill and eat those who had been in favour of this hazardous course, starting with Swan. The captain later jokingly pointed out to Dampier that though he, too, had been on the crew's menu, he would probably have been quite safe: he was so thin that he 'would have made them but a poor meal'.

In the midst of the captain's difficulties there came what must have been for him a welcome diversion. One of the crew was caught stealing. Lawless men often seem to have an obsession with the formalities and rituals of the law – witness the drumhead tribunals and 'people's courts' beloved of terrorist groups. Thus, this wretch had to be properly arraigned and condemned by due process of law. He was sentenced to receive three lashes from each member of the crew. There were one hundred men aboard the *Cygnet*. This was savage even by the standards of the day. Regulations in the Royal Navy limited the maximum sentence that could be handed out by a commander on his own authority. A court martial could and frequently did impose stiffer sentences but three hundred lashes seems to have been the normal limit and that was for serious crime, such as desertion. It was common practice on a man-of-war to involve the crew in the punishment of minor offenders. It was felt to be fitting that, if a man had offended against his comrades, they should have a hand in exacting retribution. The normal penalty for petty theft was running (or, more accurately, 'walking') the gauntlet. The culprit made his way between two lines of seamen, who belaboured him with knotted ropes, while two marines walked with drawn swords, one before and one behind, to prevent him running or ducking his punishment. The treatment of the thief aboard the *Cygnet*, thus, seems to have combined the most extreme elements of contemporary practice. This and the bland way in which Dampier records it shows just how brutish life was among these piratical riff-raff. Many seamen who went 'on the account' did so partly in the hope of getting rich quick and partly to escape what they regarded as the cruel, class-based tyranny prevalent on naval and even merchant vessels. What they frequently discovered was that life among the 'brotherhood' was even more violent.

Stories of keel-hauling, flogging with the 'cat' and hanging from the yardarm inevitably sicken the twenty-first century reader. Yet it is important to reflect on how difficult it must have been to maintain order on a sailing ship. The conditions were just about the worst imaginable for good discipline: a hundred or more men (most of them rough-and-ready, if not actually criminal), confined in a cramped and smelly space, with no opportunity to escape from each other for weeks on end is a state of affairs which breeds tensions. Most officers could maintain authority only by brutality and fear. That was why naval and merchant captains had extensive powers. When those powers were surrendered or made subject to common consent, as was the case on buccaneering and privateering voyages, good order – and therefore the smooth running of the ship – usually suffered.

Most modern yachtsmen who have experienced long periods at sea have stories to tell of how strains, tensions and person- ality clashes almost inevitably arise. John Ridgway, for example, during the 1977–8 Whitbread Race had difficulties on the Cape to Auckland leg:

> 'F' troop under Bob are another handicap; as the oldest watch they could have set an example, but instead they're a

divisive influence. Forty days is a long time at sea in such a small, cramped, confined space .

Tom is trying to keep communications open with Bob, Noel, Roger and J. C. There are mumblings that they will all get off at Auckland. I would be delighted if I never had to see any of them again.

[After arriving at Auckland] Noel and Roger jumped off the boat on to *ADC Accutrac* as soon as we were alongside, and hardly had their feet touched the deck than they started chain-smoking.

I can well understand how Sir Francis Drake came to execute his best friend on his voyage round the world![12]

It was on 20 May, when there were three days' provisions left in the barrels, that Swan's men sighted Guam. Swan had been lucky: the fresh ENE trades had brought his ships across the Pacific in fifty days. It was one of the best crossings made up till that time.

Dampier kept a careful log, noting the daily course, the distance travelled and latitude (calculated by astronomical observation or dead reckoning). The conclusions he drew only serve to show how inaccurate were the navigational methods available to seventeenth century mariners:

. . . the South Sea must be of a greater breadth by 25 degrees than it's commonly reckoned by hydrographers, who make it only about 100, more or less. For, since we found . . . the distance from Guam to the eastern parts of Asia, to be much the same with the common reckoning, it follows by way of necessary consequence from hence that the 25 degrees of longitude, or thereabouts, which are under-reckoned in the distance between America and the East Indies westward are over-reckoned in the breadth of Asia and Africa, the Atlantic Sea, or the America continent, or all together . . .[13]

Dampier was absolutely right in his general thesis but wrong in

his calculations. The distance from Cape Corrientes (the
Cygnet's point of departure from Mexico) to Guam was underestimated on all existing charts. It is not 100° of longitude. But
neither is it 125°, as Dampier suggested. It is, in fact, 110°18′.
Yet such an over-adjustment should not obscure the achievement of this self-taught navigator. Few contemporaries
mastered the techniques of astronomical observation and
course-plotting more thoroughly. Transoceanic navigation was
still in its infancy. A further ninety years were to pass before the
width of the Pacific was accurately calculated and then it would
take a trained astronomer to arrive at the correct figures.

Guam had a small garrison which was maintained by the
Spaniards for the benefit of their ships passing between Mexico
and the Philippines. How was Swan to persuade them to give
him supplies? His men counselled force but that did not at all
suit the captain's book. If he was to escape the clutches of the
pirates he might, at some point, need the goodwill of the
Spaniards. As it happened, fortune favoured him once again.
His ships arrived at dusk at the principal anchorage on the
south-west side of the island. Soon after dark a boat came
alongside with a friar aboard demanding that the newcomers
identify themselves. One of the pirates, who knew some
Spanish, called out in that language that they were of the same
nation, *en route* from Mexico to Manila. While this exchange
was going on some sailors slipped over the side and took
command of the boat. The priest was taken to the great cabin,
where Swan informed him that he was now a hostage. No ill
would befall him as long as the governor satisfied their reasonable demands.

Whether or not the governor was worried about the fate of
the priest, he was in no position to refuse Swan provisions. He
had a garrison of only twenty or thirty soldiers and was faced
by two shiploads of well-armed buccaneers. Such men had
never before broken through the barrier of the Pacific and their
arrival now was a considerable shock. Furthermore, any
conflict with these *other* white men would almost certainly

spark off a revolt among the islanders, who were only with difficulty kept in subjection. Thus, all the voyagers' needs were met and they passed an agreeable twelve days on Guam. Dampier spent every possible moment ashore making notes of everything he saw. Here are his observations about bread fruit:

> The bread-fruit (as we call it) grows on a large tree, as big and high as our largest apple trees. It has a spreading head full of branches, and dark leaves. The fruit grows on the boughs like apples: it is as big as a penny loaf, when wheat is at five shillings the bushel. It is of a round shape, and has a thick tough rind. When the fruit is ripe, it is yellow and soft; and the taste is sweet and pleasant. The natives of this island use it for bread: they gather it when full grown, while it is green and hard; then they bake it in an oven, which scorcheth the rind and makes it black: but they scrape off the outside black crust, and there remains a tender thin crust, and the inside is soft, tender and white, like the crumb of a penny loaf. There is neither seed nor stone in the inside, but all is of a pure substance like bread: it must be eaten new, for if it is kept above 24 hours, it becomes dry, and eats harsh and choaky; but 'tis very pleasant before it is too stale. This fruit lasts in season eight months in the year; during which time the natives eat no other sort of food of bread kind. I did never see this fruit anywhere but here. The natives told us that there is plenty of this fruit growing on the rest of the Ladrone Islands; and I never heard of it anywhere else.[14]

Swan had to weather another crisis during the stay at Guam. An argosy from Acapulco approached the harbour but was warned off by the governor, who sent a canoe out to tell the captain about the pirates. In trying to get away the Spaniard managed to wedge his vessel on the reef, where she stuck for three days before floating free. For three days, therefore, she was a helpless prey and the men of the *Cygnet,* naturally, wanted to capture her. Swan refused, determined to abandon his life of crime and not to give unnecessary offence to the Spaniards. What arguments he used Dampier does not tell us. Now that he had reached the safety of Asian waters he had become more authoritarian. A few weeks later Dampier noted that he 'had his men as much under command as if he had been in a king's ship'.[15] At Guam and, later, Mindanao he enjoyed hobnobbing with the local rulers and the gap between him and his crew steadily widened. If he could maintain control all would be well for him but if he pushed the men too far there could only be trouble ahead. He had persuaded them to cross the Pacific with promises of rich prizes. Letting the Acapulco ship slip from his clutches could only sow mistrust and anger among his followers.

On 2 June the *Cygnet* and her consort sailed for the Philippines. Swan chose the southern island of Mindanao rather than Manila because the Spaniards had given up all pretence of control and the Dutch had failed to extend their rule there. According to information gained in Guam, the people of Mindanao were warmly welcoming of any Europeans who did not come from Spain or Holland. So it proved: the Englishmen were well received and spent six months at Mindanao.

The island was divided into a number of Muslim sultanates. The one the visitors had dealings with was centred on the city of Mindanao (Davao) in the south. Dampier had plenty of opportunity to observe its social and political structure. He found it a poor community ruled over by a despot who had the power of life and death over his subjects. The sultan, a little man in his fifties, lived in an impressive palace on 180 poles, well defended with cannon, and only went among his people carried in a palanquin, surrounded by bodyguards. His need for protection was obvious, for he exploited the people mercilessly:

If the sultan understands that any man has money, if it be but twenty dollars . . . he will send to borrow so much money, pretending urgent occasions for it, and they dare not deny him. Sometimes he will send to sell one thing or another that he hath to dispose of to such whom he knows to have money, and they must buy it and give him his price. And if, afterwards, he hath occasion for the same thing, he must have it if he send for it . . . [16]

Dampier found the citizens very lazy but this, he assumed, was the result, not of inbred idleness, but of the disincentives of the system. There was little point in a man earning more than a bare subsistence if the sultan was likely to relieve him of his spare cash.

Mindanao's principal exports were tobacco, beeswax and rice and its main customers were the Dutch, who were welcomed but also viewed with suspicion. The sultan was well aware of how the foreigners had come to dominate the Spice Islands and he was determined to preserve his independence. That was why he made much of his English visitors and pressed them to stay. There were exchanges of presents, and feasts, and ceremonial visits to the *Cygnet* and colourful festivals in honour of the Englishmen. Dampier was particularly captivated by the gorgeously-arrayed dancing women whose sinuous movements were quite unlike anything he had seen before:

Their feet and legs are but little employed, except sometimes to turn round very gently. But their hands, arms, head and body are in continued motion, especially their arms which they turn and twist so strangely, that you would think them to be made without bones.[17]

Dampier was the first Englishman to describe this art form which is now more associated with Bali and other parts of Indonesia. On another occasion, he described with fascinated attention to detail the ceremonies accompanying the Muslim circumcision rite:

. . . most of the men, both in city and country being in arms before the house, begin to act as if they were engaged with an enemy, having such arms as I described. Only one acts at a time, the rest make a great ring of 200 or 300 yards round about him. He that is to exercise comes into the ring with a great shriek or two, and a horrid look; then he fetches two or three large stately strides, and falls to work. He holds his broad sword in one hand, and his lance in the other, and traverses his ground, leaping from one side of the ring to the other; and in a menacing posture and look, bids defiance to the enemy, whom his fancy frames to him; for there is nothing but air to oppose him. Then he stamps and shakes his head, and grinning with his teeth makes many rueful faces. Then he throws his lance, and nimbly snatches out his cresset [i.e. *creese,* a dagger], with which he hacks and hews the air like a madman, often shrieking. At last, being almost tired with motion, he flies to the middle of the ring, where he seems to have his enemy at his mercy, and with two or three blows cuts on the ground as if he was cutting off his enemy's head. By this time he is all of a sweat, and withdraws triumphantly out of the ring, and presently another enters with the like shrieks and gestures. Thus they continue combating their imaginary enemy all the rest of the day . . .[18]

The sultan and his leading men gave every inducement to Swan and his crew to stay. Embassies from nearby islands also came to offer the sovereignty of their sultanates to these foreigners with the big ships and powerful guns. Some of the men were very attracted by the prospect of becoming oriental princes, attended by harems of dusky Filipinos. Some of them simply deserted and disappeared into the forest. But Swan gave no clear lead.

He was rapidly letting the situation slip out of his control. Flattered by the attentions of his hosts, enjoying the sultan's lavish hospitality, he spent all his time ashore and neglected his men. The crew split into two factions; those who could afford to live in the city and were in no hurry to leave, and those who remained on board, being too poor to enjoy the delights of Mindanao and therefore anxious to resume the voyage. Friction between these groups became worse when Swan subordinated the dignity of his own company to the demands of the islanders. When a crew member was found guilty of some minor offence against one of the locals, the captain had him flogged in front of the natives. A few weeks later the pirates' second ship, the barque, was found to be so wormy as to be of no more use. How long would it be, the men grumbled, before the *Cygnet* also had to be scuttled and with her their last chance of reaching home? The final coal laid upon the smouldering fire of discontent was the discovery of Swan's journal. It was kept inside his locked cabin but when he sent a man aboard to fetch something, one of the crew slipped in and appropriated the book which contained the captain's private thoughts and plans. It was inflammatory reading. Swan's opinions of his piratical shipmates and his determination to ditch them at the earliest opportunity were read aloud to everyone on board.

Nothing could now stop a mutiny. Captain Teat took over the *Cygnet*. He sent boats ashore to round up all those who wished to sail. Swan made no attempt to regain the initiative. Instead of returning to his ship he sent threatening and cajoling messages by subordinates. On 14 January 1687, the *Cygnet* sailed away from Mindanao, leaving behind Swan and thirty-six others. The ex-captain's temper was not improved by this incident. Dampier later discovered that he had fallen out with his hosts, although he stayed at Mindanao for several months or years after most of his companions had died or left. At last he decided to take passage on a Dutch ship but, while he was being rowed out to it, his boat was intercepted by two canoes of warriors who hacked him to death.

From the time of the departure from Mindanao the piratical cruise disintegrated into factionalism and conflicting objectives. Teat was soon displaced as captain by a rival. Some of the crew wanted to set course for Europe. Others were for lingering in the Philippines until the Manila galleon set sail for Mexico laden with porcelain, silk, spices and other rich oriental wares. Dampier who, by his own account, had been opposed to deserting Swan, was increasingly disenchanted with his companions. He tells us that he asked them to return for the deposed captain and that, having failed in this, he looked for an opportunity to leave the ship. He recorded his disapproval of his colleagues' frequent drunkenness and noted, with prudish satisfaction, how some of them had been poisoned in Mindanao for making too free with the local women. Whether or not this high moral tone was for the benefit of his readers in England we cannot know. Certainly, for some eighteen months he was content to stay aboard the *Cygnet,* his justification being that 'the farther we went, the more knowledge and experience I should get, which was the main thing that I regarded'.

Those eighteen months certainly enabled him to fill his journal with a catalogue of novelties and strange events. For an aimless set of buccaneers the men of the *Cygnet* made a remarkable tour which took them across the South China Sea to Canton, into the Gulf of Siam for a brief stay on the Cambodian coast, to the Spice Islands, and, through the dangerous channels around Celebes, southwards to the shores of Australia. Everywhere the fascinated chronicler went he made notes of what he saw: a man buried alive for theft in Formosa; the brilliant cockatoos and parakeets of Pulau Butung; a waterspout off Celebes; a boy with four rows of teeth on Butung; the Australian aborigines – 'the miserablest people in the world'. Within the space of a few months Dampier encountered representatives of one of the world's oldest civilisations and also the Stone Age aboriginal culture. He bought dishes of tea from silk-robed ladies in the streets of Canton and admired exquisite Chinese lacquer work. He ate roasted locusts in Bashi (south of Formosa). He visited ancient temples. He was particularly interested in the customs of the Chinese, or, at least, he devoted several pages of his memoir to them. Europe was currently in the grip of the chinoiserie craze. Fashion decreed that furniture, wall-hangings and tableware should reflect oriental influence. East-Indiamen brought home lacquered cabinets and fine porcelain for wealthy customers. For those whose pockets were not so deep, factories at Delft, Bristol, Lambeth and other provincial centres produced passable imitations. Dampier pandered to this fascination with all things Chinese by describing in detail their dress, their junks, their manners and such curiosities as the way the women bound their daughters' feet to keep them small and dainty. Nor was he above exaggeration:

> The Chinese are very great gamesters, and they will never be tired with it, playing night and day, till they have lost all their estates. Then it is usual with them to hang themselves . . . The Spaniards, themselves, are much addicted to gaming and are very expert at it, but the Chinese are too subtle for them, being in general a very cunning people.[19]

Dampier's book, published in 1697, was the first world-spanning travelogue in English. It was so packed with incident and observation that it is not surprising that it ran to four editions in two years.

Through the catalogue of rare knowledge ran the exciting narrative of Dampier's own adventure and that adventure reached a high point on 5 May 1688. That was the day that the *Cygnet,* having coasted to the south of Sumatra, anchored off one of the Nicobar Islands to take on water. Dampier decided that this was the moment to break with the pirates. His, roughly formed, plans were to remain in the islands until he had collected a large amount of ambergris, the principal export; then to make his way to the English factory of Achin (modern Banda Atjeh), at the north-west corner of Sumatra. There he hoped to find a homeward passage, trade his precious ambergris for a large profit and return to his native land a wealthy man.

The scheme almost foundered before it had begun. The captain, at that time, John Read, agreed readily enough to set

Dampier ashore and had him rowed to the island with his bedding, his gun and the sea chest carrying his few possessions. But while Dampier was still on the beach taking stock of his surroundings, the boat returned, full of armed men to carry the castaway back to the *Cygnet* by force. The reason for Read's change of mind was the threat of further desertions. As soon as Dampier had gone, several other men had demanded to share his fate. When Dampier climbed back aboard he found a violent argument going on between the captain's faction and the would-be castaways, the most vociferous of whom was the surgeon, Mr Coppinger. Read knew that his men would not sail without a doctor and so he refused to let *anyone* leave the ship. At that, Coppinger leaped down into the boat which was still alongside, grabbed up Dampier's gun and threatened to shoot anyone who tried to stop him. But, before he could cast off, three of Read's men jumped into the boat and overpowered him. With the surgeon under lock and key, Read was now ready and anxious to rid himself of other troublesome members of the crew. He allowed Dampier to return to the island along with two Englishmen, four Malays and a Portuguese.

It was not what Dampier had wanted. As he later reflected, 'there are no people in the world so barbarous as to kill a single person that falls accidentally into their hands',[20] whereas a group of armed strangers automatically poses a potential threat. Although the people of Nicobar proved friendly, escape now became the castaways' only concern and Dampier was obliged to abandon his mercantile plans. The eight men decided to row the two hundred miles to Sumatra. They bartered an axe for one of the local canoes, loaded aboard their possessions, together with enough fruit and water for the voyage, climbed in, and pushed away from the shallows. Within yards the unstable craft, not designed for such lading, turned turtle.

The voyagers now had to spend three days drying out their belongings and doing some rethinking. Dampier was especially concerned about his precious journal and carefully exposed it, page by page, to the warmth of one of the fires lit on the beach.

Meanwhile the Malays were busy fitting outriggers to the canoe and hoisting a mast and sail. When all was ready, the voyagers made a fresh start. This time the boat proved more seaworthy and they were able to achieve steady progress towards the south-east corner of the island where they proposed to await favourable conditions for the hazardous crossing. But now, a fresh problem presented itself: they were followed by a fleet of native canoes. Dampier and his companions feared that this might mean trouble. If nothing else the locals might tell the other islanders all about them and make it hard to obtain supplies on favourable terms. To discourage their pursuers, one of the Englishmen raised his gun and fired a shot over their heads. It was a mistake. In an instant friendly curiosity turned to hostility. Word spread rapidly throughout the island and every time the mariners went ashore they had to contend with groups of spear-brandishing warriors.

However, they eventually reached the south end of Nicobar safely, replenished their provisions and, by 15 May, when the south-west monsoon began, they were ready for the perilous crossing. They had food and water for two or three days, some very rough sketch charts and a pocket compass. If they erred a few points to the north or south they would be carried into the wide western end of the Straits of Malacca or into the emptiness of the Indian Ocean. In either event, they would all be dead long before they reached land. Dampier was doing the navigating; constantly estimating the effects of wind and current. He knew he could not afford a mistake.

For the first two days there was little or no breeze to fill the sail. To make progress the little crew had to paddle continuously, taking their turns to work under the equatorial sun. The strain was intense. They were soon tired but dared not stop rowing. They were thirsty but had to ration their water strictly. At dawn on 17 May they saw land to the west-north-west. It was Nicobar, which they had left almost forty-eight muscle-tearing hours before. Their canoe, like a piece of helpless flotsam, had been carried westwards by a strong contrary current, despite all their endeavours. But the next day the perils of too little wind were replaced by the perils of too much. Soon after noon it built up to storm force, accompanied by rain, thunder and lightning. Dampier reduced sail but even under light canvas every gust thrust the canoe's bow deep into the waves and threatened to snap her outriggers. There was nothing to be done but take in the sail and let the boat run before the wind, even though this carried them too far to the north. The men were cold, wet, hungry, thirsty and exhausted. To make matters worse some of them were suffering from dysentery. Self-preservation alone kept them working. Dampier and another Englishman took turns at the helm. Everyone else was constantly baling. The canoe was remarkably buoyant and pliable. It twisted with the pressure of the waves but did not split. Yet its passengers expected every moment to see it disintegrate:

The sea was already roaring in a white foam about us; a dark night coming on, and no land in sight to shelter us, and our little ark in danger to be swallowed by every wave; and, what was worst of all, none of us thought ourselves prepared for another world. The reader may better guess than I can express, the confusion that we were all in. I had been in many imminent dangers before now, some of which I have already related, but the worst of them all was but a play-game in comparison with this. I must confess that I was in great conflicts of mind at this time. Other dangers came not upon me with such a leisurely and dreadful solemnity. A sudden skirmish or engagement, or so, was nothing when one's blood was up, and pushed forwards with eager expectations. But here I had a lingering view of approaching death, and little or no hopes of escaping it; and I must confess that my courage, which I had hitherto kept up, failed me here; and I made very sad reflections on my former life, and looked back with horror and detestation on actions which before I disliked, but now I trembled at the remembrance of. I had long before this repented me of that roving course of life, but never with such concern as now. I did also call to mind the many miraculous acts of God's providence towards me in the whole course of my life, of which kind I believe few men have met with the like. For all these I returned thanks in a peculiar manner, and thus once more desired God's assistance, and composed my mind as well as I could in the hopes of it, and as the event showed, I was not disappointed of my hopes.[21]

In fact, the storm may well have saved them. It provided them with fresh drinking water and it carried them fast in the general direction of their destination. As the wind abated Dampier adjusted the steering in the hope of bringing them back on course. On the morning of 19 May one of the Malays pointed excitedly across the starboard bow and shouted what Dampier at first thought was 'Pull away!'. In fact, what he was saying was 'Pulau We', 'We Island', one of a group of islands lying off the western end of Sumatra. He was mistaken, as became clear later in the day. What had appeared to be an isolated chunk of land in the midst of the sea was the tip of Peusangan Pasai, a mountain on the mainland. With salvation in sight it was cruel that the wind now suddenly dropped away again. The weary voyagers had to spend another thirty-six hours paddling before running their brave craft ashore at the mouth of the Peusangan river.

The local people treated their strange visitors with a mixture of kindness and reserve. They supplied all the Europeans' wants but, being Muslims, would not eat with them or keep close company with them (even their Malay fellow-travellers now separated themselves from the four white men). This meant that they had to prepare for themselves the food brought daily to their hut. Since they were now all suffering from dysentery this could only be disastrous. For twelve days they lay weak and feverish. Then their hosts took them by canoe to Achin. Here, two of Dampier's colleagues died and Dampier, himself, had almost given up hope of life. He was placed in the hands of

a Malay doctor and slowly recovered, though whether because
of or in spite of his medication is not clear. The physician
prescribed a strong purgative which:

> . . . wrought so violently that I thought it would have ended
> my days. I struggled till I had been about twenty or thirty
> times at stool. But it working so quick with me, with little
> intermission, and my strength being almost spent, I even
> threw myself down once for all and had above sixty stools in
> all before it left off working. I thought my Malayan doctor,
> whom they so much commended, would have killed me
> outright . . .[22]

Dampier's arrival at the East India Company's Achin depot
marked his return to respectability. He had, at last, turned his
back on the buccaneering life. However, he did seek out
information about his erstwhile companions during his subsequent voyaging. Gradually he was able to piece together the
story of Captain Read and his men. It was a story of continuing squabbles and desertions. Some men left the ship to take
service with the Great Mogul of India. Others, like himself,
escaped to East India Company factories. A few linked up
with various pirate bands. The *Cygnet* spent several months
cruising back and forth across the Indian Ocean but the pickings were not good, probably because the region was dominated by Arab pirates operating out of Persian Gulf ports. At
last Captain Swan's ship was scuttled in a Madagascar
harbour.

The officials at Achin asked few questions about Dampier's
previous nefarious activities. It was more important to them
that they had in their midst an experienced mariner and navigator. On a station where climate and disease took a terrible
toll of the men sent out from England that was important.
Doubtless this was why they went to such lengths to try to
nurse the new arrivals back to health. After recovering,
Dampier received several offers from captains and merchants.

Over the next couple of years he made three merchant voyages which took him as far afield as Madras in the west and the Gulf of Tonkin in the east.

In July 1690 he was appointed master gunner at Bengkulu, an English fort on the south-west coast of Sumatra. At the same time he acquired half shares in two people. These were a young man called Jeoly and his mother, and they came from an island to the south-east of Mindanao. Their story is a sad one. They had been taken prisoner in a raid by the sultan of Mindanao and subsequently sold to an English merchant named Moody. He had taken them to Madras, which was where Dampier first encountered them. Moody and his slaves travelled to Bengkulu on the same ship as Dampier and there the two men struck a deal by which Dampier acquired a stake in Jeoly and his mother. The understanding was that he would take them back to their own people, among whom Jeoly claimed to be a prince, and, using this as a means of ingratiating himself, establish trading relations with an island which (like so many unvisited eastern islands) was supposedly rich in gold and spices. But it had already occurred to Dampier that Jeoly might prove profitable in another way. It was eleven years since he had left home with his head full of money-making schemes. And he had nothing to show for those eleven years except a wealth of adventures, recorded in his journal – and Jeoly. For the young man was no ordinary Philippine islander. He was tattooed all over his body from his chest and shoulders to his ankles. Travellers in Malaysia and Indonesia were fairly familiar with the practice of tattooing but Jeoly obviously provided a remarkable example of the art and Dampier believed he could make a small fortune exhibiting in London the man he called his 'painted prince'.*

For some months Dampier lived at Bengkulu but his stay was not a happy one. He found the governor despotic and unreasonable. Then his two slaves fell ill. The picture he paints

*The word 'tattoo', which is of Tahitian origin, did not enter English until the 1770s when Captain Cook visited Polynesia.

of their life is a sad one. They had no skills or interests to occupy them in this alien environment. The woman filled her time sewing, at which she was very clumsy, while Jeoly 'busied himself in making a chest with four boards and a few nails that he begged off me. It was but an ill-shaped, odd thing, yet he was as proud of it as if it had been the rarest piece in the world'.[23] Then they went down with a fever and the mother died. Jeoly was so distraught that it seemed he had neither the strength nor the will to recover. Only ardent nursing by Dampier, for whom the young man was both a friend and an investment, restored him to health.

By the end of 1690 Dampier had had enough of Bengkulu. He asked to be released from his contract so that he could take passage on the next homeward-bound ship. The governor agreed and, early in January, Dampier conveyed Jeoly and his sea chest aboard the East-Indiaman *Defence,* commanded by a Captain Heath. But the governor then went back on his word. Several stormy interviews followed but the man proved quite intractable. Eventually the master gunner of Bengkulu was obliged to escape by night through one of his own gun ports. One of the *Defence*'s boats met him on the beach and he was hidden aboard the ship until she sailed on 25 January 1691.

They had a wretched crossing to the Cape. Contrary winds prolonged the voyage, and scurvy, thus, took its inevitable toll. Several of the crew died and the rest were too weak to work the ship whenever she was not running before the wind. At length the captain had to offer a month's extra pay to any man who would be constantly on call. This incentive dragged the last ounces of energy from those who were still on their feet and the *Defence* reached the Cape in early April. This Dutch port had now become a thriving, pleasant town and a favourite stopping place with all sailors. Moreover, now that peace was restored with Holland, English ships were very welcome there. Much had happened in Europe since Dampier had left. He had been absent for the entire reign of James II. While the traveller had been lying sick at Achin, the Glorious Revolution had gathered momentum and, eventually driven the last Stuart king from his throne. That seat was now occupied by William of Orange, who ruled with his English-born wife, Mary.

Dampier found his Dutch hosts very hospitable. Although the charges for liquor were exorbitant, other commodities were reasonably priced and the officers of the Dutch East India Company went to some lengths to entertain their guests, even to the extent of providing a pleasant garden for them to walk in:

> This garden is full of divers sorts of herbs, flowers, roots, and fruits, with curious spacious gravel walks and arbours; and is watered with a brook that descends out of the mountains: which being cut into many channels, is conveyed into all parts of the garden. The hedges which make the walks are very thick, and nine or ten foot high: they are kept exceeding neat and even by continual pruning. There are lower hedges within these again, which serve to separate the fruit trees from each other, but without shading them: and they keep each sort of fruit by themselves, as apples, pears, abundance of quinces, pomegranates, etc. These all prosper very well, and bear good fruit, especially the pomegranate. The roots and garden herbs have also their distinct places, hedged in apart by themselves; and all in such order, that it is exceeding pleasant and beautiful. There are a great number of negro-slaves brought from other parts of the world; some of which are continually weeding, pruning, trimming and looking after it. All strangers are allowed the liberty to walk there; and by the servants' leave, you may be admitted to taste of the fruit: but if you think to do it clandestinely, you may be mistaken, as I knew one was when I was in the garden, who took five or six pomegranates, and was espied by one of the slaves, and threatened to be carried before the governor: I believe it cost him some money to make his peace, for I heard no more of it.[24]

During his six-week stay Dampier travelled widely in the Cape, employing his descriptive pen for the last time. It was his first visit to the African mainland and he found much to interest him, including:

> . . . a very beautiful sort of wild ass . . . whose body is curiously striped with equal lists of white and black; the stripes coming from the ridge of his back, and ending under the belly, which is white. These stripes are two or three fingers broad, running parallel with each other and curiously intermixed, one white and one black, over from the shoulder to the rump. I saw two of the skins of these beasts, dried and preserved to be sent to Holland as a rarity. They seemed big enough to enclose the body of a beast as big as a large colt of a twelve month old.[25]

Zebras had been written of before in bestiaries, along with unicorns and griffins. Dampier was one of the first to essay a more scientific description.

The local people were equally fascinating though, in Dampier's opinion, far less attractive:

> The Hottentots do wear no covering on their heads, but deck their hair with small shells. Their garments are sheepskins wrapped about their shoulders like a mantle, with the woolly sides next their bodies. The men have beside this mantle a piece of skin like a small apron, hanging before them. The women have another skin tucked about their waists, which comes down to their knees like a petticoat; and their legs are wrapped round with sheeps-guts two or three inches thick, some up as high as to their calves, others even from their feet to their knees, which at a small distance seems to be a sort of boots. These are put on when they are green; and so they grow hard and stiff on their legs, for they never pull them off again, till they have occasion to eat them; which is when they journey from home, and have no other food; then these guts

which have been worn, it may be, six, eight, ten or twelve months, make a good banquet: this I was informed of by the Dutch. They never pull off their sheepskin garments, but to louse themselves, for by continual wearing them they are full of vermin, which obliges them often to strip and sit in the sun two or three hours together in the heat of the day, to destroy them.[26]

Captain Heath's problem was hiring enough seamen to make up his depleted crew. He hoped to obtain some from other homeward-bound vessels but they were in as dire a case as the *Defence*. Eventually, he had to resort to stealth, contracting with outward-bound men who wished to break their contracts. These would abscond, having arranged a secret, night-time rendezvous with Heath, who then sent his boat for them and concealed them aboard his ship.

The *Defence* left the Cape on 23 May in convoy with two other English ships and reached the Downs on 16 September. Dampier's plans to make a fortune as a travelling showman, like so many of his commercial enterprises, soon collapsed. He had hardly landed in London before financial necessity forced him to part with his share in the painted prince. Alas, Jeoly did not long survive to enrich his new owners. They paraded him before an amazed public in many towns and issued handbills telling his colourful – and totally spurious – life history. But at Oxford he caught smallpox and died.

But Dampier did have his journal. He spent six years, interspersed with mercantile voyages, preparing his manuscript. At last, in 1697, it was published with this impressive and intriguing title page:

A

New Voyage

ROUND THE

WORLD.

Defcribing particularly,

The *Ifthmus* of *America*, feveral Coafts
and Iflands in the *Weft Indies*, the
Ifles of *Cape Verd*, the Paffage by *Terra
del Fuego*, the *South Sea* Coafts of *Chili,
Peru*, and *Mexico*; the Ifle of *Guam* one
of the *Ladrones, Mindanao*, and other
Philippine and *Eaft-India* Iflands near
*Cambodia, China, Formofa, Luconia, Ce
lebes*, &c. *New Holland, Sumatra, Nicobar*
Ifles; the *Cape* of Good Hope, and *Santa
Hellena*.

THEIR
Soil, Rivers, Harbours, Plants, Fruits, Ani-
mals, and Inhabitants.
THEIR
Cuftoms, Religion, Government, Trade, &c.

By *William Dampier*.

Illuftrated with Particular Maps and Draughts.

LONDON,
Printed for *James Knapton*, at the *Crown* in St *Paul*'s
Church-yard. M DC XCVII.

The *New Voyage* was one of those rare books that catch the
imagination of a whole generation and win immortality for
their authors. People clamoured to buy it – captains, merchants
and would-be adventurers, as well as armchair travellers. In his
mid-forties Dampier achieved the fame and fortune he had so
long craved.

It was impossible for a man like Dampier to lead an uneventful
life. The eighteen years remaining to him were crowded with incident and controversy and included two more circumnavigations.

His fame and achievements had won him patrons and friends in high places. Thus, when he put forward proposals for a government-sponsored voyage of discovery he was taken seriously. His plans, as described in a letter to the Admiralty, were clear and detailed. He proposed to travel via the Cape to New Holland (Australia) to see if it was part of the unknown southern continent, *Terra Australis*. He would, he declared, run across the Indian Ocean from Madagascar:

> to the northernmost part of New Holland, where I would water if I had occasion, and from thence I would range towards New Guinea. There are many islands in that sea between New Holland and New Guinea . . . and it is probable that we may light on some or other that are not without spice. Should I meet with nothing on any of these islands, I would range along the main of New Guinea, to see what that afforded; and from thence I would cross over to the island Gilolo, where I may be informed of the state of those parts by the natives who speak the Malayan language. From Gilolo I would range away to the eastward of New Guinea, and so direct my course southerly, coasting by the land; and where I found a harbour or river I would land and seek about for men and other animals, vegetables, minerals, etc., and having made what discovery I could, I would return home by the way of Tierra del Fuego. [27]

What is interesting is that Dampier here proposes an cast-about circumnavigation. If he had carried his plans into effect he would have achieved something truly remarkable and changed the history of long-distance sailing. As it was, another seventy-six years were to pass before the globe was successfully circumnavigated from west to east.

The voyage Dampier *did* make was a fiasco. He set out in January 1699 in command of the twenty-one gun *Roebuck* and he *did* successfully reach Western Australia. But by then the whole enterprise had begun to fall apart for a variety of reasons. The ship was not up to a long voyage. The crew were decimated by scurvy. Some of the officers were mutinous and Dampier, who had learned his seamanship among pirates, lacked the qualities of a naval commander. The voyage ended in chaos and recriminations. The *Roebuck* turned for home and got as far as Ascension before having to be scuttled. Back in England, in 1702, Dampier faced a court martial for over-harsh discipline. He was found guilty and declared 'not a fit person to be employed as commander of any of his majesty's ships'.

The prohibition was scarcely serious, for within ten months Dampier was preparing to put to sea as captain of the privateer *St George,* having also under his command the *Cinque Ports.* Once again quarrels soon broke out between Dampier and his subordinates. Charges of drunkenness, brutality and cowardice were levelled against Dampier. Such dissensions were common on privateering/piratical voyages and, since the only account to survive is one hostile to Dampier, it is difficult to know how much truth there is in the criticisms. The voyage was a failure and *sauve qui peut* was the motive of all the officers called to account by the Admiralty on their return. What is clear is that Dampier and Captain Stradling who took over the *Cinque Ports* when her captain died off Brazil did not see eye to eye. As soon as the ships rounded the Horn they separated. The *St George* was involved in several indeterminate actions along the coast of Peru and Mexico which culminated in Dampier's failure to capture the Manila galleon. At this point, several of his men defected and made their way westward in a prize ship. Dampier and his depleted crew were obliged to abandon the *St George* and make their way across the Pacific in a captured Spanish barque. In Amboyna they were imprisoned as pirates by the Dutch and it was only in December 1707 that Dampier reached England to discover that Stradling and others had already savaged his reputation. The most interesting point about this, otherwise sordid, expedition is that Stradling fell out with his sailing master, Alexander Selkirk, and abandoned him on Juan Fernandez in September 1704.

Dampier did not have to spend long ashore. In August 1708 he sailed as pilot and sailing master in the *Duke,* a privateer under the command of Woodes Rogers, a tough but good-humoured seaman and an excellent captain. The *Duke* and her consort, appropriately named the *Duchess,* were pretty foul vessels and manned by the usual riff-raff supplied to privateers and it is to Rogers's credit that he maintained discipline throughout the voyage. A mutiny in mid-Atlantic was swiftly suppressed and the captain had the ringleader flogged by a fellow conspirator, to break 'any unlawful friendship amongst them'. He could be ruthless when necessary but he also saw that the men's wages were paid promptly and he took his officers into his confidence. Dampier's advice he found particularly valuable, since Rogers, himself, had never been into the South Sea. Rounding the Horn in January 1709, the ships ran into severe storms and were driven far to the south. By Rogers's reckoning they reached 61°53´, which was probably the highest latitude any mariners had reached in the southern hemisphere. The men suffered terribly during those weeks through being incessantly soaked to the skin and frozen by biting winds. Rogers, on Dampier's advice, decided to put in at Juan Fernandez. Approaching the principal anchorage, he was surprised to see smoke rising from a signal fire on the beach. A boat was sent ashore and brought back, much to Dampier's amazement, Alexander Selkirk. The lank-bearded, goatskin-clad creature was scarcely recognisable, especially as after four years of solitary confinement, he had almost lost the use of his native tongue. Selkirk's story was included by Woodes Rogers in his account of the voyage and this became the basis for Daniel Defoe's classic *The Life and Strange Surprising Adventures of Robinson Crusoe of York,* which was first published in 1719. A hundred and sixty years later the castaway's tale had not lost its appeal, for Robert Louis Stevenson almost certainly took Selkirk as his model for Ben Gunn, in *Treasure Island.* Yet neither Defoe's resourceful hero nor the half-crazed pirate of Stevenson's yarn come as close to the original as the desperately lonely mariner imagined by the poet William Cowper in his *Verses Supposed to be Written by Alexander Selkirk*:

I am monarch of all I survey,
    My right there is none to dispute;
From the centre all round to the sea
    I am lord of the fowl and the brute.
O solitude! where are the charms
    That sages have seen in thy face?
Better dwell in the midst of alarms
    Than reign in this horrible place.

I am out of humanity's reach
    I must finish my journey alone
Never hear the sweet music of speech;
    I start at the sound of my own.
The beasts, that roam over the plain,
    My form with indifference see;
They are so unacquainted with man,
    Their tameness is shocking to me.

Society, friendship, and love,
    Divinely bestowed upon man,
Oh, had I the wings of a dove,
    How soon would I taste you again!
My sorrows I then might assuage
    In the ways of religion and truth,
Might learn from the wisdom of age,
    And be cheered by the sallies of youth . . .

Ye winds, that have made me your sport,
    Convey to this desolate shore
Some cordial endearing report
    Of a land I shall visit no more.
My friends, do they now and then send
    A wish or a thought after me?

O tell me I yet have a friend,
  Though a friend I am never to see

Many visitors have eulogised about the remote beauty of Juan
Fernandez but to the man who had spent fifty-two months of
solitude there the island was indeed a 'horrible place'. Selkirk
was frantic to be taken off and pathetically grateful to
Dampier, who persuaded Rogers to appoint him mate aboard
the *Duke*.

A marauding trip along the Pacific coast of South and
Central America culminated in the capture of one of the Manila
galleons. Thus, when Dampier returned in October 1711 from
his third circumnavigation it was as a member of an extremely
successful voyage. The profit amounted to some £200,000.
Unfortunately Dampier was not destined to receive his share.
The wheels of the Admiralty ground slowly and though
Dampier lived for another three and a half years the distribution of the booty had not by then taken place. This extraordinary man died at his London lodgings in March 1715,
'diseased and weak of body but of sound and perfect mind', as
his will declared. It would be unwise to attempt a summary of
a life so full of contradictions. It is not only later generations
who have been hard put to it to understand William Dampier.
On 6 August 1698 a meeting took place between Samuel Pepys
and John Evelyn, the greatest diarists in the English language.
Dampier was also present, as Evelyn noted:

> I dined with Mr Pepys, where was Captain Dampier, who
> had been a famous buccaneer, had brought hither the painted
> prince Job, and printed a relation of his very strange adven-
> ture, and his observations. He was now going abroad again
> by the King's encouragement, who furnished a ship of 290
> tons. He seemed a more modest man than one would imagine
> by the relation of the crew he had assorted with.[28]

5

'ENOUGH TO DESTROY A MAN'

For many years privateers and pirates continued to be the most persistent circumnavigators. Driven by the basest human motives – greed, violence and the desire to shake themselves free of society's restraints – they scavenged the seven seas in single ships or packs and, in doing so, made themselves masters of the oceans. But it was not much of a life; certainly it lacked any of the romance with which later writers were to invest voyages 'under the skull and crossbones'. Rather did it qualify for Hobbes' definition of the existence of primitive savages:

> No arts; no letters; no society; and, which is worst of all, continual fear and danger of violent death; and the life of man, solitary, poor, nasty, brutish and short.[1]

Nothing illustrates more clearly than the list[2] opposite the varied and terrible risks that any seaman ran who signed on with a privateer. It is a catalogue prepared for the Admiralty showing the fate of 83 men out of a crew of 115 who sailed in the *Speedwell* in the years 1719–1722.

The captain of the *Speedwell* was George Shelvocke, as shifty a man as ever trod upon neat's leather. He was a naval officer of some thirty years' experience who was down on his luck when it was proposed that he might take command of the *Speedwell* in an expedition under the leadership of Captain John Clipperton in the *Success*. Naturally, he accepted but he had no intention of carrying out the instructions of the little group of idle gentlemen and money-grubbing traders promoting the enterprise. For one thing he was not prepared to take orders from a mere merchant captain like Clipperton. For another, this would probably be his last chance to provide comfortably for his old age. He had given the best years of his life to the service only to find himself, at the age of 38, retired without pay. Now he had an opportunity to get what he felt was only his due. Throughout the forthcoming cruise everything was to be subordinated to Shelvocke's personal profit.

His first move was to lose contact with the *Success*. An obliging storm when they were six days out provided the ideal opportunity. Rendezvous orders had, of course, been issued to cover just such an eventuality, but Shelvocke avoided the meeting place in the Cape Verde Islands. He seems to have carried his crew with him in this deliberate disobedience. Doubtless, he persuaded them that the pickings would be richer if they went it alone. He could also offer a more immediate incentive: the *Speedwell* carried the expedition's entire stock of wine and spirits.

A LIST OF SUCH OF MY SHIPS COMPANY AS DIED, DESERTED, OR WERE TAKEN OR KILLED BY THE ENEMY DURING THE VOYAGE, VIZ.:

April 7th 1719	Andrew Pedder	} Discharged at the Isle of
	Turner Stevens	May.
	Edmund Haveys	Died at sea.
April 17th 1719	William Parsons	
	Henry Chapman	} Deserted at St. Jago.
	Cornelius Colson	
	Christ^r. Terry	
April 19th 1719	William Symons	Died at the same place.

July 7th 1719	Henry Hudson	Discharged at St. Catharine.
August 5th 1719	William Marinier	⎫
	Laurence Blanche	
	Abraham Dittore	Deserted at the Island of
	Jno. Williams	St. Catherines on the
	William Leveret	Coast of Brazil.
	William Kitchen	
	Anthony Wood	⎭
October 1st 1719	William Campbell	Drowned at sea.
December 17th 1719	Robert Morrice	Deserted at the Island of Chloe.
December 27th 1719	Jno. Adie	Killed by an Ambuscade of
	Jno. Delly	the enemy in the Bay of
	Geo. Alderdash	Herradura.
January 3rd 1719/20	Joseph La Fontaine	Deserted at Conception.
February 25th 1719/20	Capt. Sim^n. Hatley	
	Capt. William Betagh	Deserted, and endeavouring
	Jno. Sprake	to go off the Coast of Peru
	Gilbert Hamilton	with 3 valuable prizes
	Robert Copps	they had taken in the
	Nicolas Laming	*Mercury* (a small vessel
	Mat^w. Appleton	I had fitted for cruising in
	Jno. Wilson	shore) were in the attempt
	Jno Panther	taken by the *Brilliant* one
	Christ^r. Preswick	of the enemy's men of
	Martin Hayden	war, near Cape Blanco in
	Robt. Bowman	Latt^d. 4° 00′ on the Coast
	Edward Nubely	of Peru.
	William Dobson	
	Richard Gloins	
	Thomas Barnet	
March 21st 1720	James Hopkins	
	Robert Rollings	
	Th^s. Wilkinson	Taken in our prize called
	Jno. Nicholson	the *St. David* by the
	Jno. Condie	*Brilliant* as aforesaid near
	Jno. Robjohn	Payta in lattitude 5°00′
	Samuel Obridge	S. on the Coast of Peru.
	Jno. Polton	
	Charles Weatherly	
	James Rowe	
March 24th 1720	Richard Baving	Deserted at Payta.
May 25th 1720	Jno. Hannah	Drowned when the ship was cast away on the Island of Juan Fernandez.

October 5th 1720	Jn°. Wisdom	
	Thomas Hawks	
	Jn°. Riddleclay	Could not be prevailed
	Jos^h. Manero	upon to come off the
	William Coon	Island of Juan Fernandez
	William Blew	with us after I had built
	William Giddy	the *Recovery,* nor when
	Louis Dassort	I departed from thence.
	Edward Osting	
	Jacob Boudan	
October 10th 1720	Gilb^t. Henderso	Killed in the engagement with the *Margarita.*
December 28th 1720	Rich^d. Phillips	Died at sea.
January 27th 1720/1	James Hendry	Discharged into the *Success*
	Thomas Dodd	
March 14th 1720/1	Willm. Murphy	Ditto.
April 5th 1721	Edward Brooke	
	Fred^k. Mackenzie	Taken prisoners by the
	William Taully	Governor of Sonsonnate
	Danial Hanny	on the Coast of Mexico
	Richard Bond	under a Flag of Truce.
	Edmund Phillips	
	William Sutton	
May 20th 1721	Jn°. Giles	Murdered on board a
	Jn°. Emblin	vessel called the *Holy*
	Jn°. Williams	*Sacrament* by the Spanish
	Geo. Chappel	crew.
	Robert Davenport	
	Jn°. Pearson	
	Thos. Benedict	Died between California
	Jn°. Popplestone	and China.
	William Clarke	
	Jn°. Norris	
December 1st 1721	David Griffith	Imprisoned by the Chinese at Canton.

W. G. PERRIN.

Off Brazil Shelvocke made a completely unjustifiable attack on a Portuguese merchant ship and took off money and silk. Part of the rich cloth was devoted to making an exotic suit of black and silver for the captain. His next move was to use *agents provocateurs* to stir up a 'mutiny' among the men. They were manipulated into demanding a more egalitarian share-out of loot, to be paid before the ship returned to England. Shelvocke's objective was to secure more for himself at the owners' expense, while giving the impression that he had only agreed to new arrangements under duress. Raiding along the Pacific coast of South America yielded considerable plunder and, in May 1720, Shelvocke retired to Juan Fernandez to rest his crew. While the men were camped ashore, the *Speedwell's* anchor cable parted in a storm. She was driven onto rocks and completely wrecked. The privateers were able to recover sufficient timber and canvas to build a smaller craft but most of the bullion was lost. Accident or another example of Shelvocke's greed and trickery? Anchoring the *Speedwell* in that particular spot was an uncharacteristic example of poor seamanship and an action taken against the advice of the officers. The loss of the ship had two immediate results: it deprived the owners of any share in the profits of the voyage and it enabled Shelvocke to put the expedition on a completely new footing. His crew now accepted the 'Jamaica discipline', that is they formed themselves into a sort of piratical co-operative in which all major decisions were, theoretically, taken by democratic vote. At a stroke, Shelvocke had transformed the entire operation into one in which he alone had any authority and could make the rules. It is difficult to avoid the suspicion that he had also secretly removed all easily-portable treasure from the *Speedwell* before her wreck.

Off Peru in November the brigands made good their loss by capturing a 200-ton merchantman, the *Jesu Maria,* and renamed her the *Happy Return.* They sailed on to the Isle of Coiba, off Panama, to lie low. And there Shelvocke had a nasty shock. Who should be already anchored there but John Clipperton in the *Success.* Inevitably, there was a scene. Clipperton upbraided his disobedient subordinate and demanded the immediate handover of the proceeds of his activities which were the property of the expedition's backers. Shelvocke maintained that, since the loss of the *Speedwell,* the owners had no claim upon him or his men. His adversary was in no position to press the point and the two once more – and finally – parted company.

Higher up the coast Shelvocke discovered a superior vessel, the *Sacra Familia* and boarded her. The Spanish captain drew his attention to the fact that peace had recently been signed between their respective countries. Such technicalities were of little consequence to Shelvocke. He transferred his crew and stores to the new prize and sailed on. In May 1721 he encountered his best victim of the entire expedition. From the *Concepcion de Recova* he took ample provisions and $100,000 in coin.

After a period of recuperation on the Californian coast, Shelvocke took the *Sacra Familia* across the Pacific to Canton, where he had agreed with the crew to sell the ship, cash up the voyage and distribute the spoils. Here the unscrupulous captain played his last – and perhaps meanest – trick on the men who had shared with him all the dangers of the previous two and a half years. He did a deal with the Chinese customs officials. They billed him for harbour dues of £2,166.13s.4d. The appropriate charge, which his men could not know, was about £350. Shelvocke divided the difference with his Cantonese accomplice. The *Sacra Familia* was sold for £700 and the proceeds put into the common pot. The thirty-two surviving crewmen were shown the cooked books and took what they, presumably, believed to be their fair shares (varying between £220 and £1100 per man). Shelvocke's official portion was £2,642. 10s. In fact, thanks to the various frauds he had perpetrated, he cleared at least £7,000.

With his ill-gotten gains, Shelvocke returned in a Company ship to England in July 1722. He was immediately arrested on a charge of piracy, but subsequently released for lack of evidence. But he immediately found himself back in prison awaiting trial on charges brought by the owners of the *Speedwell*. Shelvocke decided not to brazen this matter out in the courts. He escaped – probably by bribery – and fled to the Continent.

George Shelvocke did return home when the dust had settled. He even wrote his own account of his circumnavigation in an attempt to silence his critics. And when the time came, twenty years later, for him to lay his aged bones in his native earth, loving relatives raised a monument over them which proclaimed the deceased to have been 'one of the bravest and most accomplished seamen of his time'.

There is a postscript to the story of this notorious circum-navigation. It concerns an incident which happened while the *Speedwell* was rounding the Horn – an incident small in itself but destined to win immortality. The ship was driven to 61°30′S by violent winds and seemed quite unable to make any northing. The men were cold, depressed and scared. The likeli-hood of ever escaping from that desolate region seemed remote. It was a situation in which mariners' superstition easily gained control of half-crazed minds:

> . . . one would think it impossible that anything living could subsist in so rigid a climate, and indeed we all observed that we had not had the sight of one fish of any kind since we were come to the southwards of the Straits of Le Mair; nor one sea-bird excepting a disconsolate black albatross, who accompanied us for several days, hovering about us as if he had lost himself, till Hatley (my second captain) observing, in one of his melancholy fits, that this bird was always hovering near us, imagined, from his colour, that it might be some ill omen. That which, I suppose, induced him the more to encourage his superstition, was the continued series of contrary tempestuous winds, which had oppressed us ever since we had got into this sea. But be that as it would, he, after some fruitless attempts, at length shot the albatross, not doubting (perhaps) that we should have a fair wind after that . . . [3]

Seventy-six years later this would become the incident around which was constructed the most famous of all poems of the sea:

At length did cross an Albatross,
Thorough the fog it came;
As if it had been a Christian soul,
We hailed it in God's name . . .

In mist or cloud, on mast or shroud,
It perched for vespers nine;
Whiles all the night, through fog-smoke white,
Glimmered the white Moon-shine.

'God save thee, ancient Mariner!
From the fiends that plague thee thus!
Why lookst thou so?' With my cross-bow
I shot the ALBATROSS![4]

A voyage round the world could be a worse experience than even Coleridge's imagination could conceive. And this was so, not primarily because of the hazards of tempest or concealed reef (although these continued to claim countless lives) but because two problems remained to be solved – scurvy and longitude. On a diet of biscuit and salt meat sailors could not avoid suffering the effects of vitamin deficiency after about four weeks. And the calculation of westing and easting were so complex and inaccurate that a captain could not know his position in badly-charted seas. But the eighteenth century *had* dawned – the century that later historians would call the Enlightenment or the Age of Reason. The spirit of enquiry would drive men of science and men of the sea to seek and eventually find answers to these problems. Yet, many were the tragic deaths and great the suffering among mariners before ships could find their way round the world with confidence and survive long spells at sea without the inevitability of disease.

One of the many English lads who must have thrilled to read the broadsheets announcing Woodes Rogers's return in 1711 was a fourteen-year-old Staffordshire boy called George Anson.

Within weeks this 'sea-struck' young man with no family naval connections had engaged himself as a volunteer to Captain Chamberlen aboard HMS *Ruby*. Thus began a long and extremely distinguished naval career. Anson served throughout a quarter of a century of peace and war and, by 1739, had reached the rank of commodore. That was the year he was appointed to command an expedition which lifted him above the level of devoted but unremarkable officers and ensured him a place in history.

While Anson had been establishing his career relations between Britain and Spain had continued to deteriorate. The year 1711, which saw Dampier's return from his third voyage round the world, witnessed also the incorporation, in London, of the South Sea Company. It was modelled on the great overseas trading monopolies, the British and Dutch East India companies and, like them, took its stand upon the 'right' of all maritime nations to engage in trade with colonial regimes and foreign merchants in distant lands. The floaters of the new company believed that in 1711 the War of the Spanish Succession was entering its last phase and that under the peace terms the defeated nation would be obliged to concede trading privileges to the victors. This was, in fact, what happened and in 1713, in accordance with the Treaty of Utrecht, the South Sea Company achieved what European statesmen, captains and merchants had sought for over a century and a half: commercial concessions in the Spanish Americas and freedom to ply the seaways between Europe and the New World. Obsessed by the vision of sharing the fabulous mineral wealth of Peru and Mexico and the transpacific trade in oriental wares, investors stampeded to buy stock in the new venture. It became vastly oversubscribed and in 1720 the South Sea Bubble burst and many people were ruined.

One reason for the collapse was over-optimism in the commercial possibilities of the company. The concessions extracted from Spain were very limited. They did not, for example, include access to the Pacific coast colonies. Moreover, they had been obtained under duress and the government in Madrid winked at violations of the agreement. After two centuries of domination in the New World the Spaniards could not bring themselves to admit rivals to their markets. So the state of cold war continued, constantly exacerbated by acts of piracy on the one hand and high-handed officialdom on the other.

In 1739 open hostilities once more broke out between Britain and Spain. The insecure government of Robert Walpole decided that some spectacular naval victories would enhance its prestige and also bring the war to a speedy conclusion. With these ends in view the Admiralty launched a two-pronged attack on the Spanish colonies. A large fleet under Vice-Admiral Edward Vernon was despatched to the Caribbean and, in 1740, a smaller force was sent round the Horn in what was projected as an audacious raid on Manila, the centre of Spain's Orient trade. The instructions actually given to the leader of this latter expedition were vague. He was to 'annoy and distress' Spanish shipping and Pacific coast settlements. Specifically he was to seek out and capture the galleon which sailed annually from Acapulco, laden with silver to be exchanged for porcelain, silks and spices. If, in addition, he could take Manila and leave it garrisoned with British troops this would crown his endeavours. The man chosen to command the convoy was the forty-three- year-old George Anson.

Anson was a man made by the service. Subjected himself to hard discipline and rigid rules, he had become firm, strict and detached in the exercise of command. Those who fell foul of him regarded him as unfeeling, a 'cold fish', but Anson knew, like every other occupant of the quarter deck, that the only sure way to survive in the Royal Navy was to go by the book. That was certainly true of the voyage which now faced him.

He was being sent into the Great South Sea, the most daunting prospect for any captain. But the state of his ships and crews made his problems ten times worse. The navy was badly run down after several years of peace and Vice-Admiral Vernon had the pick of the best vessels and men for his Caribbean fleet. Of Anson's six ships of the line only the flagship *Centurion,* the fourth-rate *Gloucester* and the little sloop *Tryall* were of recent construction. The *Severn* (683 tons), *Pearle* (559 tons) and *Wager* (559) were old or rebuilt vessels. In addition the convoy had two merchantmen for carrying supplies, the *Anna* and the *Industry.* But Anson must have been more concerned about the men who mustered at Portsmouth during the summer of 1740 than he was about his ships. Of the 1,223 sailors under his command, half were pressed men; some unwilling conscripts from prisons and dockside taverns, others dragged from fields and workshops by rough recruiting officers with numbers to make up. If the prospect of his crews worried him, the sight of his marines, the fighting men who would have to board enemy vessels and storm coastal fortifications, might well have given him nightmares. The 529 'soldiers' consisted of a batch of untrained recruits, whose numbers were made up by Chelsea Hospital veterans forced out of retirement. All of the latter were over sixty, some were over seventy and many were infirm. Some had to be helped aboard, others were carried on stretchers. It was a farce, but the regulations stipulated a regiment of marines for the expedition and a regiment would be sent, whatever casuistry had to be employed in cobbling it together. Even when Anson, on the doctors' recommendation, sent two old men to shore hospitals as unfit for service, his order was countermanded. Within days of putting to sea the two 'fighting men' were dead. They were lucky. They were spared the rigours of a voyage which killed every one of their Chelsea colleagues, and many more besides. Of the 1,939 officers and men (excluding the two merchant crews) who embarked, 1,051 died on the voyage. A further 700 or so deserted or came home on the two ships which were forced to turn back. Those statistics have to be borne in mind in any retelling of the remarkable, brave and 'successful' voyage of the *Centurion.*

The fleet got under way on 20 September but could not

immediately set forth on its westerly course because the Admiralty, determined to extract the last ounce of duty from ships and men, had encumbered Anson's instructions with distractions. He had to escort merchant ships across the Bay of Biscay and force all foreign vessels he came across to identify themselves. Because members of the convoy were frequently being sent to chase after unidentified craft, it took five weeks to reach Madeira, the first revictualling point.

On 3 November they set out on the Atlantic crossing, having loaded as much provisions as the holds could carry. That meant that as the ships, sitting low in the water, encountered the light airs and humidity of the Doldrums their lower gun ports had to be kept closed. This turned the crews' living quarters into floating slums. Sailors and marines lived in cramped conditions anyway, their hammocks slung in the confined spaces between the cannon, but the oppressive heat and lack of ventilation, coupled with the rapid spread of disease turned the gun decks into filthy, creaking, airless hovels, where the stench was unimaginably foul. Ship's fever and dysentery seeped along the vessels from stem to stern. Men too weak to crawl to the 'heads' urinated and emptied their bowels where they lay. The only treatment the surgeons and their assistants could offer was the distribution of laxatives among the sick, which only made conditions worse. For the sufferers death must have seemed a welcome alternative to pain, delirium and the inescapable stink of vomit and excrement. Burials at sea became almost daily occurrences:

November 26th 1740 . . . Richard Pearce an invalid
    deceased . . .
November 29th 1740 . . . Amos Gordon and Edward
    Major, seamen, departed this life . . .
December 12th 1740 . . . Mr Robert Weldon our purser
    being quite worn out departed this life . . .
December 15th 1740 . . . David Redman a marine departed
    this life . . .[5]

It is, of course, true that the homes ashore from which many of the men came were dank and insanitary. But, even when due allowance has been made for that, it remains a fact that, for the lower ranks, life aboard a man-of-war was ghastly even by contemporary standards.

It was 21 December before they could make landfall at St Catherine's Island off the Brazilian coast (where the modern city of Florianopolis is situated). Here those well enough enjoyed fresh meat, fruit and vegetables, while the sick were carried ashore and housed under canvas. It was a hazardous place to stay any length of time, for, though the colony was Portuguese, there was a Spanish base only six hundred miles away on the Plate estuary. An enemy convoy, alerted by the treacherous governor of St Catherine's, did in fact set out in search of Anson's fleet and only the incompetence of its commander prevented a confrontation. The English were detained a whole month by the need for extensive repairs to their ships. The enforced rest did not help the stricken crews. The humid atmosphere sapped their energy and they were plagued with disease-carrying mosquitoes. Moreover, some men bartered the clothes off their backs for gold and silver ornaments. St Catherine's was a haven for pirates and brigands and the markets were well-stocked with stolen property at temptingly cheap prices. Parting with a jerkin or a shirt did not seem to matter much in the subtropics but warm clothing would be sorely missed when the ships were sailing within ten degrees of the Antarctic Circle.

Anson left St Catherine's on 18 January, made one more rendezvous with the fleet at desolate Port St Julian and, on 27 February, led his ships towards Cape Horn:

> . . . from this time forward we met with nothing but disasters and accidents. Never were the passions of hope and fear so much exercised; the very elements seemed combined against us. I had to endure such fatigues from the severity of the weather, and the duty which the nature and charge of the

sloop brought upon me, that really life is not worth preserving at the expense of such hardships.[6]

So wrote Philip Saumarez, recently promoted to command of the *Tryall,* on the death of her captain. Anson had missed the best weather and for over two months his weak and dwindling crews had to work the ships against storms which beat down almost relentlessly out of the west and north. Snow, hail, fog and mountainous seas beset the fleet as it steered well to the south, hoping to give the spiny edge of the continent a wide berth:

> March 11th 1741 . . . at 4 p.m. had set weather foresail, in doing which our men suffered extremely. The vessel frequently rolling them under water as they lay upon the yard, several of them were so benumbed as to be obliged to be helped in . . .
> March 19th 1741. The whole part squally with snow . . . Our people much began to grow sickly and impatient at the long run of tempestuous weather . . .
> March 23rd 1741. Blew very hard with a large, hollow sea breaking continually over us. Our masts and rigging all coated with frozen snow and ice . . .
> April 24th 1741 . . . at 5 a.m., the wind increasing, attempted to hand the main topsail but, being at the time weakly manned and the clew lines and buntlines breaking and the sheets half flown, . . . the sail soon split, and by its violent shakings endangering the head of the mast, we were obliged to cut him from the yard. At 8 brought to hand the foresails, but then at the first shake split and beat about the yard in such a manner as rendered it impracticable to go out and hand him. It soon beat to pieces. Our mainsail at the time blowing loose and the clew grommets, buntlines and leech lines breaking, were obliged to lower the yard down to secure the sail. On lowering the fore-yard down likewise, the ship falling broad off in the hollow of the seas, laboured

exceedingly, taking prodigous deep rolls and shipped a great quantity of water. At noon had no sight of the squadron .
May 13th 1741. Gales, rain and squalls on this day with a large hollow sea . . . Arthur James, Vernon Head, seamen, deceased. The latter died suddenly . . .
May 17th 1741. A continuation of stormy, surprising weather, the elements seeming all confused. In the height of the squall had several violent claps of thunder, before the explosion of which a quick, subtle fire ran along our decks which, bursting, made a report like a pistol and struck several of our men and officers, who with the violence of the blow were black and blue in several places . . .[7]

It says much for the discipline and navigational skills of the officers and senior mariners that the ships held together for much of this appalling passage. The fleet frequently had to heave to, taking advantage of temporary lulls in the weather, to help one or other of their number which had lost a mast, damaged a rudder or become disabled in some other way. In mid-April the captains of the *Severn* and the *Pearle* gave up the struggle. Having insufficient men to work their crippled ships they turned back and eventually reached England with battered vessels and skeleton crews. The rest of the fleet, eventually scattered, broke through into the Pacific still at the mercy of shrieking winds, rearing seas and racing currents. The *Wager* survived till, six hundred miles up the ragged coast of West Patagonia, she was caught on a lee shore and driven hard upon the rocks. A hundred and forty of her crew escaped the waves only to be confronted by the likelihood of starvation on a friendless beach. What followed was one of the most remarkable stories of survival in maritime history. After mutinying against their incompetent and pig-headed captain, the majority set out by boat on a three-thousand-mile journey through the Straits of Magellan and up the east coast to the mouth of the Rio Grande. Captain Cheap and his small band of supporters, including Midshipman John Byron, of whom we shall hear more, had a scarcely less adventurous escape. A hazardous rescue by Indians, who took them up the coast in flimsy canoes, was followed by their arrest by Spaniards who took them to Valparaiso. But their captors treated them well and eventually sent them back to Europe.

What makes it even more remarkable that most of Anson's ships got round the Horn was the fact that their captains had imprecise and inaccurate information. The charts compiled by early mariners – usually under appalling conditions – bore little relation to reality. It was still impossible to calculate longitude accurately and some chart markings were as much as two hundred miles out. Anson, knowing how unreliable his information was, bore well to the south so as to avoid being driven on-shore. But he was still deceived by the lie of the land – with almost fatal results:

> April 13th 1741 . . . Squally. At 1 a.m., providentially clearing up, discerned land right ahead about 2 leagues . . . This was a most unexpected sight, esteeming ourselves at that time near 200 leagues off . . . The Commander immediately made the signal to stand to the south West.[8]

While the other vessels encountered all manner of difficulties, the flagship eventually cleared the Horn. Anson made for Juan Fernandez and anchored there, hoping that the rest of his fleet would rejoin him. Between 12 June and 17 August the *Tryall*, the *Gloucester* and the *Anna* reached the island. They were in a pitiable state. The storeship was almost completely rotten below the waterline and had to be burnt. Dead bodies lay all over the decks of the sloop, 'it being impossible to conceive the stench and filthiness which men lay in or the condition that the ship was in between decks'.[9]* When the *Gloucester* appeared a boat was put out to her with provisions. She was found to be in 'a most deplorable condition, nearly two-thirds of her men being dead but very few of the rest able to perform their

*Saumarez had by this time transferred back to the *Centurion*.

duty.'[10] Rats were everywhere, feeding on the corpses and even gnawing toes and fingers from the sick. The *Gloucester's* crew was so weak that, although they had brought their ship within a couple of miles of the anchorage, they could not prevent her being carried offshore by winds and current. It took them another six days to wear back into the harbour.

The pleasant island which had succoured Alexander Selkirk for four years now restored the health and spirits of such of Anson's men as had been tough enough or lucky enough to survive thus far. Philip Saumarez was anxious to see the island which had already gained a place in the mythology of the sea:

> On the first appearance, [he recorded] strangers would naturally conclude it to be a barren inhospitable island affording a prospect of broken inaccessible mountains and rocky precipices, but on nearer approach are easily reconciled to it when surprised with the discovery of trees and verdure with which it is clothed, with several streams of water discharging themselves from below into the seas and forming agreeable cascades in their falls . . .

For the desperate crewmen the principal attraction of Juan Fernandez was fresh food:

> We found great relief from our feeding on fish which this bay is plentiful stored with in great variety. There are cod of prodigious size, cavallies, groupers, large bream, silver fishes, congers, albacores with many others, and a black fish, somewhat resembling a carp, called by our predecessors a 'chimney sweeper', with great quantities of big fish of a voracious kind which often interrupted our fishing, it being observable that no fish would approach the baits while they were near to these, and I may also add sharks of an enormous largeness which often accompanied our boats and seemed exceedingly ravenous. The craw fish was likewise found in the greatest plenty conceivable and beyond any like

I ever saw in largeness or goodness. We generally caught close to the sea side, often striking them with our boat hooks. Nor were the sea lion and seals excluded from our table. Through satiety or wantonness or depraved appetites we found them excellent food. The former bearing some affinity with beef and the latter not to be distinguished from mutton . . .[12]

Sometimes the travellers enjoyed the rare luxury of goat meat, which to their deprived palates tasted like venison. The remnants of the little herd introduced by the first Spanish colonists had bred freely and would by 1742 have covered much of the island had another species of animal not been introduced by some passing ship:

The place is covered with dogs of an enormous size resembling . . . grey hounds. These with the advantage of level surface have effectually destroyed the goats on this side, whose refuge consists of steep rocks and precipices, and probably in time will destroy them on the other, the dogs likewise having contracted an agility and swiftness almost equal to the goats.[13]

Foraging parties found it difficult to track down and shoot the nimble goats and Saumarez calculated that there were only about a hundred and fifty left.

The most important element in the diet, however, was not fish or flesh, but vegetables. As we have seen, mariners had long since observed that fresh-grown produce was one remedy for scurvy. In 1734 the Dutch writer, John Backstrom, went so far as to suggest that vegetable deficiency was the *only* cause of this appalling disease. Anyone who had made a long sea voyage could not have failed to notice the near-miraculous recovery sick men made as soon as their diet could be properly regulated. This makes it all the more astonishing that naval authorities did so little to promote dietary regulations on board their ships.

Throughout the eighteenth century when British naval vessels were committed for the first time to frequent long voyages, more men died of scurvy than were killed in action. Yet old-fashioned ideas, such as the belief that citrus fruit caused enteritis and fever, persisted. Anson, for all the suffering of his men, made no attempt at a landfall on the Patagonian coast in search of more fresh produce. Some of his officers even seemed to share a quarter-deck conviction that scurvy was essentially a disciplinary problem, an opinion challenged by one member of the expedition:

I shall endeavour to remove a very great prejudice from which persons who labour under this affliction have most unjustly suffered which is that none but the indolent are ever sick of this disease. This mistaken opinion has caused many poor sufferers to endure more from their commanding officers than from the distemper itself; being drubbed to do their duty, when incapable of it. Our experience has abundantly testified that the most active, stirring persons are oftenest seized with this disease; and the continuation of their labour only helps to kill them the sooner.[14]

It was, undoubtedly, the natural vegetation on Juan Fernandez which saved Anson's expedition from total disaster.

As to what regards the refreshments it seems providentially calculated for the relief of distressed adventurers who find such vegetables as are particularly adapted for curing the distempers contracted on long voyages and bad diets, especially those of the scorbutic kind; it abounding in great quantities of water and wood cresses, excellent wild sorrell, a great profusion of turnips, the tops of which we generally preferred to the roots, with great quantities of clover and oats . . .[15]

The emaciated sailors began to put on weight. Aching limbs

and limp muscles regained their strength. Soon the men were working eagerly recaulking their vessels and making good damaged spars and torn sails.

It was not just the appalling sufferings of the previous two years which made Juan Fernandez appear so delectable. Anson's men were neither the first nor the last to be captivated by its wooded valleys, open grassland and varied foliage. Even in the southern winter the island, lying close to the thirty-third parallel enjoys a mild climate. Dampier had estimated that it would easily support four or five hundred families and another visitor a hundred and fifty years later would eulogise, 'Blessed island of Juan Fernandez! Why Alexander Selkirk ever left you was more than I could make out.'[16]

The commodore noted its qualities and, on his return, urged the government to set up a British settlement and garrison there. In view of the problems which have beset the Falkland Islands perhaps it is as well that no one in London took up his suggestion.

With three ships at least partially serviceable and a body of men who, though greatly reduced in number (the *Centurion* alone had lost 280 men out of a total complement of 531) were for the most part restored to health and vigour, Anson now embarked on what was the strategic objective of the voyage: marauding Spanish settlements and shipping. The Admiralty's plan had been to clamp the Isthmus of Panama between the two jaws of a naval vice but Anson soon discovered, to his immense chagrin, that the plan had failed. Vernon's well-equipped Caribbean fleet was supposed to have established a strong British presence on the Atlantic coast of Darien and opened up a corridor across the Isthmus along which men and supplies could be sent for activities in the South Sea. Anson now learned from Spanish captives that the whole operation had been bungled (thanks to incompetent leadership of the land forces, as we now know) and that the British army, more than halved by fever, had given up and gone home over a year before. Anson's three ships were, thus, all alone and the commodore was faced with the prospect which had confronted Drake over a century and a half before: he had to inflict as much damage on the Spanish empire as possible and then return home, either by going back or by going on.

Another similarity between Anson and El Draco was the terror both men inspired along the Pacific seaboard. Anyone who successfully braved the terrors of the Horn had to be in league with the devil. How could mere men survive against those who had spat in the face of death? Wildly exaggerated tales of the Englishmen's exploits flew before them along the coast of Chile and Peru. Merchant vessels yielded almost without a struggle. The Chilean town of Payta put up no resistance and, over three days, was systematically and unhurriedly looted. By the time Anson's convoy reached the Mexican coast it consisted of five vessels of which three were Spanish prizes (the *Tryall* had by now been scuttled). All were laden with food, wine, livestock, naval supplies and an assortment of merchandise, including a large amount of bullion. But the best was yet to come.

Anson hoped to emulate his illustrious predecessor in yet another way; by capturing a treasure galleon off the Mexican coast. It was not to be. The vessel he stalked, outward bound for Manila, took refuge in Acapulco harbour and stayed there till the sailing season was so well advanced that Anson had to make haste and embark on the Pacific crossing. It was Hobson's choice. His ships were in no fit state to face Cape Horn again. Furthermore, his orders were to go on and invest Manila. Anson knew that with his depleted force he could achieve little in the Philippines but he also knew what happened to commanders who wilfully deviated from their instructions. He had no intention of ending up, like other 'failed' captains, removed from the active list and whiling his time away ashore on half pay or no pay. So he now put his vessels into the best possible trim for the westward voyage.

He made for Chequeton, further up the coast because Dampier had reported, 'A mile and a half from the shore there is a small key and within it a very good harbour where ships may careen. There is also a small river of fresh water and wood enough.'[17] For the last time before embarking on the empty Pacific the men availed themselves of fresh meat (mainly from birds shot in woodland close to the shore) and limes and other antiscorbutic fruits. They filled the water butts and carried out all possible repairs. Ropes, sails, spars and tackle were brought from the prize ships to the *Centurion* and *Gloucester* for Anson decided to scuttle the Spanish vessels and take from them whatever was usable for his men-of-war. The decision was not well received by his officers. Cutting down the fleet deprived some of them of command and that, in turn, deprived them of major shares of prize money. In fact, the commodore had no alternative. The total complement was now so depleted that he had scarcely enough men left to man two ships, let alone five.

Seven thousand miles lay between the voyagers and the Marianas when they set sail on 6 May 1742. It was a frightening prospect. One traveller had described the Pacific crossing as 'enough to destroy a man or make him unfit for anything as long as he lives'.[18] With favourable winds and good weather they could have made the crossing in seven or eight weeks. In fact, they were at sea for 114 days. Once again it was ignorance which was their worst enemy. Anson had calculated on picking up the NE trade winds. What he did not know was that the anticyclonic pattern producing these winds moves with the seasons. In the northern summer it shifts to the north, leaving the equatorial region in the grip of the doldrums. The *Centurion* and the *Gloucester* made course virtually due west in about 13°N. and soon ran into the depressing region of light airs, sultry heat and occasional thunderstorms. Within a month scurvy and fever had returned and the log once more became a mournful catalogue of deaths. By July it was only just possible to maintain the routine running of the ship. No one had the energy to cope with emergencies. Thus, when the *Gloucester's* rotten foremast splintered she had to be taken in tow. And when the top of the *Centurion's* mainmast snapped, it was left hanging in a tangle of ropes and broken wood.

On 14 August Saumarez recorded:

> . . . ½ past noon the *Gloucester* came under our stern, when Captain Mitchell acquainted the Commodore that his ship had sprung a leak and had then seven foot of water in her hold, his men with incessant pumping being all fatigued, as were likewise the officers and no longer able to hold out, having had 9½ feet of water within her; all the full water casks were entirely covered and the people had no water to drink. The ship rolled and laboured and was under no command of the helm . . .[19]

The 866-ton, 50-gun ship was only five years old but sun, wind and wave had prematurely aged her. She was literally falling apart. The next two days were spent ferrying her crew and stores to the flagship. Saumarez recorded that when a boatload of forty-six sick men arrived at the *Centurion,* three died while trying to drag themselves aboard. Then fires were laid on the *Gloucester,* and Anson's ship drew away to a safe distance while her men watched the warship's end. She burned for several hours before the flames reached her magazine and blew her to pieces. The silent sailors could only regard the warship's end as an omen. Half a world away from home, one ship left out of the eight which had left Portsmouth, nearly all their comrades dead: it could only be a matter of time before they, too, were in Davy Jones's locker. No wonder Saumarez described the spectacle as, 'as melancholy a scene as ever I observed since I have been in the navy'.[20] Then, her decks littered with casks and lumber hastily brought from the *Gloucester,* and dead and dying men who fouled the running lines, *Centurion* hoisted sail and lumbered westwards.

Ten days later she anchored off Tinian in the Marianas with only seventy- one men still fit for duty. Although this area was frequently patrolled by Spanish warships, the voyagers were obliged to spend another seven weeks reviving the sick and patching up their leaky vessel. But at last Anson had every reason to hope that the worst was now behind him. If he could make the Portuguese trading post of Macao on the China coast he doubted not that he could see his ship properly repaired in a well-equipped dockyard, buy all the provisions he needed and, through the good offices of the resident British agent, hire men to bring his depleted crew up to strength. Everyone aboard the *Centurion* was excited at the prospect of meeting some of their fellow countrymen for the first time in over three years, looked forward to hearing news of home, and expected to receive a warm welcome in Macao.

The reception they received when they dropped anchor in the Canton river in mid-November, therefore, came as a shock. The arrival of a British warship filled the commercial and diplomatic community with alarm. Chinese officials, the Portuguese governor and East India Company factors were united in their urgent desire to be rid of the *Centurion* as quickly as possible. They flatly refused Anson's request for stores, repairs and men and brought every pressure to bear to persuade him to depart. The commodore was dismayed and angry. Only slowly did he come to appreciate the reasons why his arrival had caused such alarm. Peaceful trade at Macao was enormously profitable to all concerned but it depended upon a very delicate balance of interests. China was still a closed country. She tolerated the western trading community as long as it gave no trouble. The appearance of a British warship, even one in an obviously distressed state, meant trouble. If Anson's requests were granted there was little doubt that the *Centurion* would soon be looking for Spanish prizes. The residents at Macao were horrified at the prospect of naval engagements in Chinese waters. It took weeks of argument, bribery and threats for Anson to get what he wanted. At last he succeeded, through frightened interpreters, in making his reluctant hosts realise that they would not be rid of him until he had a seaworthy, well-provisioned, properly-manned ship under his command.

In mid-January a hundred Chinese workmen came aboard and, at long last, the *Centurion* had the complete overhaul she so desperately needed. She was beached for careening. Rotten planks were replaced. She was completely recaulked and resheathed. New masts, spars, rigging and sails had to be made. The boats needed to be repaired. Anchors, chain and cable lost during storms had to be replaced. Anson made sure that the refit was thorough. He left nothing to chance. The work took two months, during which the *Centurion*'s crew, cargo, cannon and movables were lodged in huts specially constructed nearby. When she was ready the commodore had her fully provisioned. But in one respect he failed: he could not obtain the men he needed. The East India Company captains refused to part with any of their sailors and strenuous recruiting ashore resulted only in a motley bunch of twenty-three Indians, Dutchmen and Lascars. These brought the *Centurion's* strength up to 237 officers and men. She should have carried a complement of 400.

By the beginning of April the nervous authorities were growing very impatient:

April 3rd 1743 . . . Two Mandarin's boats anchored here from Macao, being very urgent with us to go away and refusing to assist us with any more necessaries or refreshments, forbidding all the Chinese from coming on board or even selling us anything in the market . . .[21]

But Anson had his reasons for waiting and it was another eight days before the *Centurion* weighed anchor. She was a 'new' ship and her crew was in better spirits than they had been at any time since leaving England. They were now on the way home and there actually seemed to be some prospect of reaching their journey's end. Only when they were safely at sea did Anson assemble the crew and tell them that they were not going home – not immediately. They had some unfinished business to attend to: the little matter of the Manila galleon.

Having failed to take her at Acapulco, they would lie in wait for her off the Philippines. This was the plan that had been forming in the commander's mind as he put his ship into the best possible trim at Macao. He knew the route the annual treasure ship took through the Philippine channels to reach Manila. He knew she usually arrived around mid-June. He therefore had an excellent chance of intercepting her.

The *Centurion* sailed south-eastwards and gunnery practice became a part of every day's routine. By 20 May she had taken up station in the straits to the south of Luzon. Now all she had to do was wait. Exactly one calendar month later the lookout reported a sail coming up from the south-east. It was the *Nuestra Señora de Cobadonga,* the unescorted galleon from Mexico, carrying a treasure in bullion, plate and specie worth (as was later revealed) over £50,000,000 in modern terms. The two vessels sighted each other at dawn and closed steadily. The Spanish captain knew the identity of the approaching ship; he had been warned that the *Centurion* was skulking in Philippine waters. But not for a moment did he seek to evade the conflict. He had at his command 530 men and a 60-gun armament. His latest intelligence about Anson's ship was that she was in poor condition and manned by a dwindling, dying crew. He, therefore, felt more than able to look after himself. Certainly, the *Cobadonga* should have been more than a match for her adversary. What made the difference was that aboard the *Centurion* every man was possessed of a determination, fine-honed by suffering. Before the crew was a prize that would make them all rich. To find her they had come through every manner of earthly hell. Nothing would induce them to let her escape.

The two ships came broadside on and began to pound each other with cannon fire. The *Centurion's* guns were loaded with grapeshot and men stationed in the yards kept up a steady fusillade with small arms. The objective was to shred sails and rigging and drive men from the *Cobadonga's* decks without causing serious damage. This quickly demoralised the Spaniards. Saumarez 'could observe the officers running about confusedly as if they were preventing the desertion of their men from their quarters, which accordingly proved so'.[22] In a couple of hours it was all over. The Spanish captain struck his colours and was soon a prisoner aboard the *Centurion*. He had lost about fifty men and a further 170 were wounded. British casualties were three dead and sixteen wounded.

Philip Saumarez was put in charge of the prize and much of his time over the next few hours was devoted to clearing up the debris of battle, repairing damage, burying the dead, making provision for the wounded, shipping prisoners across to the *Centurion* and getting the *Cobadonga* under way. But he was able to start inventorying the cargo. What he discovered must have taken his breath away, though he recorded it laconically enough:

> at 6 p.m. sent a launch away [to the *Centurion*] loaded, having to the value of 55,000 pounds sterling on board her in chests of silver . . . From our first beginning to ship off to this instant esteem by a general calculation that I have sent on board 1,300,000 dollars, besides some wrought plate . . .[23]

But that was not all. Over the ensuing days the prize captain continued to find caches of treasure. As well as the chests packed with new-minted coin and other consignments catalogued in the *Cobadonga's* bill of lading, there were, as usual, scores of concealed private caches of gold and silver. Money was hidden beneath cabin floors, in the false bottoms of passengers' trunks, and even in the middle of a cheese.

The two vessels made their way back to Macao. Anson knew that his reception there would be unfriendly but there was nowhere else that the battle damage could be made good. Here the *Cobadonga* was sold, being unequal to the long haul back to Europe. From the point of view of circumnavigation there is little else worth recording about the voyage of the *Centurion*. On 15 December she made sail for England. She took the shortest route to the Cape, following a course which was now well-charted, sailed with the SE trades across the southern Atlantic, and picked up the prevailing westerlies of the northern hemisphere to reach Spithead on 15 June 1744. Stories of her exploits had gone before her so that Anson and his men were welcomed as heroes. Crowds turned out to gaze in wonder at the thirty-two well-guarded cartloads of treasure which lumbered along the main road from Portsmouth to London. Amidst the public celebrations many were the lusty perform-ances of the most popular song of the day – *Rule Britannia*. Thomas Arne had written it only weeks before Anson's expedi-tion set out and the *Centurion*'s triumphant return seemed to confirm – to patriotic landsmen, at least – that Britons really did rule the waves. In course of time every survivor received his share of prize money, divided according to rank. For all of them it was more wealth than they had ever seen before. Whether they felt it adequate compensation for five years of living with death and terror we cannot know.

In the story of circumnavigation the voyage of the *Centurion* marks the end of an era. It was the last of the great buccaneering expeditions whose objectives were plunder and the raiding of enemy bases. In that regard it was by far the most successful of such ventures. No commander ever returned to port with such a vast treasure as that which Anson delivered to a grateful British government. But no commander ever returned from a circumnavigation voyage having lost so many men. Of the 1,939 who set sail under his leadership, fewer than 500 survived. The vast majority were victims of scurvy. The tale of the *Centurion* and her sister ships had a moral: if the Great South Sea was ever to be conquered some means would have to be found of enabling mariners to survive more than four weeks away from land without falling victim to debilitating disease.

6

CONQUERING THE GREAT SOUTH SEA

Among those who read the published accounts of the *Centurion's* voyage was Dr James Lind, a naval surgeon. During several voyages he had had plenty of opportunity to observe and to try to treat cases of scurvy but it was the appalling loss of life during Anson's expedition that drove him to make a serious study of the disease. Between 1748 and 1754, when he was living in Edinburgh, he gathered information from mariners and other doctors and experimented with various possible remedies. The result was *A Treatise on the Scurvy* which was dedicated to Anson and published in 1754. It was soon reissued, was translated into French and aroused great interest in the international maritime community. Lind followed it three years later with *An Essay on the most effectual means of Preserving the Health of Seamen in the Royal Navy,* which contained observations on the prevention and treatment of scurvy, typhus and malaria as well as pioneering ideas on hygiene and disinfectants. Lind's work sets him firmly in the top rank of eighteenth century medical researchers and it is little short of a tragedy that the Admiralty did not adopt his recommendations until 1795, the year after his death.

This, however, did not prevent individual captains and ships' surgeons from trying the new methods. Lind knew nothing about vitamin C deficiency but he did realise that scurvy was the result of poor diet and he deduced that it could be avoided by ensuring that seamen were plentifully supplied with citrus fruit, onions, vegetables or lemon juice. As his ideas filtered through to naval commanders of various nations the incidence of scurvy fell dramatically and other shipboard diseases were brought under greater control.

It was as well that this was so, for, at about the same time, the governments in London and Paris became obsessed with sending naval vessels on long voyages of discovery to the Great South Sea. This was the age of the Enlightenment, when scientists, philosophers and political thinkers threw off old religious and philosophical restraints, sought knowledge for its own sake and worked for the perfection of human society. It would be pleasant to believe that the various captains now sent to explore the uncharted regions of the Pacific were despatched in the pure quest for truth The motives of politicians are seldom so unalloyed:

> We have reason to believe the French to be in a fair way of getting . . . spices in their plantations, as Mr de Poivre has actually planted at Isle de France some hundreds of clove and nutmeg-trees.* Every true patriot will join in the wish, that our English East India Company, prompted by a noble zeal for the improvement of natural history, and every other useful branch of knowledge, might send a set of men properly acquainted with mathematics, natural history, physic, and other branches of literature, to their vast possessions in the Indies, and every other place where their navigations extend, and enable them to collect all kinds of useful and curious informations; to gather fossils, plants, seeds, and animals, peculiar to these regions; to observe the manners, customs, learning, and religion of the various nations of the

*Cf. below, p.194.

East; to describe their agriculture, manufactures, and commerce; to purchase Hebrew, Persian, Braminic manuscripts, and such as are written in the various characters, dialects, and languages of the different nations; to make observations on the climate and constitution of the various countries; the heat and moisture of the air, the salubrity and noxiousness of the place, the remedies usual in the diseases of hot countries, and various other subjects. A plan of this nature, once set on foot in a judicious manner, would not only do honour to the East India Company, but it must at the same time become a means of discovering many new and useful branches of trade and commerce; and there is likewise the highest probability, that some unsearched island, with which the Eastern Seas abound, might produce the various spices, which would greatly add to the rich returns of the Indian cargoes, and amply repay the expenses caused by such an expedition.[1]

Those words were written by a Polish scientist and traveller who had made England his adopted country. John Reinhold Forster was a scholar of natural history and, in the same year that he wrote these words (1772), he embarked as naturalist on Captain Cook's second great circumnavigation. To this we shall return. What interests us immediately is the light Forster sheds on the motivation for promoting voyages of discovery. Scientific enquiry might be the declared objective of some of these endeavours, but national prestige and commercial advantage were seldom absent from the minds of their promoters.

The Spanish and Dutch explorations in the South Seas had kept alive interest in the possible existence of a vast continent somewhere to the west of America and to the south of China. Around the middle of the eighteenth century several writers made detailed studies of the existing accounts of Pacific voyages and put forward their own conclusions. Dr John Campbell, a prodigiously industrious Scottish author, published his monumental *Navigantium atque Itinerantium Bibliotheca* in 1744 and such was the demand for it that it was reissued in parts. Campbell, who was something of a tub-thumper, urged British captains to take up the challenge of discovery before their foreign rivals did so and thereby increase the size and competence of the navy, establish valuable new colonies and enhance national prestige. Charles de Brosses, whose *Histoires des navigations aux terres australes* appeared in 1756, had a more scientific interest. He was the first to suggest that the island chains comprising Polynesia were quite distinct from the southern continent and its offshore islands. He, too, urged persistence in the quest for *terra australis,* though he, naturally, wanted it to be discovered and settled by the French. De Brosses was the first to suggest that any newly-discovered distant territory would be the ideal place to send the unfortunates of European society such as the poor, orphans and – criminals. These and other works had a wide circulation and frequently ran to new editions and foreign translations. Most of the writers were armchair geographers. Not so Alexander Dalrymple.

Dalrymple joined the East India Company in 1752 at the age of fifteen. He served at Madras and made two voyages to China and the East Indies. These experiences and his wide reading of ancient travels stirred in him a passion for the extension of British commerce and colonisation. He returned to England in 1764 to urge the directors of the Company to commit men and ships to Pacific exploration. Not content with private persuasion, he carried his ardent campaigning to a wider public with *An account of Discoveries Made in the South Pacific Ocean Previous to 1764* (1767) and followed this up three years later with *A Historical Collection of Voyages . . . in the South Pacific Ocean.* He 'proved' the existence of a southern continent, vast and populous which had:

> a greater extent than the whole civilised part of Asia, from Turkey, to the eastern extremity of China. There is at present no trade from Europe thither, though the scraps from this table would be sufficient to maintain the power, dominion

and sovereignty of Britain, by employing all its manufactures and ships.[2]

All that was needful, in Dalrymple's view, was for brave captains of the stamp of Magellan to come forth, men spurred on, not by material considerations, but by passionate curiosity and the spirit of adventure.

Scientists, philosophers and zealous patriots might campaign for new expeditions to be sent forth but if they expected the mercantile companies to finance such enterprises, they were baying for the moon. Even the prospects of the legendary isles of gold, the Solomons, and trade with a whole new continent could not induce the wealthy burghers of London, Paris or Amsterdam to put their hands in their purses. Their ships and men were sufficiently occupied in lucrative trade with the known parts of the Orient; they had no need to engage in speculative ventures to find new markets. So it was left to government-sponsored naval expeditions to solve the riddles still posed by the Great South Sea.

If we ask why politicians should be any more anxious than merchants to squander money, men and ships on Pacific exploration, the answer lies largely in national prestige and maritime supremacy. Throughout much of the century Britain and France were in a sporadic state of either cold or hot war. Clashes occurred both in Europe and the colonies. Both nations had extensive overseas commercial interests. It was, therefore, important to make occasional demonstrations of nautical prowess. Moreover, since neither side was prepared to scale down its navy, work had to be found for captains and crews when there were no war manoeuvres to execute. Whatever the problematic mercantile advantages to be derived from opening up new territories, there were usually more quantifiable nautical and navigational spin-offs from long voyages: charts became more accurate; officers more skilled, new instruments could be tested; new islands and harbours might be discovered where ships could take on water and fresh food. The stage was thus set for new feats of endurance and the transportation of European rivalries to distant parts of the globe.

The main strategic prize which still attracted imperialistically-minded officials in London and Paris was control over the western access to the Pacific. It was to achieve this that they revived their interest in the seas and islands of the southern Atlantic and also the old quest for a north-west passage. It was these objectives which gave the impetus to a flurry of momentous voyages in the 1760s and 1770s, voyages which provided fresh fuel for Anglo-French rivalry and sometimes brought the two nations close to war.

The first location of that rivalry was a troublesome group of islands in the far South Atlantic known to the French as the Maloumes, to the Spaniards as the Malvinas and to the British as the Falklands. The uninhabited isles had first appeared on European charts in 1592, when John Davis discovered them. But it was not until the second half of the eighteenth century that their potential importance was appreciated. When the French and British governments determined to have their respective flags carried all over the broad Pacific they realised that that task would be made much easier by the existence of a staging post where ships and men could be fully prepared for the storms of the Horn or the Straits. The Falklands possessed in abundance what the hostile Patagonian coast conspicuously lacked: safe anchorages, anti-scorbutic plants, fresh water, fish and the meat of seals, sea-lions and birds.

In 1763 a thirty-four-year-old French soldier proposed to his government the founding of a settlement in the Falklands. Since Louis Antoine de Bougainville offered to furnish this at his own expense, the ministers in Paris eagerly supported the scheme.

To the urbanity and dash of a French aristocrat and officer Bougainville added a genuine passion for scientific discovery. Not only had he served with distinction in Canada during the Seven Years War, principally as ADC to General Montcalm, but he was also a fellow of the Royal Society. He had taken up a naval career in 1756 and the change of direction seems to have been largely inspired by de Brosses, whose writings Bougainville greatly admired. Since the French had been ousted from Canada and India they must seek new lands whereon to plant the Bourbon *fleur de lys,* and in the search they would make discoveries about untravelled oceans and the flora and fauna of distant lands which would add lustre to the reputation of French philosophy and science. Bougainville wanted to be in the forefront of this new enterprise. As soon as he received permission for his settlement, he set about recruiting colonists and accumulating grain, cattle and other necessaries. On the following 5 April, having established and provisioned his little settlement on East Falkland, he claimed the islands in the name of the French crown and returned to Europe for fresh provisions.

All this activity had not been lost on France's rivals. Early in 1764, the Admiralty commissioned two ships, the *Dolphin* and the *Tamar*, ostensibly for a voyage to the East Indies by way of the Cape. But the expedition's commander received secret instructions of a very different nature.

They represented the conviction, urged since the 1740s by George Anson and now enthusiastically taken up by the Earl of Egmont, First Lord of the Admiralty, that the Falklands provided the key to the Pacific. In a long, chauvinistic preamble the instructions laid claim on extremely tenuous grounds to various, for the most part unspecified, distant territories and affirmed the desirability of adding newly-discovered land to the British Empire:

Whereas nothing can redound more to the honour of this nation as a maritime power, to the dignity of the Crown of Great Britain, and to the advancement of the trade and navigation thereof, than to make discoveries of countries hitherto unknown, and to attain a perfect knowledge of the distant parts of the British Empire, which though formerly discovered by his majesty's subjects have been as yet but imperfectly explored; and whereas there is reason to believe that lands and islands of great extent hitherto unvisited by any European power may be found in the Atlantic Ocean between the Cape of Good Hope and the Magellan Strait, within latitudes convenient for navigation, . . .[3]

The leader was instructed to claim the Falklands formally for Britain, seek out any other promising islands in the southern Atlantic, explore New Albion, on the west coast of North America, renew Francis Drake's claim thereto and travel into the North Pacific in seach of the Straits of Anian. If he found no prospect of return via a north-west passage, he was to make for home via the Dutch East Indies or China and the Cape of Good Hope. The vessels made available by the Admiralty for this extended voyage were two well-fitted frigates. The *Dolphin,* in particular, was protected against the ravages of worm by having her hull sheathed in copper plates.*

The man appointed to lead this expedition was none other than the Honourable John Byron, erstwhile midshipman of the *Wager* who, if his own account is to be believed, had experienced an amazing number of exciting and amorous adventures during his return to England after being shipwrecked on the coast of Chile. This rumbustious captain, known to his men as 'Foul-Weather Jack', had enjoyed an eventful naval career and received steady promotion. Now he was elevated to the rank of commodore and in June he hoisted his broad pennant in the *Dolphin.* As the only surviving officer of Anson's expedition, Byron was the obvious choice to lead a new Pacific venture. But he knew full well how hazardous that venture was. So did his superiors. That was why they had authorised Byron to keep his plans secret from his officers and men until the last possible moment and then to offer them the choice of continuing with the voyage on double pay or being shipped home on the first available vessel. The inducement worked. When, somewhere in the South Atlantic, Byron called his ships' crews together and

*This experiment proved extremely successful, though Byron attributed the crew's failure to catch fish to the *Dolphin's* copper bottom.[4]

presented them with the facts, only one man opted to return to England.

Had Byron made a serious attempt to carry out his instructions, his ships, which left Portsmouth on 2 July, would have been at sea for several years. In fact, Byron's expedition entered the record books as the fastest circumnavigation so far achieved. He was back in England after only twenty-two months, having made no attempt to explore the South Atlantic, visit the coast of California or search for the North-West Passage, and having crossed the Pacific in a hundred and thirty days. Two factors seem to have influenced him in treating his orders so cavalierly: he was concerned for the health of his crew and he wanted to rediscover the Solomon Islands.

Byron was a humanitarian and popular with his crews but, even had he not been, efficiency would have demanded that he took every precaution to prevent his sailors falling sick. The nightmare memory of weak, dying men lashed into action to force the *Wager* through the storms of Cape Horn must have been vivid to him even after a quarter of a century. Little though he understood the causes of scurvy and fever, he took every precaution to avoid them. Foremost among those precautions was the constant provision of fresh food and water. The equipment the *Dolphin* took on board at Woolwich included a machine for sweetening 'stale and noxious water'. This apparatus, invented by a Lieutenant Orsbridge, apparently worked by forcing air through the water and, when it was used during the voyage, Byron 'found it answer very well'.[5] Another innovation recommended by the Admiralty was 'portable soup', a kind of glutinous cake made up of meat extract which, when boiled up with peas and legumes provided a tolerably palatable substance which, if it had little nutritional value, at least was a welcome change from salt meat and weavily biscuit. The ships set out with bulging larders and the usual complement of penned animals for slaughter. They put into Rio de Janeiro for restocking and subsequently made landfalls as often as possible, where they experimented with whatever foodstuffs were available. Birds, fish, wild pig, berries, grasses, fruit – it was all trial and error. Some substances proved poisonous; others made the men sick; some were just inedible; but there were items that Byron and his surgeons found to be, or believed to be, excellent remedies for various ailments, notably, of course, scurvy. Reading the nautical journals of this period, it is interesting to see just how absorbed captains were in exploring the healing possibilities of strange plant and animal foodstuffs. Each made his own discoveries and swore by them. For Byron, coconuts appeared to be a sovereign remedy:

> It is astonishing the effect these nuts alone had on those afflicted with that dreadful disease [scurvy]. Many that could not stir without the help of two men, and who were in the most violent pain imaginable, their limbs as black as ink, and thought to be in the last stage of that disorder were in a few days by eating those nuts (tho' at sea) so far relieved as to do their duty, and even go aloft as well as they had done before.[6]

Byron, therefore, kept to a minimum the length of time that his ships spent at sea or tacking off barren coasts, and this helped to determine his route.

His reasons for seeking the long-lost Solomons were both exotic and pragmatic. The El Dorado whose rumoured existence had excited captains and geographers since the voyages of Mendaña and Quiros supposedly lay close to the Pacific route which a ship would take if borne along by the trade winds. Byron could, therefore, make a crossing which would avoid those hideous experiences which had befallen the *Centurion* and still solve one of the great puzzles of South Sea exploration. Given the choice between searching for either of two places which might not exist, the Solomon Islands must have seemed preferable as an objective to the Straits of Anian.

When Byron set out at the beginning of July he made course for the west coast of Africa. Having rewatered at the Cape Verde Islands, he tried to pick up the trade winds which would carry him across to Brazil. But, like thousands of other sailors before and since, he found himself trapped by the variable equatorial winds and currents. Whole days were spent becalmed or on long tacks and only after six weeks at sea, in heat so sweltering that fresh meat was putrid within a couple of hours of being slaughtered, did the *Dolphin* and *Tamar* thankfully drop anchor in Rio roads. There was some sickness aboard the *Tamar* but the men quickly recovered after a few days ashore.

The situation was far worse aboard another English ship which put in while Byron's ships were there. This was the East-Indiaman *Kent*. She had left her home port a month before the *Dolphin* and *Tamar* and made a direct Atlantic crossing. Yet she arrived off Brazil a month after Byron's ship, by which time many of her crew were down with scurvy. Her most prestigious passenger was Robert Clive, returning to India for the third time to crown a dazzling career in the service of the East India Company. Much to Byron's embarrassment this public hero now applied to transfer from the *Kent* to the *Dolphin,* believing that the naval vessels were bound for the East and would reach India long before the Company ship. A request from Lord Clive was virtually an order. Probably Byron was able to extricate himself only by sharing his secret instructions with the would-be passenger.

Rio de Janeiro was now a highly civilised port of call where all the needs of Byron's ships and men could be met and the commodore himself was received with a fifteen-gun salute and granted an impressive audience by the viceroy:

> . . . he received me with great form. About 60 officers were drawn up before the palace, as well as a captain's guard, all extremely well clothed and very well looking men. The vice king with a number of persons of the first distinction belonging to the palace received me at the head of the stairs . . .[7]

But the city had its hazards. One was the local version of the press gang:

> . . . as the Portuguese carry on a great trade from hence, they make it their business to attend every boat's landing in order to entice away some of the crew. By this means I lost five seamen, who were made drunk and immediately sent away into the country, and care enough taken they should not return till after I sailed. The *Tamar* had lost 8 or 9 of her people, but by great good luck heard where they was detained and in the night sent and surprised them and got them every one back.[8]

Despite such setbacks, the six weeks' respite in Rio proved beneficial to Byron's men though doubtless they would have made greater use of it had they realised that it was to be their last Europeanised port of call for over a year and that they were bound for some of the world's emptiest and most inhospitable regions. Certainly they would not have sold their warm clothes and spare bedding to buy liquor and trinkets, as many now did (they were later issued with extra clothing – 'slops' – from the ships' stores).

The two frigates stood out from Rio on 21 October and set a southerly course through the squally, fog-laden waters off Patagonia. Around 43°S the entire ships' companies fell prey to a rare group hallucination. At 4 o'clock on a stormy afternoon the cry 'Land ho!' went up. On the lee bow a long projection from the coast with two hills clearly appeared, contrary to the charts. Not wanting to find himself embayed, Byron altered course several points to the south-east. As they neared the supposed shore, officers and crew clearly discerned trees and waves breaking on the beach. Then, suddenly, the sea was empty. What must, in reality, have been a fog bank dispersed. 'Though I have been at sea now 27 years,' Byron recorded, 'never saw [I] such a deception before, and I question much if the oldest seaman breathing ever did . . .'[9]

Byron had a hard job of it bringing his ships into the next haven, Port Desire. He found his charts and rutters 'too deficient'. The *Dolphin,* lacking adequate ballast, was riding high in the water and very prone to being driven onto a lee shore. To add to his problems the weather in this region lived up to its reputation of unpredictability, as the commodore colourfully recorded:

> It is certainly the most disagreeable sailing in the world, forever blowing and that with such violence that nothing can withstand it, and the sea runs so high that it works and tears a ship to pieces . . . It continued to blow very hard till between 4 and 5 p.m. when the wind in a minute or two went once or twice all round the compass and then fell flat calm for about half an hour, the sea running very high, all in heaps.[10]

John Byron had a fine way with words, even when writing an official log. Perhaps he possessed in lesser measure those gifts that were bestowed so abundantly on his grandson, Lord Byron, the poet. The captain also seems to have possessed something of the imaginative powers of his famous descendant. This emerges clearly from the bewildering episode of the Patagonian giants.

The south-east coastal region of South America was originally populated by scattered Amerindian hunting communities. They were well-built people rather above average European height. Though theirs was basically a Stone Age culture, they had absorbed, probably from Spanish settlers to the north, the use of horses and, perhaps, some metal artefacts. Undoubtedly they welcomed the occasional visits of white men to their shores and saw them as bringers of prestigious and useful tools, weapons and decorative adornments. Early European visitors, ever ready to astonish their countrymen with tales of great marvels, had circulated exaggerated stories of these simple people. Pigafetta, the chronicler of Magellan's voyage, had given the name *patagones* ('big-feet') to the people of this region and claimed that they were of remarkable stature. Later visitors had either confirmed or denied the existence of a Brobdingnagian race and the truth of the matter had become something of considerable speculation in scholarly circles. Byron had promised Lord Egmont that he would try to make contact with the Indians and establish their size once and for all.

But that is precisely what he did *not* do. The report he sent home of his encounter with the Indians and the published accounts of the voyage which soon appeared gave rise to still more wildly inaccurate stories of 'enormous goblins' and 'frightful Colossuses'. What happened was this: anchoring in a bay close by Cape Virgins (or Cape Virgin Mary as it was by now named on the charts), at the eastern end of Magellan's Straits, the Englishmen saw a large group of the local people waving and beckoning to them. Byron landed two boatloads of men, drew them up in impressive battle order on the beach, then went forward alone to meet the strangers. There were men and women of all ages, some of whom were on horseback. They were loosely covered in animal skins worn 'as a Highlander wears his plaid', their faces were vividly painted, and they seemed nervous but friendly. Like all European travellers to 'savage' lands the Englishmen carried a supply of such baubles and gewgaws as were believed to appeal to primitive peoples. Byron distributed some beads. Then he motioned the people to sit down in a line, stretched a length of green ribbon along the row as far as it would go, cut it into lengths of about a yard and tied these strips round the men's heads like bandanas. What the Indians made of all this is impossible to say but one did manage to make clear by signs that they would rather have tobacco and so Byron sent for some. He and the Patagonians conversed some more in sign language, then the commodore ordered a return to the boats and the encounter was over.

It is intriguing that Byron never committed himself to a

measurement of these people; all the statements in his journal were vague: '. . . one of the most extraordinary men for size I had ever seen till then'; 'these people . . . in size come the nearest to giants I believe of any people in the world'.[11] In a private letter to Lord Egmont he was a little more specific but, strangely, quoted a second-hand observation: 'Our people on board who were looking at us through their glasses said we looked like mere dwarfs to the people we were gone amongst.'[12] It is as though he was providing his superiors with the kind of information they could develop and use in the way that best suited their purposes. Apparently the British government had reason to encourage the spread of fanciful tales about 'Patagonian giants', probably as a means of deflecting attention from their real interests in the region. Whatever the official motivation, returning members of the expedition and pirate authors soon cashed in on popular interest to publish wildly inaccurate accounts – and pictures – of a race of people varying from eight to twelve feet in height. This created a contentious debate in scholarly circles and did little to enhance the reputation of Foul-Weather Jack.[13]

But that was all in the future when *Dolphin* and *Tamar* entered the Straits on 21 December. Byron devoted two weeks to an exploration of the eastern end of the straits, noting anything that might be of value to future settlers on the Falklands and to ships visiting them – tides, winds, anchorages, vegetation, animal and bird life, etc:

> Here is great plenty of wild celery and many herbs that must be excellent for seamen after a long voyage . . . here are abundance of ducks, geese, teal, snipes, etc – I thank God our ship's company are all extremely healthy; this cold air has given them such voracious appetites that they could eat three times their allowance . . .[14]

On 6 January 1765 Byron set off in search of the Falklands which no British mariner had visited for eighty years. He was in some doubt of his ability to locate the islands but six days' sailing brought him to their northern shores. He discovered a well-sheltered, broad bay on Saunders Island and, while anchored there, he wrote to Lord Egmont, to inform his lordship that he had named the place Port Egmont. Byron vigorously praised the latest colony which he had now formally claimed in the name of his Britannic Majesty, King George III. It had fish and fowl in abundance. Fresh water was plentiful. The soil was excellent. 'The land is all covered with wood sorrel and wild celery, which are the best antiscorbutics in the world.'[15] Byron informed his lordship that he had proved their efficacy by having them boiled up and served with the portable soup (a process which robbed the vegetables of any efficacious properties they possessed). John Crosier, the *Dolphin's* surgeon, planted a small garden for the benefit of the British settlers who were expected to be arriving within a year. To crown all, Byron said that he had dug in several places and discovered iron ore. He doubted not that experts would discover other metals on the islands.

Ideal though the Falklands were in Byron's estimation, he was anxious to get away. He had arranged to rendezvous at Port Desire with a storeship from England. By 6 February, therefore, he was back on the Patagonian coast where he found the *Florida* waiting for him. Unfortunately, she was badly damaged, though Byron's description of her as 'little better than a wreck' is probably an exaggeration. It took all the expedition's carpenters four days to effect the necessary running repairs. Then the convoy made its way into the Straits to find a quieter anchorage for the transfer of stores, for Port Desire was too exposed.

It was here, in the eastern end of the Straits, that Byron had an odd encounter with no less a person than Louis Antoine de Bougainville. The faithful French coloniser had just returned to the Falklands with a fresh batch of settlers and was visiting the mainland for timber to build houses and store huts. Spotting the British 'interlopers', he shadowed them for several days, never coming close enough to exchange signals or making any attempt to send a boat across to his rivals. The nearest the two circumnavigators ever came to direct contact was when the *Florida* ran aground. The French captain sent off a couple of boats to render assistance but Byron immediately despatched his own men to forestall them and politely decline their help. It is strange to picture these two fine captains circling each other suspiciously like wily and uncertain lions on the veldt. Neither had instructions covering the situation and, therefore, did not know what to do. Eventually, Bougainville found an anchorage and proceeded with his logging operation and Byron passed him on his journey westward. At about the same time the store-ship was sent home with a detailed report for Lord Egmont.

On 9 April *Dolphin* and *Tamar* reached the Pacific and made for the island of Más Afuera, rather than the larger Juan Fernandez so as to be less likely to be detected by the Spaniards. They found the shore-line rocky and pounded by a heavy surf, so that bringing off water was a hazardous enterprise. To minimise the risk Byron had his boatmen dressed in cork jackets, another innovation he was trying out for the Admiralty. Even thus equipped, one sailor refused to wade out through the waves to a waiting boat. His shipmates shouted to him that he would have to be abandoned if he refused to brave the breakers, since the boat could get no farther inshore. He replied that he would prefer a lonely life to certain death by drowning. At that point a midshipman jumped into the water with a rope's end and swam ashore. Before the hesitant seaman knew what was happening, the officer threw a prepared noose round his waist and signalled the other sailors to pull. Byron laconically chronicled the end of this affair:

> . . . when they got him in he was both speechless and motion-less, for he had swallowed such a quantity of water that he was to all appearance dead. They held him up by the heels till he came to himself and he was perfectly well next day.[16]

Byron's next quest, since he had no intention of heading for New Albion, was the trade winds which would carry him as swiftly as possible across the Pacific. For several days progress was slow thanks to squally and variable weather. By the time he did, at last, pick up the south-easterlies he was becoming anxious. When the ships left Más Afuera on 30 April the crews were in good health. By 31 May he was reporting 'my people fall down daily in the scurvy. The heat is excessive'.[17] The ships were then in about 15°S. Had they pursued a more westerly course they would have discovered Tahiti. As it was they only encountered a few atolls which make up the northern limit of the Tuamotu Archipelago, of which Tahiti is a part. There was no anchorage and Byron, naming these seductively attractive places the Isles of Disappointment, sailed on.

The travellers fared little better with the next pair of islands in the chain, to which Byron gave the name King George's Isles. Not only was there no anchorage; the people were also hostile, crowding to the beach to brandish their spears and chasing after the ships' boats in their canoes. Byron was in a dilemma – he did not want to provoke an incident which would lead to deaths on both sides but he desperately needed to bring off some boatloads of fresh food. Making signs to denote friendship had little effect, so Byron eventually resorted to a show of force. A single shot from one of his cannon proved sufficient to drive the islanders from the beach and into the palm groves beyond. Then, he was able to send his boats ashore to collect coconuts and scurvy grass.

Byron continued due west in quest of the Solomons. But he had not forgotten that there were other potential objectives to Pacific exploration – the great south continent, for example:

For a day or two before we made the Islands of Disappointment till this day we saw vast flocks of birds which we observed towards evening always flew away to the S°ward. This is a convincing proof to me that there is land that way, and had not the winds failed me in the higher latitudes as mentioned before, I make no doubt but I should have fell in with it, and in all probability made the discovery of the S° Continent. Indeed if it had not been for the sickness in both ships, I would still have attempted it by hauling away to the S°ward immediately from those islands. I remarked before that all the islands we have seen are well peopled. Now if there are not a chain of islands reaching to the continent how can we account for these peoples being here, situated we may say in the middle of this vast Southern Ocean?[18]

Had Byron turned southwards he would not have found Australia but he would have made some of those discoveries which were now reserved for later, more single-minded explorers.

The commodore was more concerned about the safety of his men. As well as illness he now had to contend with the navigational hazards of an ocean dotted with uncharted reefs, shoals, atolls and islands which offered no safe havens and were more dangerous than the empty sea. Night-time sailing was particularly difficult. The ships could only proceed cautiously with few sails set, trying not to lose sight of each other and ever on the watch for broken water ahead. Off-duty watches were frequently brought on deck in the small hours by the warning boom of the consort's cannon or the cry of a nervous lookout who had confused the glint of moonlight on water for waves breaking over coral. And lost sleep was especially irritating to men weakened by scurvy, as most of them now were. On 29 June Byron abandoned his search for the Solomons and steered a north-westerly course in the general direction of the Philippines and that section of the Pacific which was, by now, well charted.

For a month the ships crawled slowly over the ocean, the heat and humidity making it difficult for the men to work and lacklustre breezes scarcely stirring the sails. On 21 July Byron was prompted to make the exaggerated observation in his journal: 'certainly this is the longest, the hottest and most dangerous run that was ever made by ships before'.[19] By the time the expedition reached Tinian, in the Marianas, on 30 July there was scarcely a member of it who was not suffering from scurvy or enteric disorders.

Tinian had been the salvation of Anson's voyage. He had spent seven weeks there restoring his men and repairing his ship. His emaciated, debilitated crew gorged themselves on plentiful food and water which seemed to them the most delicious victuals they had ever tasted. Perhaps conditions had changed in twenty-three years. Perhaps Byron's expectations were too high. Perhaps, being in a less desperate situation than his predecessor, he was more disposed to be critical. Whatever the reason, Foul-Weather Jack did not like Tinian at all. The water was brackish and full of worms. The centre of the island was overgrown with brush which tore shirts and trousers to pieces. Cattle were not plentiful as the *Centurion's* journal had claimed and were to be found only at some distance from the anchorage. Because of the heat, meat was stinking before it could be got back to the camp. Fowls were plentiful 'but the best of them are very bad tasted'. Some of the men were badly poisoned by eating the local fish. Flies and mosquitoes swarmed everywhere and two men died of fevers inflicted by insect bites. Scorpions and ants were scarcely less of a menace. The anchorage was so exposed that during one rough seven-day spell *Dolphin* and *Tamar* had to stand out to sea to prevent being driven onto the shore. As for the climate:

> I take this to be one of the most unhealthy places in the world, at least at this season. The airs are extremely violent and the sun so scorching that it is difficult breathing . . . I have been upon the coast of Guinea [the West African coast, known with good reason as 'the white man's graveyard'] and West Indies and even the island of St Thomas's under the line [Sao Tomé, an island on the equator off the coast of Gabon]. I don't remember to have felt it anything near as hot as it is here.[20]

Yet, for all these complaints, the nine-week stay on Tinian proved highly beneficial. The sick, lodged ashore under canvas, revived quickly on a diet of fresh meat, coconuts, limes, sour oranges, guavas, bread fruit and paw-paw; And, before leaving, Byron was able to lay aboard a store of coconuts and fruit and also some wild boars some of the men had snared.

Like so many others who had reached this point half a world away from home, Byron and his men could only think now of completing the voyage. The work which the commodore had been set or had set himself was behind him. He had done all he could at the Falklands. He had not found his islands of gold. He had crossed the Pacific with the loss of only two men. He had recorded all there was to record for the benefit of mariners who would follow after. It was enough. He was not an explorer at heart. The empty spaces on his charts did not lure him as they would lure Carteret and Cook. The Admiralty might send men to the Pacific but it could not make them explore. From the Marianas Byron made a north-westerly course around the Philippines and thence by way of the coast of Sumatra to Batavia. Here he received what must have seemed like a welcome back to civilisation; a thirteen gun salute from an East-Indiaman anchored in the roads.

Batavia was the Dutch mercantile capital in the Orient, a place where Europeans of all nationalities mingled with Malays and Chinese. It had all the virtues of a well-laid-out modern city and all the vices of a cosmopolitan seaport. Broad tree-lined avenues shaded elegant houses. Company merchants, officials and even tradesmen lived in luxury. Byron noted that if a tailor paid a professional call he would do so in his own carriage, accompanied by two servants. No European, he observed, would so demean himself as to be seen *walking*. Batavia boasted a magnificent hotel which had 'more the appearance of a palace than a tavern'. It was very expensive and was owned by a Frenchman who, it seems, was operating a lucrative racket with the Dutch governor general. The latter levied a fine of five hundred dollars on any Batavian resident who received a guest

Above: Allegory of Magellan sighting Tierra del Fuego and the Straits named after him. Engraving by Jean-Théodore de Bry, c 1590.

Left: Sir Francis Drake, 1591. Painted by a follower of Marcus Gheeraerts the Younger.

Left: The *Golden Hind* engaged with *Cacafuego*. Engraving of 1603.

Below: Thomas Cavendish, engraving by Jodocus Hondius from *Franciscus Dracus redivivus*, Amsterdam, 1596.

One of the drawings made by Peter Munday,
an Englishman who visited China in 1637.

Byron landing on the coast of Patagonia, 1764. From
Account of Voyages. . ., 1773 by John Hawkesworth.

Tahitians attacking Wallis in the *Dolphin*.

John Harrison's first chronometer, 1735.

John Harrison's fourth pocket chronometer, 1759. Cook took one of these on his second voyage and called it 'his never-failing guide'.

Captain James Cook, 1776. Painted by Nathaniel Dance.

Louis XVI at Versailles commissioning La Pérouse's expedition.
Painted in 1817 by Nicolas-André Monsiau.

A Maori war canoe attacking Cook. Watercolour
by Sydney Parkinson, 1769.

James Forbes's *Marco Polo*. Painted by T. Dove.

The version of Slocum's conversation with President Kruger
published in the Cape Town *Owl*, 5 March 1898.

in his own home. Visitors, therefore, had no option but to pay *monsieur le patron*'s high prices which doubtless included the governor general's commission. Batavia was a place of bustling markets, brothels, cheap arrack – and death. Because of the swampland on which it was built it teemed with mosquitoes and other disease-bearing insects. Byron noted that Europeans died there 'like rotten sheep'. He lost four of his own men from fevers contracted in this delusory paradise. He, therefore, kept his stay as short as possible and on 10 December he weighed anchor.

If the crews felt cheated out of their indulgence in the flesh pots, Byron made it up to them two months later when, after an uneventful crossing of the Indian Ocean, *Dolphin* and *Tamar* reached Cape Town. The men enjoyed three weeks' shore leave and took every opportunity to get drunk on the local wine. After this the expedition enjoyed a trouble-free run for home waters, though the *Tamar* was deflected to Antigua for her rudder to be rehung. The *Dolphin* reached home on 9 May 1766, and Byron hurried to the Admiralty to make his report.

Their lordships declared themselves well pleased with a voyage which had demonstrated British maritime supremacy and paved the way for the occupation of the Falklands and further Pacific exploration. Moreover, the *Dolphin* had lost only six out of her complement of 153 officers, sailors and marines – and not one of those six had died of scurvy. The Pacific ghost had been laid.

Byron was immediately involved in urgent Admiralty plans for a follow-up expedition. Anglo-French colonial rivalry had grown to a new intensity and there could be no backing off. When the *Florida* storeship had returned in June 1765 with Byron's report on the Falklands, Captain John McBride had been despatched to the islands to land a party of marines at Port Egmont and thus establish a British colony. McBride had reached the Falklands in January 1766. During the course of his survey of the islands in the frigate *Jason* he had encountered the

French inhabitants, informed them that they had no right to be in his Britannic majesty's territory without permission, and offered to convey them to a French port of their choosing. Naturally, they declined to move and McBride, who had no authority to use force, had to content himself with dark threats. By this time the Spanish government had become alarmed. They saw the security of their fragile American empire severely threatened by the activities of more powerful maritime nations. They, accordingly, claimed the Malvinas as their own sovereign territory. Their French allies willingly conceded the point, since this seemed the best way of keeping the strategic Falklands base 'in the family'. Bougainville was, therefore, instructed to hand over his settlement to a representative of Spain. In December 1766 he set out on this mission.

By the time Byron returned, the diplomatic situation had become very delicate. French and Spanish representatives were protesting about British naval activities and the Cabinet was divided. The 'doves' were unwilling to provoke open war over a handful of distant, bleak islands and urged the impossibility of defending Port Egmont against an enemy who could easily send a large contingent of ships and men from South America. The 'hawks' insisted that, at all costs, British rights to the Falklands and free navigation in the southern hemisphere must be defended.*

The Earl of Egmont was, of course, one of the 'hawks'. In Cabinet he vigorously defended the actions of his captains and at the same time he hurriedly and secretly prepared a new expedition to reinforce the British settlement and carry out further Pacific exploration. The summer months passed in frenzied activity. Dock workers at Deptford and Chatham hastily prepared vessels for a long sea voyage. Angry letters passed between Paris, Madrid and London. No one, not even Egmont's government colleagues, knew his plans in any detail. The Cabinet wavered. The expedition was on; then it was off; then on again. The little fleet was manned, provisioned and

*These arguments surface again during the Falklands War in 1982.

moved to Plymouth, where it awaited instructions. On 13 August Egmont, frustrated by opposition to his plans, resigned as First Lord of the Admiralty. But, before his resignation could take effect, he sent instructions to Plymouth for his ships to set sail immediately. On 21 August, the *Dolphin,* accompanied now by the *Swallow* sloop and the storeship *Prince Frederick* weighed anchor. They were well past the Scillies before anyone who might want to recall them knew that they had put to sea.

The expedition which now set out turned into two expeditions and is of interest because it shows how two very different captains handled the problems of circumnavigation. Egmont had intended to refit the *Dolphin* and the *Tamar* for a second voyage but, because the *Tamar* was away in the West Indies undergoing repairs, his subordinates had to cast around for another vessel. They chose a twenty-year-old, sixth-rate, fourteen-gun sloop, the *Swallow,* which had never been out of home waters. She was a sluggish craft, dependable in heavy seas but not a fast mover under full sail. Nor was her limited below-deck space adequate for the amount of supplies necessary for a long voyage. She proved to be a nuisance to the expedition's leader, Samuel Wallis, but to her commander, Philip Carteret, she was like a millstone, hindering his chances of a successful voyage and also his career prospects.

Wallis was a thirty-eight-year-old, conventional, competent officer whose entire life from the age of twenty had been devoted to the Navy. He served in peace and war and commanded his first ship at the age of twenty-eight. He seems to have been quite popular with his men and, if he was unimaginative, he was conscientious. He went by the book, kept his own counsel, did not readily confide in his officers and was jealous of his authority. In all his years of service he had never sailed farther than the Atlantic. Carteret was thirty-three and the *Swallow* was his first command. Promotion had come more slowly, perhaps because he had not been present in a major theatre of war. Yet he was a good officer. At least, that was the opinion of Captain the Hon. John Byron. Carteret had served several times under Foul-Weather Jack and Byron had specifically asked for him to be appointed to his 1764 expedition. He returned from that voyage as first lieutenant in the *Dolphin*. By temperament Carteret was adventurous, impatient, intolerant and quick to take offence. The two captains were thus as different from each other as the ships they commanded. Carteret, doubtless, expected that his superior would take him into his confidence and rely heavily on his experience as a circumnavigator. Wallis seems to have been determined to keep his junior in his place. There were several officers and men who had sailed on the Byron voyage and their new commander probably felt that he had to stamp his authority on the new expedition. He may even have regarded Carteret as something of a threat.

Whatever the reasons for their estrangement, the two men did not get on. At the outset Wallis refused to reveal his secret instructions to the captain of the *Swallow*. Carteret, like everyone else on board the three ships, assumed that they were going to provision and equip the Port Egmont settlement, where he was to relieve McBride and the *Jason*. Only after they had been at sea for three weeks and it was necessary to make plans for a rendezvous in the event of the convoy being split up, was Carteret made privy to Wallis's real intentions. These were to make for Magellan's Straits where the *Prince Frederick* would be despatched to the Falklands and the other two ships would sail westwards to continue the work of Pacific exploration. Carteret was stunned when he realised that he was expected to sail his inadequate craft round the world. Wallis was scarcely less annoyed when, day after day, the progress of his fleet was held up by the ill-named *Swallow*.

But the frustrations of the Atlantic crossing were as nothing compared with what befell the expedition in the straits. They reached Cape Virgin Mary on 16 December and Wallis ordered Carteret to go ahead and act as pilot. So, into the confusion of narrows, shoals, contrary currents and changeable winds the young captain steered his lumbering sloop. It was a ridiculous situation. Given a more manoeuvrable craft Carteret could have accomplished what was demanded of him, but the *Swallow* simply could not cope. Tacking in limited space was almost beyond her. When the wind was ahead she could only turn through it by being rowed and towed by two of her boats. It took ten days for the *Swallow* to lead her companions to safe anchorage at Port Famine, 150 miles within the Straits.

After three weeks during which the *Dolphin* and *Swallow* took on wood and water and stocked up with victuals from the *Prince Frederick,* the storeship was sent off to Port Egmont. Carteret employed part of the time contriving makeshift modifications to improve his ship's performance. He widened the rudder in the hope of making her more responsive to the helm. But as soon as they left harbour on 18 January and sailed out into the teeth of the westerlies Carteret discovered that his ship was just as unmanageable as before. It was obvious that if Wallis persisted in using *Swallow* as his guide through the twisting, rock-strewn waterway he ran the risk of reaching the Pacific when the best of the summer weather had passed. There had to be a change of plan. Over the next few days, Carteret assailed his commander with written suggestions. Wallis rejected them, one after another. The letters between the two men just managed to remain within the bounds of civility:

Dangerous passages lay ahead and the *Swallow* was unreliable. Would Wallis abandon the present scheme in favour of a more prudent one?

No. It was vital the two ships stayed together 'lest any accident befall either'.

Supposing the *Swallow* were to be anchored in a suitable cove and Carteret were to use the ship's boats to lead *Dolphin* through the straits.

No. Wallis' instructions were to keep his ships together.

Carteret would willingly come aboard the *Dolphin* as first lieutenant and make his knowledge of the South Sea available.

No. Wallis could not depart from his Admiralty instructions. Two ships were essential for voyages of exploration.

If Wallis would not sail a single ship across the Pacific, Carteret would. Perhaps the commander would prefer to return home with the *Swallow* while he went on in the *Dolphin*?

No!

The two ships limped from anchorage to anchorage. Sometimes *Swallow* led the way. Sometimes she had to be towed. Often she and *Dolphin* had to remain in harbour for days or weeks together. The end result was that the passage of the Straits, which Magellan had made in thirty-seven days and Drake in seventeen, took Wallis's expedition 115 days. Then, to crown all, and despite his protestations about the necessity to proceed in tandem, Wallis *did* leave the consort behind. It happened on the night of 10–11 April when the ships were approaching Cape Pilar at the outlet to the Pacific. They were sailing before a favourable wind and the *Swallow* was in the lead. Soon after dark the *Dolphin* put on sail and passed her companion. By morning she had broken through the barrier of cross currents and variable winds at the Straits' mouth and was standing out to sea with all sails set. About nine o'clock she disappeared over the western horizon and that was the last the men of the *Swallow* saw of her.

Such are the facts. The explanations of those facts given by the two captains differed widely. Wallis claimed that only weather conditions forced his reluctant separation from the consort:

> . . . it falling little wind was obliged to make all the sail we could to get without the Strait's Mouth. At 11 would have shortened sail for the *Swallow,* but could not, and was obliged to carry to clear the Isles of Direction the current setting us strong down upon them, and the wind westing. We soon after lost sight of the *Swallow,* and never saw or heard of her after. I would have gone back into the Straits but the

weather coming on thick and dirty we were all of opinion that we had nothing to do but get an offing as soon as possible, for the sea raising fast and the weather greasy, that the ship could not weather Tierra del Fuego on one tack nor, the land off Cape Victory on the other unless we pressed her with sail before the sea rose to too great a height.[21]

Carteret, by contrast, was convinced that his superior had deserted him as soon as he had outlived his usefulness by bringing *Dolphin* within sight of the Pacific. His version of events on the fateful night portrays Wallis as doing everything possible to disembarrass himself of the sluggish sloop:

The *Dolphin* had all along before much outsailed us, but now as our bottom was grown much fouler, and hers by being coppered, kept always clean, we found now that she sailed faster with only topsails, with a reef in them, than the *Swallow* did with all the sails we could set. At 6 o'clock in the evening . . . the western entrance of the Straits fairly open, and the Great South Sea in sight. I had all the time before this, been made to keep ahead, but soon after it was dark, we observed the *Dolphin,* who was nearly abreast of us, set her foresail, by which she soon shot ahead of us, and before 9 o'clock (as she did not carry, nor during the whole night, did she show us any lights) we had quite lost sight of her. All this night, we had a fine light eastern breeze, of which we endeavoured to make the best use we possibly could, by carrying even our topgallant-studding sails, a conduct, which people who are acquainted with the sudden squalls, and the variableness of the winds, which reign, with so much violence in the Straits of Magellan, may be apt to censure, and think rather imprudent. . . but I always determined to keep up with the *Dolphin,* and to be as little hindrance in delaying of her, as possible . . . but notwithstanding all my endeavours, I could not keep up with her. . the next morning . . . about 7 o'clock we discovered the

Dolphin, bearing W½ N, but was so far ahead we could but just see her topsails, above the horizon; and we observed that she had likewise studding sails set; by which it is not to be wondered, that she should be at so great a distance from us; and by 9 o'clock she was entirely gone out of sight of us.[22]

Carteret tried to follow *Dolphin* but was driven back into the shelter of the Straits by contrary winds. It was another four days before he was able to break out into the open sea.

We shall never know to what extent Carteret's suspicions were justified. Both he and Wallis blamed the limitation of their subsequent success on the 'desertion' of the other. In fact, neither was probably altogether sorry about the separation. Wallis was no longer hampered by the 'dull *Swallow*' (as George Robertson, master of the *Dolphin* called her) and Carteret could, at last, be his own master.

Wallis's ship was very soon in a desperate plight. The men 'began to fall down very fast in colds and fevers, in consequence of the upper works being open and their clothes and beds continually wet'.[23] The unnecessarily long sojourn in the dank and chilly atmosphere of the Straits, added to the normal debilitating effects of a long voyage, had weakened the crew, and Wallis, himself, suffered bouts of illness. Nor could he make for the shelter of some Chilean cove or offshore island. Violent storms threw the *Dolphin* out into the Pacific. For almost two months she bucketed her way through empty seas. Occasionally the masthead lookout had tantalising glimpses of islands which were inaccessible because the wind was wrong and the crew weak.

Then, on 6 June, land was sighted dead ahead:

The joy which everyone on board felt at the discovery can be conceived by those only who have experienced the danger, sickness and fatigue of such a voyage as we had performed.[24]

The hitherto untravelled WNW course had brought *Dolphin* to the undiscovered Tuamotu archipelago. Wallis now threaded his way cautiously westward through the labyrinth of reefs and islands, sending a boat ashore whenever possible to negotiate for food and water with the natives. The Englishmen received a mixed reception but were able to collect fresh water, coconuts and scurvy grass.

On 19 June the voyagers came upon a larger island, which proved to be their most important discovery. Since Wallis was confined to his bed he was obliged to send his second lieutenant, Tobias Furneaux, ashore to claim the land for his sovereign and to name it George III Island. But the title was not destined to stick; later visitors gave it an anglicised form of the name the local people used for their home – Tahiti. The natives of this populous island were wary of the white strangers in their big canoe. Naturally, they could not know the desires or intentions of the newcomers. The flotilla of craft which made its way out to the *Dolphin* indicated these doubts and hesitations very clearly: some boats were loaded with produce. Others bore a cargo of young women, who 'made all the wanton gestures that can be conceived'. But a third of the fleet was loaded with stones. An initial attempt at long-distance parley failed. *Dolphin* was subjected to a hail of missiles. Other well-armed canoes quickly paddled out to the anchorage. The local chief came forth in his own impressive barge. Soon Wallis's men reckoned they could count about 300 boats and 2000 men, rapidly closing on their ship. Wallis had no alternative but to order a salvo. One shot, more by luck than judgement, swamped the chief's canoe. The Tahitians rapidly withdrew.

It took a few days for Wallis to persuade the islanders that he came in friendship but once they understood this, their eagerness to trade knew no bounds. They were desperate for iron, which they could turn into tools or, more likely, weapons and were willing to give anything in exchange for nails, pots and implements. Soon the visitors were living sumptuously on fruit, vegetables, and the meat of fowls and pigs. But it was not only food that the Polynesians had to offer. As had been noticed at the first encounter, many young women (doubtless egged on by their seniors) were prepared to offer sexual favours in return for much-prized metal. The sailors, of course, entered readily into this commerce – too readily. Those who had no iron goods to offer took to stealing tools and prising nails from various parts of the ship. As a result there was a breakdown in discipline which almost led to mutiny. Wallis tried without success to track down the culprits. He became frustrated and angry and the men grew surly at repeated questioning. Worse was to follow. The insatiable sailors began defrauding their bedfellows by such tricks as paying them with lead cut to resemble nails. This threatened the good relations Wallis's officers were carefully building up with the Tahitians. On the other hand, when culprits were caught and publicly punished, the whole crew felt humiliated and resentful. After about three weeks the situation was getting out of hand and Wallis seemed unable to bring it under control.

. . . it was discovered that Francis Pinckney, one of the seamen, had drawn the cleats to which the main sheet was belayed, and, after stealing the spikes, thrown them overboard. Having secured the offender, I called all the people together upon the deck, and after taking some pains to explain his crime, with all its aggravations, I ordered that he should be whipped with nettles while he ran the gauntlet thrice round the deck: my rhetoric, however, had very little effect, for most of the crew being equally criminal with himself, he was handled so tenderly, that others were rather encouraged to repeat the offence by the hope of impunity, than deterred by the fear of punishment. To preserve the ship, therefore, from being pulled to pieces, and the price of refreshments from being raised so high as soon to exhaust our articles of trade, I ordered that no man, except the wooders and waterers, with their guard, should be permitted to go on shore.[25]

Wallis now decided to make haste to quit the island. A week later (27 July), having thoroughly overhauled the ship and filled her with all the water and fresh food she could hold, he gave the order to weigh anchor. *Dolphin* pulled away from the shore amidst manifestations of great distress from the natives. Their feelings were, no doubt, echoed by many aboard.

Wallis could well feel pleased with the progress of the expedition. He had added considerable information to the Pacific chart. Not by nature an explorer, he doubtless felt that he had done all his superiors required of him. Accordingly, he set course for the Marianas and the conventional route home. But, because the course he was following lay for the most part to the south of that followed by earlier expeditions, he was able to put several more island discoveries on the chart before he arrived at Tinian on 19 August. By this time most of his men had recovered and a month spent completing their recuperation and restocking the larder enabled him to leave with a healthy ship.

Batavia changed all that. Though Wallis kept his visit as short as possible, forty of his men went down with smallpox and dysentery. Many died. Others were unfit for duty on the Indian Ocean crossing. So the *Dolphin* was obliged to spend a month at Table Bay while the crew once more came up to strength. She finally reached the Downs on 18 May 1768 after a circumnavigation of one year and nine months.

When Wallis set foot on English soil Carteret was still in Celebes, having endured an eight-month Pacific crossing and become embroiled in an angry dispute with Dutch colonial officials. The points of interest about the *Swallow's* laboured passage around the world concern the character of Carteret and his contribution to the exploration of the random scattering of Pacific islands.

He was already a bitter man when he left the Patagonian coast. He believed himself to be the victim of a conspiracy which had condemned him to cross the wide ocean with an unsuitable ship and an inadequate crew. He recorded in his journal that for some days his men fully expected to come upon the *Dolphin* searching for her consort but that he laboured under no such delusion. Yet, angry and frustrated though Carteret was, he never once thought of turning back. He was determined to show the Admiralty and Wallis and anyone else who despised the *Swallow* and her mariners that they could accomplish what supposedly 'better' ships and men could not. There was more of the committed explorer in Carteret than in either Byron or Wallis. Yet even he was to be frustrated by the prevailing winds of the South Sea and the need to seek out supplies of fresh food and water.

His first disappointment came at Juan Fernandez. He made straight for this delectable island from Cape Pilar with the intention of making a leisurely stay there to prepare his ship and crew for the Pacific crossing. For three weeks the little *Swallow* battled her way towards this haven through hideous seas which gave her a chance to reveal her more impressive qualities.

. . . about 5 o'clock, the wind all of a sudden shifted from NW, to SW, and for the space of about an hour, it blew, I think stronger than ever I had seen it at sea. This wind made that the ship come up with her head, right against this great and mighty sea, which the NW wind had raised. It was now, I thought all our masts would have been carried away, and at that instant, I would willingly have compounded with the loss of the topmasts, (to have insured the lower ones) to have eased the ship, which I was much afraid would have foundered, for at every pitch she made, against this terrible high sea, it was with the end of her bowsprit under water, over which (and the forecastle) these mighty great seas broke in as far aft, as the main mast, and as if it had been over a rock; so that we were quite under water, and had not the ship been an extraordinary good sea boat (which was the only good quality she had) she could never have outlived this storm . . . it was really wonderful, how well this little vessel rose and cleared herself, from these high mountainous seas, which broke so furiously, occasioned by the sudden shifting of the wind, from one quarter of the compass to the other, without ceasing blowing with the same violence, that no canvas could withstand its force. Notwithstanding this was a fair wind, yet I did not dare to put the ship before the wind, for to make use of it; for if in wearing, any of those raging mountainous seas had broke on her side, it unavoidably would have carried all away before it and would probably have been of the most fatal consequence.[26]

Having survived such appalling conditions Carteret and his men thankfully reached Juan Fernandez on 10 May. But relief turned to frustration as they approached the main anchorage of Cumberland Bay:

I was not a little surprised to observe a great number of men all about the beach, with a house and four pieces of cannon over the waterside with two large boats lying off of it, a fort about two or three hundred yards up on the rising of the hill and on which they hoisted Spanish colours . . .[27]

Unknown to any of her European neighbours, Spain, alarmed by news that Anson had projected an English colony on Juan Fernandez, had settled the island in 1749. Despite the expense and the almost complete destruction of the settlement by earthquake in 1751, the Spaniards had been driven by English activity in the Falklands and the Pacific to maintain a garrison. It now proved its worth, for Carteret was forced to retreat and make for the only other port of call, the rocky island of Más Afuera. Here he fared little better than on the previous occasion when he had stopped there with Byron. There was no safe anchorage and getting watering parties ashore through squalls and breakers was hazardous. Three naked sailors had a particularly uncomfortable time. They were stranded on a tiny beach when their boat was forced to withdraw by a sudden storm.

With no shelter of any kind they survived the night by taking it in turns to lie on top of each other. Next morning, because there was no way to reach the main camp by land, they had to swim out through the surf, risking rocks and sharks, in order to reach their companions who had a tent and could share their clothes with them. Carteret regarded it as a miracle that he lost no men or boats during the two weeks he spent at Más Afuera. Storms were severe and intermittent, blowing up with great suddenness and every trip ashore was fraught with danger. When, on 31 May, the *Swallow* weighed anchor she had still only replenished some of her water casks. Apart from a few birds and fish, this was all the succour she obtained from Más Afuera.

Carteret hoped to strike out westwards and cross the ocean in a more southerly latitude than any captain had attempted before. But this was no more possible for him than it had been for his predecessors. The prevailing winds simply did not allow of an east-west crossing between Chile and New Zealand. Carteret was forced to sail northwards in search of the trade winds. He found them just south of the tropics, and, turning westward followed a course which was at times more than five hundred miles to the south of that followed by Wallis. This proved to be another misfortune. In conscientiously attempting to chart unknown regions Carteret missed Tahiti and other islands where he could have gained refreshment. He discovered lonely Pitcairn and described it with some justification as 'scarce better than a large rock in the ocean'.[28] (He never knew that his description of this forested isle far distant from any inhabited land would commend it to Fletcher Christian and the *Bounty* mutineers twenty-three years later, when they were looking for somewhere to hide.) *Swallow* encountered some of the outlying, barren islets of the Tuamotu archipelago but her crew found no evidence of a continent or even some of the islands marked on earlier charts.

After six weeks, Carteret had to bow to necessity:

The ship's company growing sickly, the scurvy making great progress among them, and seeing that in spite of all endeavours we could not keep in any high south latitude . . . that, from the badness of the weather, variableness of the winds and ill sailing of the ship, I advanced and made but slow progress on the voyage, it was now absolutely necessary to fix on some determined point for the future safety of the ship and crew . . . in consequence of the above said reason and circumstances, I bore away to the northward and got into the strong trade wind, keeping in such track as I was made by the charts to hope I should meet with some island from which I flattered myself I should procure some refreshments.[29]

There can scarcely have been an unluckier Pacific voyager. Had Carteret continued on a westerly course he might well have fallen in with islands of the Tonga or Fiji groups. Turning northwards where he did carried him through empty sea to the west of the Society Isles and to the east of Samoa.

In 10°S 167°W Carteret again turned westward, looking for the Solomons that Byron had missed two years before. He sailed right through the region where they had been located on charts since the Spanish voyages of the sixteenth and seventeenth centuries. Then, by a cruel irony, he came, seventeen days and thirteen hundred miles later, to the island of Santa Cruz, the easternmost of the Solomon group – and did not recognise it. Quiros had described the island carefully, and indicated that it possessed a good harbour in Graciosa Bay (where he had established a settlement) and was well stocked with animals, fruit and vegetables. But Quiros had also located Santa Cruz twenty degrees east of its true position, and that explains why Carteret failed to identify it.

That failure gave birth to a complete brood of further disasters. The scurvy-weakened crew were desperate for fresh food and water so Carteret anchored in a bay on the desolate northern coast and sent out a reconnaissance party to see what benefit the island offered. To their delight, the men came upon Graciosa Bay and its more abundant hinterland. They also found a large group of friendly natives. All was going well until the leader of the party, anxious to gather a boatload of coconuts, ordered one of the trees to be cut down. This broke a local taboo and the mood of the islanders changed. To dissuade them from making an attack, the *Swallow's* master fired a pistol. This had the exact opposite of the desired effect. In the subsequent affray, seven of the Englishmen were wounded (four later died of tetanus). After that it was impossible to re-establish good relations or to gather supplies. The *Swallow's* men took on fresh water but only by frightening the natives away with musket salvoes.

Carteret now gave way to depression and inertia. His ship needed a complete overhaul. Most of his men were sick. He had only one lieutenant fit enough for duty. There was no prospect of obtaining fresh food. He would have to abandon his plans of resuming exploration to the south with a refreshed crew. To crown all he was himself gravely ill with an intestinal disorder – near to death, if his own lugubrious account is to be believed. He bitterly blamed the master, Alexander Simpson, for provoking the hostility of the islanders. He blamed his crank and now leaky ship. He blamed his lack of officers. In fact, as he lay weak and sweating in his cabin, he blamed everyone but himself:

My ill state of health; the little regard that had been given to my orders, the incensing and falling out with these people . . . the loss of so many of my best men . . . the great number of sick . . . the little likelihood there was of getting any refreshments for them, the want of officers . . . were dispiriting incidents that at once blasted and damped all my hopes, from being again in a condition to pursue the voyage any farther, and this at the time when I had flattered myself I was at the point of doing something worthwhile towards the desired end.[30]

He summoned the master and the fit lieutenant to his sickbed and asked them what they thought it best to do. They advised him to turn northwards in order to pick up the known route which would bring them to the Marianas and thence, by using the monsoons, to Batavia. This was the way Anson, Byron and (though Carteret did not know it) Wallis had gone. It was the only known way and, therefore, the only way which offered any safety.

But Carteret did not take it. The adventurous spark, it seems, had not been entirely extinguished. By sailing on a heading west by north he hoped to reach New Britain, of which Dampier had written enthusiastically and, perhaps, on the way to make fresh discoveries. On 20 August he fell in with a cluster of islands which were part of the main Solomon group, though, of course, he did not know it. Still dispirited, he, too readily, decided not to linger. Landing looked hazardous and when the *Swallow* came close inshore the inhabitants made hostile gestures. So Carteret sailed on, having failed to write his name in the annals of exploration as the man who rediscovered the fabled and long-lost Solomon Islands. He now continued parallel to but out of sight of the archipelago and, on 28 August, he reached the large islands of New Britain and New Ireland.

At last the travellers found a cove where they could drop anchor in peace and safety, carry their sick ashore and gather food, water and timber. New Ireland was not the brimming, natural larder Dampier had represented it to be but the men were able to gather coconuts in abundance. This they did by chopping trees down rather than by the more energetic process of climbing the tall, slender palms. Carteret, like Byron, set great store by the produce of the coconut palm – not only its fruit but also its leafy crown, which he called 'cabbage':

> The milk, or rather water, of these nuts is an excellent and perhaps the best anti-scorbutic that is in the world. The cabbage part of this tree . . . is a white, juicy crispy substance,

has much of the taste, when eaten raw of our chestnuts, but when boiled eats much like a good parsnip. But you must cut down a tree for each cabbage which makes a great destruction of these useful trees.[31]

Frugal though the hospitality of this place was, Carteret's spirits revived. He named it 'English Cove' and set up a plaque claiming New Ireland and New Britain for King George.

When the *Swallow* weighed anchor, on 9 September 1767, it ended a remarkable phase in the exploration of Oceania. The, often unsung, achievements of Anson, Byron, Wallis and Carteret, were considerable. They did not clear up the mystery of the great southern continent. Their routes were dominated by prevailing winds and the search for antiscorbutics. There was still much exploration to be done and not before the end of the century would mariners and geographers have accurate Pacific charts to study. But what these four English voyages did was to indicate the general pattern of that scattering of islands which lies across the Tropics between New Guinea and Easter Island like ink spots flicked from a pen onto blotting paper, thickly clustered in the West and thinning towards the East.

Carteret, still following Dampier's narrative, decided to make for Mindanao in the southern Philippines, where the buccaneer-explorer had found the local people so hospitable. But almost a century had passed since Dampier's visit and the indigenes had learned during that time to be wary of Europeans, most of whom seemed to be bent only on conquest. Thus, when Carteret sent a cutter ashore for water the islanders, 'at the sight of our boat . . . fired two great guns and sent three boats who chased ours till they got sight of the ship'. And later, 'about 9 o'clock at night we were suddenly surprised with the hollowing of a number of men onshore abreast of the ship, intended as I imagine to have frightened us. It was exactly like the Indian war cry, which is a sudden, hideous hollow they all give the instant they attack, to dismay and terrify their enemies . . .'[32] Frustrated again, Carteret gave Mindanao a wide berth.

He now became the first circumnavigator to take the channel between Sulawesi and Borneo *en route* for Batavia. It was the shortest course and, with forty of his men totally incapacitated, he had no alternative. On 15 December 1767 and 246 days after leaving the Straits of Magellan this unfortunate captain dropped anchor off the Dutch port of Maccasar (modern Udung Panjang) on the south-west coast of Sulawesi. The long sequence of encounters with deceptive havens and hostile natives was past. Now his ship and his men could be rested for five months until the easterly monsoon began in May. Or so Carteret may reasonably have hoped. But he was doomed to drain to the dregs the cup of disappointment.

His letter to the governor, requesting permission to stay received an abrupt answer:

> he ordered me instantly to depart and be gone from this part nor to offer to approach any nearer nor to anchor on any parts of this coast or suffer any of my people to go onshore in any part of his government . . .[33]

This callous refusal of aid to mariners so obviously in distress was occasioned by fear and insecurity. The Dutch East India Company relied for the maintenance of its monopoly on alliances with local rulers. Many of these alliances, forged by a mixture of force and diplomacy, were very tenuous and might easily be upset by the agents of rival commercial nations. The governor of Maccasar, like all his colleagues in the service, was thus under strict instructions not to succour foreign merchant ships.

Carteret was furious. He told the governor's men that under no circumstances would he depart. He accused them of want of humanity. He took them on a tour of the *Swallow's* sick and dead. He threatened to run his ship ashore if they continued to deny an ally 'the treatment they would [give] to a Christian enemy'.[34] Eventually, the Dutch offered a compromise: he might rest up his ship at Bonthain, a small harbour down the coast and wait there for the monsoon season. This was agreed, amicable relations were restored and courtesy gun salutes were exchanged.

But before Carteret had been a few weeks at Bonthain relations were soured again. He was allowed a house in the town to use as a hospital but beyond that the movements of his men were strictly limited. His hosts, so he claimed, made him pay through the nose for supplies. Worst of all, Carteret became obsessed with suspicion. He persuaded himself that the Dutch were planning to massacre their unwanted guests. This fear seemed confirmed when he received a letter warning him of a plot hatched by the Dutch and one of the Sulawesi princes. The 'plot' was, in fact, a fabrication by a local faction trying to involve the English in their struggle against the Dutch. But Carteret's xenophobia and persecution mania were easily aroused. He had the *Swallow* ostentatiously guarded. He sent angry letters to the local officials and threatened reprisals at the highest diplomatic levels when he returned to England. The governor, genuinely surprised and alarmed, demanded evidence for Carteret's allegations but the Englishman refused. By the time the expedition put to sea again on 22 May relations with the Dutch had been well and truly soured and Carteret's reputation had gone ahead of him to Batavia. This involved more delays and acrimonious exchanges before *Swallow* could be repaired and reprovisioned for the journey home. The captain was not sorry to get away from Batavia on 15 September. Many of his men were sick with the inevitable malaria or dysentery and the Dutch eastern capital was, in his words, a place where 'nothing else reigns but pride, haughtiness, insolence, jealousy, suspicion and mistrust.'[35]

At his last anchorage before setting out to cross the Indian Ocean Carteret noted further evidence of what he regarded as the tyrannical rule of the arrogant Dutch. This was at the south-east corner of Java. Although it was far from any colonial settlement, the people did not flock out in their canoes to sell local produce to travellers as they had done in time past 'for fear of being seen by any of the guard boats which the Dutch keep here in the straits to speak to all shipping that go through'.[36] Only under cover of darkness did some of the Javanese venture to trade with the Englishmen.

During the two month crossing of the Indian Ocean (25 September–28 November) the *Swallow* still had to be manned by a sickness-depleted crew, despite the fact that numbers had been augmented by twenty-five sailors pressed by the Dutch who took the opportunity of escaping back to England. Seven more mariners died before *Swallow* reached the Cape. However, with the wind on her port beam or quarter most of the way, she did not require heavy handling. At Cape Town Carteret, after twenty-seven and a half months at sea, at last, found a port of call to his liking:

> Here we breathed a good air, had the wholesome food and went freely about in the country, which is extremely pleasant, and I began to think myself already in Europe.[37]

Six days into the new year, 1769, *Swallow* set out on the last lap of her ill-fortuned voyage. She made calls at the uninhabited islands of St Helena and Ascension. At the latter the men feasted on turtles. They caught eighteen of these large creatures by the simple expedient of waylaying the females at night, when they came ashore to lay their eggs, and turning them on their backs. Ascension was also an island 'post office'. Captains calling there had developed the habit of leaving messages in bottles recording their visit. It was by complying with this habit that Carteret revealed his whereabouts to a famous rival.

Three days after *Swallow's* departure on 1 February, Louis Antoine de Bougainville called at Ascension. This first French circumnavigator who had haunted Byron in Magellan's Strait in 1765 had followed Wallis and Carteret from Europe and gradually gained on them. He had called at the Cape after the Englishman and left quickly in the hope of overtaking him. Arriving at Ascension on 4 February, he discovered, to his delight, that he had already gained six days on him in the southern Atlantic. Bougainville now lost no time in pressing his pursuit and, on 19 February, he came up with the *Swallow*. He immediately sent one of his officers in a boat to enquire if the English captain needed any assistance. Carteret politely declined and questioned his visitor about the identity of his own ship. The young man, who, much to Carteret's disgust, presented himself dressed only in a waistcoat and trousers, told a cock and bull story about his ship being in the French East India Company's service and now returning from a voyage to Sumatra. He was under strict instructions to reveal nothing while keeping his eyes and ears open to everything that might be of interest aboard the *Swallow*. Thus Bougainville played with his rivals just as he had done four years before. And just as on that earlier occasion he and Byron never met, so now the French and English circumnavigators came very close together without actually setting eyes on each other. Soon the two vessels parted company, Bougainville's racing ahead. Only afterwards, when comparing notes with his officers and men, did Carteret realise the identity of the apparently solicitous Frenchman.

A month later, on 20 March, Carteret and his men came to anchor at Spithead – 'to our great joy'.

7

FILLING IN THE GAPS

Louis Antoine de Bougainville's expedition may claim to have been the first genuinely scientific voyage of circumnavigation. The scholarly Frenchman set out with the deliberate objective of making reliable charts of those parts of the Pacific through which he passed, collecting plants, and trying to master the accurate measurement of longitude. But he did not set out on a pure and disinterested quest for truth. He was following the principles laid down by de Brosses for the French colonisation of distant lands. The charts he drew up were for the benefit of his countrymen who would follow after, establishing settlements, as he had done in the Falklands. The plants he collected were nutmegs and cloves which his superiors wanted to try growing on Île de France (Mauritius). This Indian Ocean island had been ruled by the French East India Company for half a century but the government in Paris had now decided to bring it directly under crown control. While Bougainville was still on his outward voyage the new governor arrived at Île de France and began transforming what was no more than a port of call into a thriving colony whose economy was based on plantation agriculture. His objective was to grow spices there and thus make France independent of Dutch supplies from the Moluccas. Bougainville was charged, secretly of course, with obtaining plant specimens for preliminary tests. But the task to which the scientist-captain devoted most energy was experimenting on the measurement of longitude.

The correct calculation of longitude was the philosopher's stone sought by hundreds of eighteenth-century astronomers, mathematicians, inventors and cranks. So important was it that, in 1713, the British government offered the staggering sum of £20,000* to the man who could solve the problem to within thirty nautical miles of accuracy. They then set up the Board of Longitude to examine the 'solutions' which came flooding in. Despite the hundreds of ingenious ideas and mechanisms which were submitted, half a century passed without anyone winning the reward.

The key to the calculation of longitude is time. If you know what hour it is at the place where you are now and also at your original point of departure; if you subtract one figure from the other and multiply the result by fifteen, you know how far east or west of your starting point you are, measured in degrees of longitude. It only then remains for you to add or subtract the difference between the longitude of your embarkation point and the Greenwich meridian to fix your absolute longitude. That is the easy way. Unfortunately, it was not available to sailors in the 1760s. Or, rather, it was only just beginning to be available. To make the necessary calculations an accurate chronometer is essential: one that is impervious to the erratic movements of a ship and to variations in heat and humidity. Such sophisticated instruments were just on the point of being perfected.

In 1728 a thirty-five-year-old horologist by the name of John Harrison arrived in London with a design for a new clock. He devoted the rest of his long life to perfecting it. During that time he made a succession of instruments. The first was cumbersome and expensive but its successors were progressively more

*Equivalent to £1 million in modern currency.

manageable – and accurate – and a pocket chronometer tested on a trip to Barbados in 1764 enabled longitude to be calculated to within ten miles. The terms of the government's offer had obviously been met but it took the now aged Harrison another nine months to induce them to pay up. Meanwhile similar work had been done in Paris, where Pierre Le Roy produced another type of chronometer in 1765. The principles had been established but it was still a further twenty years before ships could be issued with inexpensive, standard chronometers.

Bougainville and his contemporaries, therefore, had to rely on the *other* method for calculating longitude. It was more complicated. It required careful handling of instruments and several mathematical calculations. It was also less accurate. But those experts who preferred this method (and the superiority of calculations based on chronometers was by no means proved in the 1760s) believed that it could be perfected and simplified. The astronomical calculation of longitude aimed at measuring the difference in time between different points on the earth's surface by comparing the occurrence of constant astronomical phenomena such as the angular distance between the moon and various other heavenly bodies. The marine navigator – given a clear sky and a deck that was not pitching too violently – had to take regular readings with instruments of varying sophistication. Then he had to consult his almanac, which gave him corresponding measurements in London or Paris or some other European fixed point for every day of the year. The arithmetic necessary to convert all these data into a single, accurate measurement of the angle of longitude was not simple and was certainly beyond many mariners. However, the astronomical method, like the mechanical method, was being improved. In 1766 the British Astronomer Royal, Nevil Maskelyne, published the *Nautical Almanac* which provided a new set of lunar tables and instructions for their use. Equipped with these, an accurate set of readings and more than a smattering of mathematics a naval officer could calculate longitude in about a quarter of an hour. But there were still many points in the process at which human error could insinuate itself. What was needed, in Bougainville's opinion, was to take an expert to sea and entrust all measurements and calculations to him.

Thus it was that Pierre Antoine Véron, a young astronomer, boarded the expedition's flagship, *Boudeuse,* equipped with all the latest instruments. During the voyage he took thousands of readings with quadrant, octant and megameter – devices of varying sophistication for measuring the angular distance between various heavenly bodies. Sometimes Bougainville took his own readings for the sake of comparison and noted the results in his journal. Whenever possible Véron went ashore to make his sightings under more stable conditions and twice he observed eclipses. All his calculations were checked against the ship's charts and Bougainville's readings. Always there were discrepancies and the discrepancies were not even constant. They might be several degrees or only a few minutes in disagreement. Sometimes they erred to the east, sometimes to the west. Islands shown on Bougainville's Pacific charts were, in reality, nowhere to be seen. Similarly unexpected chunks of land showed up in what should have been empty ocean. Even familiar landmarks appeared in the 'wrong' place. For example, the position of the Azores as calculated by M. Véron's methods differed by 200 nautical miles from that shown on the chart. Bougainville's scientific approach to the problems of longitude measurement was a long overdue initiative. He and Véron established for the first time the actual width of the Pacific Ocean. But overall it must be said that their work clearly illuminated the extent of the problem rather than provided a lasting solution. However, the French might with some justification claim that their first circumnavigation, unlike contemporary British ventures, was planned in a spirit of scientific enquiry

It is a measure of the importance the government placed upon it that Bougainville was equipped with a newly-built frigate, the *Boudeuse.* However, from the start, the commander was worried about his vessel. The *Boudeuse* was designed as a sleek, fast-moving warship. She was armed with twelve-pounders and carried a great deal of sail. She was a greyhound of the sea. But Bougainville needed a cart-horse, a stalwart ship that he could cram with supplies and which would stand up to the buffetings of the ocean. His worst fears were realised when the first Atlantic storm carried away the *Boudeuse's* foretop and maintop and the overloaded vessel took in too much water. Immediately he returned to Nantes, where he had the masts shortened, exchanged his twelve-pounders for smaller cannon and carried out other modifications. Still he was unhappy. He was convinced that his ship would not survive the legendary horrors of Cape Horn and, therefore, he planned to take the slower route through the Straits of Magellan.

Bougainville was an immensely cautious man – no great fault in a circumnavigator. He was determined to leave nothing to chance. Having completed his Falklands mission and returned to Rio de Janeiro to rendezvous with his storeship, the *Étoile*, he devoted another five months to recaulking and refitting his ships and cramming aboard all the victuals they could hold. He divided his crews into three groups and rotated them so that one contingent was always resting ashore. By mid-November 1767, ships and men were in as good shape as they would ever be and Bougainville had provisions for ten months' sailing. Yet, as he ruefully reported, some of his followers were not prepared to face the rigours ahead. He shared with Byron the aggravation of having some of his crew enticed away by the Portuguese: 'Notwithstanding all our care, twelve men, soldiers and sailors, deserted from the two ships'.[1] It was Bougainville's boast that, unlike the British, he had no need to offer his men financial inducements, and he later reported:

It has not been necessary to animate them by any extra-ordinary incitement, such as the English thought it necessary to grant to the crew of commodore Byron. Their constancy has stood the test of the most critical situations, and their good will has not one moment abated. But the French nation is capable of conquering the greatest difficulties, and nothing is impossible to their efforts, as often as she will think herself equal at least to any nation in the world.[2]

But it would seem that at least a dozen members of his expedition did not share their leader's ardent national pride.

Bougainville claimed that his decision to proceed via the Straits was taken on purely professional grounds. Not only did he consider his ships to be unequal to rounding the Horn; he actually professed to believe that it was safer to take the open sea route during the southern winter when there is less than eight hours of daylight. Since he was obliged to travel in summer, he insisted that the proper course was by way of Magellan's Straits. Byron concurred with this judgement up to a point. He thought December and January the best months for passing through the Straits but he believed this course *always* better than the alternative. 'I would prefer it twenty times over to the going round Cape Horn,' he honestly stated.[3] There seems little doubt that Bougainville felt the same basic fear of the 'wild Horn's hate'. His strange opinion runs so completely counter to the experience of earlier expeditions that it is difficult to avoid the conclusion that Bougainville was seeking to excuse rather than explain his actions. For example, Anson's difficulties in this region had arisen largely because he had delayed his assault on the waters of the Horn to March and April when the winter storms were at their worst. Bougainville, fully familiar with such awful precedents, simply took the safest course – and would probably have done so whatever time of year he reached Cape Virgins. No modern sailor would criticise him for such a decision but there were, at that time, many men in England and not a few in France, who questioned his bravery and insisted that the first French circumnavigation was not to be compared with the courageous exploits of Anson, Schouten and other great mariners. Bougainville was familiar with the eastern end of the Straits: he had made previous voyages there collecting timber for his Falklands colony. The devil he partially knew must have seemed infinitely preferable to the notorious devil he did not.

But the demon of the Straits played him false with a vengeance. Bougainville took fifty-two days to reach the Pacific. Although dwarfed by Carteret's mammoth 119 days his passage from ocean to ocean is still one of the longest on record. Even Magellan's tiny ships took two weeks less for the journey than the *Boudeuse* and the *Étoile*. But it was not only the strong currents and unpredictable winds which delayed the Frenchmen. Bougainville was a captain who took no chances. He preferred to keep within sight of land, even though this meant taking constant soundings and reducing sail every time the wind veered to an unfavourable quarter. He anchored frequently and sought out suitable havens in which to rest his ships and men. He took every opportunity to go ashore for fresh food and water.

It was, in fact, his desire to ensure the health of his crew which was Bougainville's chief and most convincing justification for his slow passage through the Straits. The fear of scurvy was very real and the captain wanted his men to be as fit as possible before the long Pacific crossing ahead. In this respect his caution paid dividends:

> . . . there will be some obstacles in passing the straits, but this retardment is not entirely time lost. There is water, wood and shells [i.e. shellfish] in abundance. Sometimes there are likewise very good fish; and I make no doubt but the scurvy would make more havoc among a crew who should come into the South Seas by way of Cape Horn, than among those who should enter the same seas through the Straits of Magellan. When we left it we had no sick person on board.[4]

Once in the Pacific, Bougainville's most pressing concern was maintaining the health of his crew. He intended to 'island hop', making landfalls as often as possible. Ironically, it was good fortune which prevented him making his first projected stop at Juan Fernandez. It being midsummer, the south-east trades were at their southernmost point and Bougainville had to take advantage of them. From late January to the beginning of April his ships scudded north-westwards across the ocean, while he scoured the horizon for a landfall. The *Étoile* and the *Boudeuse* sailed a parallel course keeping just in sight of each other so as to observe as wide a swathe of ocean as possible.

Within six weeks scurvy had begun to appear, despite all Bougainville's precautions: 'Each sailor got daily a pint of lemonade, prepared with a kind of powder, called powder of *faciot*'.[5] This powder was mixed with fresh water obtained either from rain or from distilling sea water in an apparatus designed by a Monsieur Poissonier. Every night the still was set in operation and it produced one barrel by morning. Although Bougainville set much store by these measures it is unlikely that they did anything to stave off scurvy. Powdered lemonade cannot have provided the vitamin C so abundant in fresh fruit and vegetables. Fortunately, the French expedition reached land before the disease became rampant.

After passing the outer islands of the Tuamotu archipelago, the voyagers came on 6 April to Tahiti which Wallis had discovered the previous year. The islanders must have thought that their British friends had returned for they rushed out by canoe in their hundreds to greet them, bearing gifts of fowls, fruit, meat and coconuts. Nor was that all.

The periaguas [canoes] were full of females, who, for agreeable features, are not inferior to most European women, and who, in point of beauty of the body might, with much reason, vie with them all. Most of these fair females were naked, for the men and the old women that accompanied them, had stripped them of the garments which they generally dress themselves in . . . The men . . . soon explained their meaning very clearly. They pressed us to choose a woman and to come on shore with her; and their gestures, which were nothing less than equivocal, denoted in what manner we should form an acquaintance with her.[6]

Small wonder that the Frenchmen enjoyed their two-week stay among the exceedingly friendly Tahitians. The Polynesians' tolerance and desire to please seemingly knew no bounds. Even when some of their men were murdered by the sailors, they did not turn against their visitors. Yet, those visitors unwittingly ill repaid their hosts. For shortly afterwards venereal disease, previously unknown, spread among the islanders and they attributed its appearance to the men of the *Boudeuse* and the *Étoile*. And when the ships, at last, prepared to sail away, one of the young men begged to accompany his new friends back to Europe.*

Bougainville sailed due westwards on about the 15°S parallel of latitude, stalked always by the spectre of scurvy. There was now no lack of land; the voyagers were in the maze of the isles and atolls that make up southern Polynesia. The French expedition, by crossing the Pacific farther to the south than its predecessors, was able to add several new discoveries to the charts. But the cautious captain rarely allowed his mariners to stop. The sight of natives brandishing spears, or breakers smashing onto jagged reefs was sufficient for him to order his helmsman to steer away into deeper water. Just what was Bougainville up to? If we were to judge his actions purely on the basis of his own written account we would have difficulty in making much sense of them. He emerges from his journal as a strange mixture of contradictory aspirations and anxieties. His perseverance in journeying due west was, he claimed, to discover the east coast of New Holland (Australia).

Yet as soon as he encountered what he believed to be

---

*Bougainville took him to Paris where for some months he was the sensation of society. Then he sent the young Polynesian on a ship bound for Île de France, together with precise instructions for finding Tahiti, in the hope that he would find a captain able and willing to return him to his people. Whether or not he regained his native land is unknown.

floating vegetation – he made the assumption that it was a barren shore and concluded, 'It would have been rashness to risk running in with a coast from whence no advantage could be expected, and which one could not get clear of, but by beating against the reigning winds.'[7] Accordingly, he altered course to the north-east (a fortunate decision, for had he continued to westward he would eventually have encountered the Great Barrier Reef).

By now (7 June 1768) hunger was adding to the miseries of his crew. Bread and pulses were strictly rationed and the salt meat was so foul that his men preferred to eat rats when they could catch them. Yet when, after three days' sailing, they reached, and named, the Louisiade Archipelago which seemed able to furnish all their needs, Bougainville declined to stop.

Long before the break of day, a delicious smell announced us the vicinity of this land, which forms a great gulf open to the S.E. I have seen but few lands, which bore a finer aspect than this; a low ground, divided into plains and groves, lay along the sea-shore, and from thence it rose like an amphitheatre up to the mountains, whose summits were lost in the clouds. There were three ranges of mountains; and the highest chain was above twenty-five leagues in the interior parts of the country. The wretched condition to which we were reduced, did not allow us, either to spend some time in visiting this beautiful country, that by all appearances, was fertile and rich; nor to stand to westward in search of a passage on the south side of New Guinea, which might open a new and short navigation to the Moluccas, by the gulf of Carpentaria. Nothing, indeed, was more probable, than the existence of such a passage; it was even believed, that the land had been seen as far as W by S. We were now obliged to endeavour to get out of this gulf as soon as possible . . .[8]

Bougainville was clearly not a coward, so how do we explain his timorousness in the face of poorly-armed 'savages'? He was concerned for the welfare of his crew, so why did he shun potentially beneficial landfalls? He was a dedicated explorer, so what reason did he have for deliberately declining to seek the coast of *Terra Australis* and refusing to sail through the Torres Strait, separating Australia from New Guinea? The answer lies in his secret instructions. His immediate objective was the Moluccas. He had to be sure of reaching the Spice Islands in order to reconnoitre the possibilities for French trade and to collect his sample plants. His cargo and his news were urgently required at Île de France, so he could not afford to take up more time in speculative forays around the coasts of the southern continent. But he had another problem: if he did not make haste to reach the Indies he would miss the monsoons which were to carry him across the Indian Ocean and this would delay by several months his arrival at Île de France. Bougainville's options had thus been reduced to one: he had to make for the Moluccas by the only known route. This meant turning eastwards in order to circle the Louisiades. This proved much more difficult than he had hoped. Day after day the lookouts scanned the reefs and islands on their port beam for some break that would enable the ships to get back on course. But, as Bougainville and his men travelled farther and farther away from their objective, there seemed no end to the shoals and the breakers. It was as though they had become embayed in a vast gulf from which there was no escape.

For over two weeks they sailed steadily eastwards, the fear of wandering among these hostile coral outcrops until hunger and disease picked them off, one by one, growing stronger by the hour. So it is easy enough to imagine the crews' relief when, on 25 June, they sighted the easternmost point of the chain and thankfully named it 'Cape Deliverance'.

A northerly course brought the Frenchmen to New Ireland where they at last found a safe anchorage. By a strange chance it was precisely the same bay, English Cove, in which Carteret and his men had sheltered. A reconnaissance party discovered nails, pieces of tent ropes and the metal plate which Carteret had fixed to a tree. This had, however, been torn down and broken by some Polynesian visitors. The haven offered fresh water and timber but little in the way of food. Thus, when the Frenchmen continued on their way after a stay of eight days their general condition was but little improved. However, English Cove was the location of an important scientific experiment. While here Véron observed a solar eclipse and from it he calculated his position accurately. Having done that he was able to do what no mariner had ever done before, make a correct assessment of his longitude and thus of the width of the Pacific.

On 24 August the master of the *Boudeuse* died of scurvy. Almost all the men and officers were now afflicted with the disease and half of them were too ill to work. But deliverance was near. The ships were cruising along the northern coast of New Guinea and on 1 September they reached the eastern edge of the Moluccas. Aided at last by accurate charts, Bougainville made for the Dutch factory of Kajeli on the island Buru:

> The aspect of a pretty, large town, situated in the bottom of the gulf; of ships at anchor there, and of cattle rambling through the meadows, caused transports which I have doubtless felt, but which I cannot here describe.[9]

Bougainville hoisted a Dutch flag and fired a gun in salute as he entered the harbour but the local ruler, who came aboard the frigate, was cautious. He had strict instructions from the Dutch governor to give no succour to foreign ships. However, when all had been explained, the Frenchman received a warm welcome. He and his officers supped that evening in the chief's house:

> One must have been a sailor, and reduced to the extremities which we had felt for several months together, in order to form an idea of the sensation which the sight of greens and of a good supper produced in people in that condition. This

supper was for me one of the most delicious moments of my life . . .[10]

But there could be no dallying in this delectable haven. There was little more than a month to the start of the north-east monsoon. In that month Bougainville had to reach Batavia and stay there long enough to obtain supplies and repairs before taking once more to the open sea. Thus, after only eight days, the *Boudeuse* and the *Étoile* weighed anchor from Kajeli. Bougainville naturally did not indicate in his journal whether he had obtained during his brief stay what he had come to the Moluccas for. Perhaps he did not; Pierre Véron certainly had to return to the Spice Islands the following year for the vital plants upon which the prosperity of Île de France was destined to be founded.

On 28 September, after a good spell of sailing weather, the expedition reached Batavia. Like other commanders before him, Bougainville was anxious to expose his men as little as possible to the fever-haunted avenues and palaces of the city. Yet it took two and a half weeks to see his ships provisioned and put in readiness for the homeward stage of the voyage. By that time malaria and dysentery were rife among his crews and four men eventually died.

The *Boudeuse* and the *Étoile* left Batavia on 16 October 1768 and after a good crossing reached Port Louis on the north-west coast of Île de France. Bougainville and his men must have been delighted to be back among their own countrymen but they found the summer heat and humidity of the little colony oppressive. They also found the inhabitants bitterly divided by quarrels between the new governor, Jean Dumas, and representatives of the East India Company (Dumas was, in fact, recalled during the *Boudeuse's* stay). Bougainville shared with the leaders of the community whatever information he had gleaned in the Moluccas and it was agreed that Véron should remain to help re-establish relations with the ruler of Kajeli. As soon as the new sailing season arrived he set out with the intendant of Île de France, Pierre Poivre, on an expedition to the Spice Islands which brought back specimens of clove and nutmeg trees for replanting.

The only remaining feature of interest about Bougainville's voyage was the incident we have already mentioned when the French ship overtook Carteret's near the island of Ascension. His offer of help to the British captain was undoubtedly genuine; he noted in his journal that the *Swallow* 'went very ill'. But it was doubtless with a distinct twinge of pride that he watched the British ship which had set out months before his own fall far behind and disappear over the southern horizon.

The French ships sailed on and reached St Malo in March 1769. Bougainville closed his account of the voyage with what he obviously considered to be its most important achievement: 'I entered it on the 16th in the afternoon, having lost only seven men, during two years and four months, which were expired since we had left Nantes.'[11] Of the seven, only two had died of scurvy. The longest period spent at sea without anti-scorbutics had been five months and Bougainville noted that, had their arrival in the Moluccas been delayed by a few more days, he would certainly have lost several more men. What this voyage demonstrated was the maximum length of time sailors could survive without a proper diet.

Louis de Bougainville's circuit of the globe was the first French circumnavigation, but it has another – and perhaps more intriguing – claim to fame: it was the first circumnavigation by a woman. When the *Étoile's* crew was embarking at Rochefort, one of her officers, M. de Commercon, was approached on the quayside by a young man, named Bare, who asked to be taken on as a servant. After a few weeks at sea certain suspicion was being entertained about young Bare. 'His shape, voice, beardless chin, and scrupulous attention of not changing his linen or making the natural discharges in the presence of anyone, other signs . . . kept up this suspicion.'[12] How a company of raucous sailors – and French sailors at that – can have kept themselves from the simple and pleasurable task of verifying such a rumour, Bougainville does not tell us. Bare was, apparently, a strong and attentive servant. Commercon was the expedition's botanist and Bare always accompanied him ashore, frequently carrying his heavy equipment over long distances. It was when Commercon landed at Tahiti to explore the local flora that all was discovered. The Polynesian men were, apparently, more observant than their French counterparts.

> Bare had hardly set his feet on shore with the herbal under his arm, when the men of Tahiti surrounded him, cried out 'It is a woman!', and wanted to give her the honours customary in the isle. The Chevalier de Bournand, who was upon guard on shore, was obliged to come to her assistance, and escort her to the boat.[13]

The story she told, amidst many tears, to the commander was that she was a country girl orphaned at a young age, who, finding herself without money or friends, had refused to turn to the only occupation open to young women in such a situation. Instead she had donned masculine attire and found employment as valet to a Swiss gentleman. When she heard that the *Étoile* was bound for a voyage round the world she had been seized by a desire for the kind of adventure denied to all members of her sex. That was why she had approached M. de Commercon.

One would love to know more about Mlle Bare. Bougainville assures us that she completed the voyage with her honour intact, which says as much for the discipline of his men as it does for her resolution. Strange that she did not become a celebrity on her return, the subject of romanticised biography or ribald broadsheet. Certainly, in terms of circumnavigation hers was a singular feat and one which would not be repeated for many years.

By the time Bougainville reached home the most famous of all

Pacific explorers was already in the South Sea on a course for Tahiti. The three voyages of James Cook belong more properly to the history of discovery than to the history of circumnavigation. Cook solved, almost singlehanded, most of the remaining mysteries of the world's largest expanse of water; he added new islands and landmasses to the charts; he familiarised himself with the wind and current patterns of previously untravelled oceans; and he kept his ships free of scurvy and fever throughout months at sea. Yet, because he made mariners more familiar with the world's oceans and opened up new routes, his travels profoundly affected the story of circumnavigation. This is particularly true of his second voyage which we will follow in some detail. But first we shall have to consider briefly the expedition of 1768–1771 which overlapped with those of Bougainville and Carteret.

James Cook was a thirty-nine-year-old ship's master who had served on merchant and naval ships for twenty years and had latterly been employed as a marine surveyor of the coast of Labrador and Newfoundland. He had a keen mind, little encumbered by formal education. This made him both eager to learn from experience and able to assimilate, evaluate and accurately record information. Add to this the facts that he was methodical in his habits and quietly authoritarian in the exercise of command and you have a character ideally equipped to lead men into – and through – the unknown.

The main objective of the voyage which began on 25 August 1768 was the continuation of the work begun by Byron and Wallis, particularly seeking out the elusive *Terra Australis* which was still believed to lie to the south of the routes taken by earlier ships:

Whereas there is reason to imagine that a continent or land of great extent may be found to the southward of the tract lately made by captain Wallis in his majesty's ship the *Dolphin* (of which you will herewith receive a copy) or of the tract of any former navigators . . . You are to proceed southward in order to make discovery of the continent above mentioned until you arrive in the latitude of 400, unless you sooner fall in with it. But, not having discovered it or any evident signs of it in that run, you are to proceed in search of it to the westward between the latitude before mentioned and the latitude of 350 until you discover it, or fall in with the eastern side of the land discovered by Tasman and now called New Zealand.[14]

So ran Cook's secret instructions. But the openly acknowledged purpose of the voyage was a purely scientific one. On 3 June 1769 the planet Venus was scheduled to pass between the earth and the sun, a phenomenon which would not recur for another 105 years. Mathematicians and astronomers were excited by this event because they believed it would enable them to calculate the distance between the two planets and between Venus and the sun, thus enabling the distance between the earth and her parent star to be determined for the first time ever. To do the job properly it was important to observe the transit of Venus from several locations. As part of the British contribution to this international scientific project, the Royal Society, supported by George III, who personally donated £4,000, proposed to send observers to the recently discovered island of Tahiti. Thus, Cook found himself making a journey to the South Sea accompanied by a scientific team led by the wealthy patron and amateur botanist, Joseph Banks.

And this time a circumnavigator was provided with a vessel specifically chosen for the purpose. The lessons of the Wallis-Carteret voyage seem to have been learned and the Admiralty, having considered and rejected several small naval ships currently available, decided to buy a Whitby-built collier, the *Earl of Pembroke,* for the task. She was small (106 feet overall), sturdy, young (laid down in 1764) and had adequate storage space for the provisions needed on a long voyage. Equipping her with new masts, six guns and an outer sheathing to her hull (wood and flat-headed iron nails, not copper) transformed this

merchant vessel into his majesty's barque *Endeavour*. The
Admiralty had learned another lesson from previous expeditions. This was that it was very difficult to keep a group of
ships, or even two ships, together on long passages. The risks
of slower vessels being separated from their flagship, lost at sea
or simply hampering the work of the commander far
outweighed any advantages which might be gained by mutual
support and strength of numbers. So, on 25 August 1768,
Endeavour sailed alone.

She took the conventional route via Madeira and the Cape
Verde Islands to Brazil. She reached Tierra del Fuego at the
height of the southern summer and Cook then took her round
the Horn. His instructions ordered him to do so. The Admiralty
had concluded from the experiences of Anson and Wallis that,
at the right time of year, it was better to risk the storms off the
Cape than the possible delays of the Straits. And Cook was
lucky. Even a giant sleeps sometimes and, though Cook had to
tack far to the south against the prevailing westerlies, he met
none of the savage gales that other mariners had experienced.
There were even days of flat calm when Joseph Banks could be
rowed away in a boat to shoot birds for his collection and the
table. Cook was able to approach within a few miles of Cape
Horn itself and describe it accurately while Charles Green, the
astronomer, correctly computed its longitude. By 13 February,
when his ship was well into the Pacific, Cook could allow an
element of self-congratulation to creep into his journal:

. . . we are now advanced about 120° the westward of the
Strait of Magellan and 3½° to the northward of it, having
been 33 days in doubling Cape Horn or the land of Tierra del
Fuego, and arriving into the degree of latitude and longitude
we are now in without ever being brought once under our
close reefed topsails since we left Strait la Maire, a circumstance that perhaps never happened before to any ship in
those seas so much dreaded for hard gales of wind, insomuch
that the doubling of Cape Horn is thought by some to be a

mighty thing and others to this day prefer the Straits of
Magellan.[15]

It would be wrong to say that Cook had dispelled that dread.
Just off the Falklands there lies the 'tall ships' graveyard', an
area of ocean floor littered with the remains of vessels so
battered by the winds and waves of the Horn that they had to
be scuttled. Hundreds of others were not so fortunate as to be
able to lay their bones where they wished. No mariner looks
forward to rounding the Horn, yet many, like Cook, have
found the experience an anticlimax. What Cook did establish
was that the dangers could be minimised. He concluded, and on
his next voyage proved, that the best way to double the Horn
was from west to east, in order to take advantage of the
prevailing winds. This, the southern summer, and that element
of luck every deep-sea man needs could rob the notorious
passage of much of its terror.

Exactly two calendar months later, after a trouble-free run
before the trades, *Endeavour* anchored at Tahiti. Three months
were spent in this South Sea 'paradise' and all the visitors
enjoyed their stay. The scientists did their work. Cook observed
and recorded the geography and customs of the island. And his
men availed themselves of all the pleasures extended to them by
the lithe, smiling natives – pleasures which, they were delighted
to discover, had not been exaggerated by Wallis's mariners.
Cook had the usual problem of theft to contend with. Tools,
weapons, clothing and scientific instruments disappeared with
alarming frequency. Even inside the well-guarded stockade
things were not safe. The Polynesians could insinuate themselves silently through the smallest spaces and make off with
their spoils. The scientist in Cook was fascinated by this very
strange culture but when it came to practical matters, such as
stealing, the Christian in him could not make allowance for a
different set of moral values. His reprisals and threats sometimes puzzled and angered his hosts. An even more serious
incident occurred as *Endeavour* was being made ready to

depart. Two of his men decided not to leave this tropical heaven. They disappeared into the hills accompanied by their Tahitian lovers and with the connivance of the girls' families and friends. If Cook had tolerated this minor desertion he could well have found himself with a serious mutiny on his hands. He had to take drastic action, even at the risk of alienating the islanders. So, he arrested some of their leading men and held them until the fugitives were delivered up. The captain only resorted to force reluctantly but his determination, when necessary, to impose his will on a people whose friendship and cooperation were important indicates the root cause of those misunderstandings which bedevilled many South Sea expeditions and eventually cost Cook his life.

Finally leaving the Society Islands behind on 9 August, the *Endeavour* set course due south into the unvisited latitudes of the Pacific. After three weeks there was still no evidence of land and Cook decided that he could not carry out a complete examination of this stretch of ocean:

> I did intend to have stood to the southward if the winds had been moderate, so long as they continued westerly, notwithstanding we had no prospect of meeting with land, rather than stand back to the northward on the same track as we came; but as the weather was so very tempestuous I laid aside this design, thought it more advisable to stand to the northward into better weather, least we should receive such damages in our sails and rigging as might hinder the further prosecutions of the voyage.[16]

But Cook was still determined to pursue his westerly course farther south than any previous captain and to seek land where European expeditions had sought it before. He even offered a gallon of rum to the first man to sight it. The prize fell to Nick Young, a ship's boy, who, at 2 p.m. on 6 October, shouted excitedly from the masthead and pointed to the horizon dead ahead. The next day *Endeavour* stood into a broad bay that was obviously part of a considerable land mass. Officers and scientists gathered in eager groups along the ship's rail pointing out to each other mountains, forests and signs of habitation. Surely, here was the long-sought continent, and they were the first to make the greatest discovery since Columbus. The captain was more circumspect. The position they had now reached was very close to that in which Abel Tasman had located a stretch of coast which he had named New Zealand. But the Dutchman had not known whether the mark newly-added to his chart represented an island or the tip of something stretching far to the South. It was Cook who, during the next six months, sailed right round the two islands, thoroughly surveyed the coastline and established that New Zealand was a landmass comparable in size to Great Britain and occupying a place in the southern hemisphere almost identical to that occupied by his homeland in the northern. More importantly it afforded him timber, water, fish, meat and vegetables – especially the invaluable wild celery and scurvy grass.

But the story of the first contact of Europeans with Maoris was not an altogether happy one. The islanders, a warlike, cannibalistic people, were naturally frightened at the strange sight of the *Endeavour,* especially when men put off from her in 'canoes' which they rowed backwards. Had these newcomers got eyes in the back of their heads? In most cases the Maoris reacted with a show of hostility. Inevitably, although Cook ordered his men to be reticent in the use of force, the end result was that the white men, just as nervous as the indigenes, opened fire, killing and wounding several of the natives. However, in many cases the travellers were able to break through the barrier of initial fear and suspicion. They established friendly relations with some communities, bought food from them and bartered freely for such curiosities as weapons, tools and the preserved heads of the villagers' consumed enemies.

Having now found a point of reference on the old charts, Cook was well placed to tidy up some more loose ends. He knew that if he steered due west he should fall in with what Tasman had named Van Diemen's Land (Tasmania) and that, by coasting it northwards, he should be able to determine its size. If he then continued in the same general direction he could discover what lay between it and New Guinea. This course should provide further information about New Holland (Australia) and, particularly, whether or not it and New Guinea were part of the same landmass. This route would also have the advantage of probable frequent landfalls and, therefore, fresh food. Cook probably expected to locate more islands in the area represented on his chart by an empty space. He certainly did not realise that the stage was set for the momentous discovery of the entire eastern coastline of the Australian continent.

Foul weather carried the *Endeavour* northward of Cook's intended course and as he approached, and then passed, the chart location of Van Diemen's land (it was marked 3° too far to the eastward), the captain grew anxious. Sea birds and drift-wood indicated a near shoreline and the storm was driving him sharply towards it. Yet it was quite invisible through the all-enveloping grey of rain, mist and cloud. The nights were particularly hazardous. *Endeavour* rolled forward under reefed sails while the leadsmen took constant soundings. On the night of 18/19 April 1770, Cook took in all sail and hove to. It was as well he did so; at dawn the south-east coast of Australia was clearly visible.

For seven weeks the voyagers followed the coast northwards, marvelling at its extent and growing increasingly excited at the significance of the discovery they were making. Banks and the other scientists had a wonderful time collecting botanical and zoological specimens though, in general, they found the coast rather barren. What neither they nor Cook realised as bays, headlands and inlets were noted and named on the charts, was that they were running into one of nature's deadliest traps. North of the Tropic of Capricorn the Great Barrier Reef begins to converge with the coast. Shoals and arms of viciously beautiful coral gradually but inexorably close the gap. As *Endeavour* sailed northwards the watch officers had to contend with wildly fluctuating soundings – 20 fathoms, 17, 12, 22, 9! Just before 11 o'clock on the night of 10 June the ship came to a sudden, jarring halt. She was stuck fast on the reef – and at high tide.

For the next twenty-four hours everything was desperate but organised action. Everyone, including the scientists, took turns at the pumps. The boats were launched in readiness to haul *Endeavour* off. Everything that could be spared, starting with the cannon, was thrown overboard. As the ship listed she took in more water. She failed to float off on the next high tide. In the afternoon the pumps were clearly losing the battle. If *Endeavour* did not float free on the next tide she might sink before the crew could get her beached. That night, at high water, with boats' crews straining at the oars the ship was brought off. The sails were run up and *Endeavour* moved towards the land. But there was no suitable place near at hand to run her ashore and water was gushing in through the rent in her bottom. Only a broken-off lump of coral lodged in the gash was slowing the inflow. One remedy remained to be tried. An old sail was lowered over the bow with ropes at each corner, manoeuvred into position over the hole and lashed tight. It worked. Most of the water was pumped out. But it could only be a temporary measure; the stricken vessel had to be hauled onshore for proper repair. But the boats, sent out to find a suitable bay or inlet, had no luck. Then the wind rose again, making manoeuvring more difficult. It was five days before Cook could run the *Endeavour* into a small estuary and bring her bows out of the water for the carpenter and his men to get to work.

But when the repairs were completed Cook's troubles were not over. How could he get away? The wind was almost continuously onshore. And when he was under sail, how to extricate himself from the maze of shoals and reefs into which he had wandered? Boats were sent north and south to look for a channel to the open sea. The results were not encouraging. And if he did get free of the reef would he be able to make sea room away from the massive breakers pounding on the outer edge of the Great Barrier? The fifteen days following 29 July, when he was at last able to take advantage of a slight breeze from the land and leave the creek, were a severe test of his seamanship and captaincy. With the wind on his starboard quarter, he moved cautiously north-eastward, preceded by the pinnace. Frequently he was forced to anchor, then turning round, seek another channel. Cook was baffled, as he honestly recorded in his journal:

> I was quite at a loss which way to steer when the weather would permit us to get under sail. For to beat back to the SE the way we came as the master would have had me done would be an endless piece of work, as the winds blow now constantly strong from that quarter without hardly any inter-mission. On the other hand if we do not find a passage to the northward we shall have to come back at last.[17]

When the wind rose, he had to put out all the anchors to hold *Endeavour* fast and, once, the ship spent three days swinging at her cables and surrounded by reefs and islands. As well as sending the boats out to reconnoitre, Cook made his own observations from the masthead and high points ashore. It was not until 13 August that he found a deep-water channel. Two days later his ship was almost smashed to pieces against the outer wall of the reef. At the last moment a cleft in that wall was observed and he slipped through into sheltered water with as much relief as he had earlier escaped seawards.

By now he was developing a knowledge of his enemy. Though his respect for the reef never diminished, the confi-dence grew that he could outwit it. He had to do so if he was to explore Torres Strait, the gulf that he believed lay between New Guinea and New Holland. So he kept, now, as close to land as possible, always preceded by one or two boats and always anchoring at night. On 21 August he identified and sailed past the northernmost point of Australia and proved that it had no connection with New Guinea.

Endeavour made a brief landfall on the island of Savu but it was under Dutch influence and Cook, like earlier British captains, experienced nothing but suspicion and hostility. So there was nothing for it but to go on to unwholesome Batavia, where *Endeavour* arrived on 11 October. Because she needed a thorough overhaul and there was no way of hurrying the Dutch shipyard workers, the ship and her complement were obliged to stay for two and a half months. The result was inevitable. Cook, who had prided himself that, up to this point he had lost only one man through illness, now had the chagrin of watching seamen, officers and scientists drop like flies. By early December, when the ship was ready, he had only a dozen men fit to sail her and he was obliged to hire nineteen fresh hands. Eventually, thirty men died of malaria and dysentery contracted at Batavia. Considering Cook's remarkable record of having kept scurvy almost completely at bay this was a cruel irony indeed. Losing a third of his men through disease was something which weighed heavily on his mind and made him on his subsequent voyages redouble his already considerable efforts to ensure health and hygiene.

The rest of the voyage proceeded much like most previous circumnavigations. The Cape provided an opportunity for the remaining sick to recuperate and for Cook to replace some of his missing crewmen. There was a brief stop at St Helena, but Cook did not choose to dally at Ascension. At noon on 10 July 1771 Nick Young, who had first sighted New Zealand, proved his keen eyesight again by pointing out Land's End.

A year and a day after setting foot on English soil, Cook went forth to circle the earth again. His voyage in the *Resolution* from 13 July 1772 to 30 July 1775 has been called the greatest maritime expedition of all time. His achievements were breathtaking: the first eastabout circumnavigation; the first penetration of the Antarctic Circle; the first voyage across the Pacific between New Zealand and South America. Perhaps even more gratifying to Cook than his many discoveries was the fact that, despite long spells at sea, not one of his 119 crew died or suffered seriously from scurvy; there was no outbreak of fever; and throughout the entire voyage only one man succumbed to disease.

Even before his return to England, Cook had formulated the plan for a second venture which would complete the exploration of the southern Pacific and establish, once and for all, whether any continent lay to the east of New Zealand. With an alacrity which seems out of character for the Admiralty's lumbering bureaucracy, Cook's superiors agreed to such an expedition and, by the end of September, had begun to make preparations for it. One reason for their lordships' enthusiasm was the evident success of the *Endeavour*'s voyage. The scientific establishment was ecstatic about the achievements of Banks and his colleagues. The profusion of specimens, data and drawings they had brought back would provide the members of the Royal Society with the raw materials for years of research. The popular journals made much of the geographical discoveries and other achievements of the voyage. Banks was received more than once by the king and fêted by London society. It would have been foolish not to ride this wave of national prestige.

But, as always, there was another motive for promoting a second expedition with all despatch. Details of Bougainville's voyage were now known and there seemed little doubt that the French would follow up his discoveries. Particularly worrying was the fact that he had stopped at Tahiti. This island had emerged as the obvious base for all further Pacific endeavours. It was centrally situated, possessed good harbours, an abundance of food, water and timber and was populated by a people almost unique among the Polynesians for their friendship. The thought of the French establishing a superior presence there was intolerable. The Admiralty, therefore, wanted Cook to return to the scene of his former triumphs as soon as possible.

They expressed the hope that all could be in readiness by the following March.

Cook was promoted to the rank of commander and the Navy Board was instructed to provide him with two ships. It was probably Cook's idea to revert to the old scheme of providing a consort vessel. His disastrous plight on the Great Barrier Reef would have been considerably eased with a second ship at his disposal which, if necessary, could have taken aboard all survivors of the shipwreck and sought another way out of the coral labyrinth. In the event, the reversion to a two-ship expedition did not work. Throughout Cook's second voyage of thirty-six months his flagship and consort were twice separated and spent only twelve months together. There was no question, now, what kind of craft was best suited to a long voyage in the southern hemisphere. The *Endeavour* had proved herself beyond a shadow of doubt. The Navy, therefore, bought two more colliers from the same Whitby yard, the *Marquis of Granby* (462 tons) and the *Marquis of Rockingham* (340 tons). Both were comparatively new and in excellent condition. After refitting, they were renamed the *Resolution* and the *Adventure*. (An early suggestion to call them *Drake* and *Raleigh* was dropped as being unnecessarily provocative to the Spanish.)

The projectors of the new voyage assumed that it would be conducted in the same spirit of cordial cooperation between scientific and naval establishments that had marked the cruise of the *Endeavour*. Accordingly, Joseph Banks's offer to lead the scientific team was happily accepted. And that lit the fuse of a series of disasters which rocked the expedition and continued to trouble Cook long after its conclusion. Perhaps because of the adulation he was receiving, Banks had begun to develop autocratic tendencies. He took it upon himself to plan all aspects of *his* new venture and when anyone remonstrated with him he relied on his intimacy with the court and personal friendship with Lord Sandwich, First Lord of the Admiralty, to get his own way.

Without reference to Cook – or to anyone else – Banks accumulated a prodigious amount of equipment and a large suite of servants and scientific assistants. Then he personally redesigned the *Resolution* to accommodate his luggage and personnel. A second deck had to be built and, atop that, a roundhouse. Cook suffered all this in the name of friendship and because Banks was so powerful but every visit to the ship-yard caused him more alarm, particularly when he observed his flagship to be swarming with sightseers: 'scarce a day passed on which she was not crowded with strangers who came on board for no other purpose but to see the ship in which Mr Banks was to sail round the world.'[18] The result of the alterations was disastrous. Charles Clerke, one of Cook's lieutenants, told Banks with brave directness, 'By God, I'll go to sea in a grog tub, if desired, or in the *Resolution* as soon as you please, but must say I think her by far the most unsafe ship I ever saw or heard of.'[19] As if to confirm this judgement, the *Resolution* behaved so badly when she was moved from Deptford down the estuary that the pilot refused to take her beyond the Nore. Her increased superstructure made her so top-heavy that hoisting a single sail threatened to turn her right over. She was returned to her dock and work began immediately on stripping away her extra deck and cabins. Banks was furious. He performed an enraged war dance on the quayside. He wrote angrily to Lord Sandwich. He questioned Cook's competence. He withdrew himself and his staff from the venture. If he thought that the Admiralty would go down on their knees to beg him to reconsider, he miscalculated. The scientific posts on the expedition were offered to others. And Banks went off on a hastily-planned visit to Iceland to salve his bruised pride.

Before many weeks at sea, Cook may well have wished that Banks was back aboard the *Resolution,* baggage and all. For the man who replaced him as naturalist soon proved to be an exceedingly troublesome travelling companion. He was John Reinhold Forster, whom we have met briefly already as the translator of Bougainville's journal. Forster was an impecunious scholar who, despite his undoubted abilities, which earned him, among other things, the patronage of Alexander Dalrymple and a fellowship of the Royal Society, never quite achieved that position in the academic world which he believed was his due. One reason was his inability to make himself agreeable to people who mattered. Indeed, he found it difficult to make himself agreeable to anybody. He was over-sensitive, censorious and argumentative. He was employed, and assisted by his talented son George, to study the flora and fauna of all seas and lands visited and to contribute to an account of the voyage which would be written on the *Resolution*'s return. The Forsters did their job well but the father managed to upset almost every single person aboard the flagship and, after his return, became involved in a bitter argument about the writing of the official account which eventually obliged Cook to undertake the task singlehanded.

However, all that lay in the future when the two ex-colliers slipped out of Plymouth on a morning tide in the middle of the hot summer of 1772. They made a leisurely progress to the Cape of Good Hope, dropping anchor in Table Bay on 30 October. Cook allowed three weeks here for revictualling and bringing ships and men to peak condition for the regions of fog and ice into which they were about to enter. Lying nearby in the anchorage were two Dutch East-Indiamen bound for Batavia. Scurvy was rife on board these vessels but there was no trace of the disease on *Adventure* and *Resolution*. What secret, then, had Cook discovered which enabled him to combat this scourge so effectively?

If by 'secret' we mean some sovereign antiscorbutic which could be kept fresh and potent for months on end, the answer is that he had no secret. It seems that he did not realise the value of fresh lemons and oranges, which were recommended by Dr James Lind, for these items do not appear on his lists of provisions. This is strange, for Banks had dosed himself with citrus fruit juice during the cruise of the *Endeavour* and Lind almost came on Cook's second voyage. (He withdrew when Banks abandoned the expedition.) The reason for this blindspot may be that he placed no confidence in another substance with which the Admiralty provided him: rob. This was a syrup made from lemon and orange juice, boiled down and mixed with sugar. Cook was, of course, right: the necessary vitamins had been driven out during the process of concentration. However, he continued to use rob and anything else that varied the diet and might prove beneficial. This included portable soup, currants, sauerkraut, a decoction of malt and spruce beer; few of which items were, in fact, beneficial in cases of scurvy. Like other good captains, he supplemented the ship's larder with fresh meat and vegetables whenever possible. In this he went further than most of his contemporaries by experimenting with whatever berries, grasses, leaves and roots were offered by even the most sparsely covered terrains. None of this set him apart as an innovator.

What made him different was a thoroughness in matters of health and hygiene which was noticed by every officer and seaman who signed on with him. As Lieutenant Clerke observed:

> Our people all in perfect health and spirits, owing, I believe, in a great measure to the strict attention of Captain Cook to their cleanliness and every other article that respects their welfare.[20]

Cook regularly inspected his men, their clothing and their accommodation. He insisted on proper ventilation and regular washing of hands and clothes. Above all, he forced everyone aboard, by a mixture of discipline and example, to take full advantage of a varied diet. One enemy of good health had always been the conservatism of the British sailor. He might grumble about an unbroken regimen of salt beef and ship's biscuit, but he was suspicious of anything new and hostile to such unpalatable innovations as sauerkraut. Cook made a point of sampling every kind of meat and vegetable he encountered. If he believed something was good for his crew he had it served regularly at the officers' table and ordered it to be consumed on the lower deck. Any man who infringed the rule suffered a cut in his rum ration. By his attention to detail James Cook combated the evils of ignorance and prejudice which were so often the midwives of disease.

Leaving Cape Town on 22 November, the two ships struck southwards, to seek land in this uncharted region. Water was rationed, the crews were provided with extra clothing and warned to prepare for hardship. Soon the animals brought aboard at the Cape began dying of cold, so the survivors were killed and eaten. On 10 December *Resolution* and *Adventure* entered a sea strewn with towering, craggy icebergs. Three days later their progress was stopped by pack ice. Cook coasted it to the eastward and southward then found himself caught in a wide bay of ice. The obvious course was to tack out of danger but now snow and fog reduced visibility sometimes to zero. And carrying out the rapid manoeuvres necessary to avoid collision with the great slabs of frozen sea, was a nightmare. When the men braced themselves to haul on the lines they lost their footing on the slippery deck and cut their hands on the ice-crusted ropes. But the ships were sufficiently clear of the worst of the ice by Christmas Day for Cook to feast his men and allow them a few hours of drunken roistering and boxing bouts – much to the disapproval of Forster.

Cook kept as close as he dared to the icefield and, as it broke up under the influence of the midsummer sun he made more southing. On 17 January he entered the Antarctic. Scarcely a day passed which did not reveal some new fact: the sea does not freeze at 32°F (0°C); icebergs are made up of *fresh* water (a very welcome discovery); the presence of birds in the high latitudes is not evidence of nearby land. Cook penetrated 75′ within the circle before being obliged to stand away to the north-east. Without knowing it, he had come within seventy-five miles of the Antarctic continent, a remarkable feat. It would be another forty-seven years before anyone actually saw Antarctica.

In thick fog on 8 February Cook lost contact with his consort. He maintained position for a couple of days, firing the *Resolution's* signal gun at regular intervals but there was no sign of the *Adventure,* which had been carried away by a current and could not bear back. Cook now made for Queen Charlotte Sound in New Zealand, the rendezvous point pre-arranged for just such an emergency, but not without taking a course as far south as the ice floes would permit. The officers, whom Cook consulted, showed little enthusiasm for a return towards the bitterly cold latitudes but their captain never forgot that his first priority was discovery. Sadly, the discomforts of the next six weeks were not repaid with any fresh significant information. *Resolution* was now in the Roaring Forties, the band of often violent westerlies which stretches southwards from the fortieth parallel. Day after day the ship raced along with the wind at her back or on her quarter, over a sea scattered with monumental boulders of ice. The stiffened sails had to be handled frequently by men balanced on the slippery yards working with numb fingers. How the offwatch crew must have cursed these seemingly senseless proceedings and what a relief it must have been when Cook, at last, ordered a change of course to the north-east and ran for New Zealand. When, on 26 March, *Resolution* anchored in Dusky Bay she had travelled over 10,000 miles in 122 days without a sight of land.

Cook allowed a month's respite in this wildly beautiful spot of fjords, steep forest-clad slopes and ribbons of falling water. He made contact with the shy local people and joined his officers on hunting expeditions. The off-duty seamen enjoyed themselves fishing and catching seals on a nearby island. Everyone ate well and enjoyed the varied diet of fish and game birds. Lieutenant Clerke, eating sealmeat for the first time, pronounced it 'very little inferior to beefsteak'. The scientists had plenty to occupy their waking hours. There were charts to be made, specimens to be collected and drawn, astronomical readings to be taken and the chronometers to be checked. The Admiralty had provided Cook with four of these instruments and he tested them stringently. Before the voyage he was a convinced supporter of astronomical reckoning but he gradually changed his opinion. Two of the chronometers failed to last the course and a third was aboard the *Adventure* but the fourth, a copy of one of John Harrison's timepieces, made by Larcum Kendall of Furnival's Inn Court, London, in his opinion 'exceeded the expectations of its most zealous advocate'.[21] All in all, despite some atrocious weather, everyone enjoyed the stay in Dusky Sound – although any haven would probably have seemed paradisal after the experiences of the last few weeks. At the end of April *Resolution* weighed anchor and set off along the west coast for Queen Charlotte Sound. On 18 May she was reunited with her sister ship.

The men of the *Resolution* found their colleagues of the *Adventure* comfortably settled for the winter. The ship was securely anchored. A shore camp had been set up and even gardens planted. Good relations had been established with the locals, who came every day to barter food. It all looked very cosy and Cook's sailors must have looked forward to a prolonged rest. Even their workaholic captain could not contemplate more Antarctic wanderings at this season of the year. If they thought thus they were in for a rude shock. Certainly there could be no question of returning to the high latitudes, but Cook was not prepared to idle away the winter. The island chains of Polynesia still presented puzzles in need of solution and he was under orders to reassert the British presence at Tahiti. On 7 June the two ships launched out due eastwards into the dirty weather of the South Pacific winter.

For almost six weeks they were driven by south-west and north-west gales, between 40° and 47°S, towards the heart of that large area shown on the charts as an empty space and where some geographers still believed a southern continent was located. They were almost half-way to South America before Cook ordered a change of course to the north. What a welcome the warmth and light airs of the Tropics must have been and with what eagerness the men must now have begun to look

forward to the delights of Tahiti. It had so far been a very hard
voyage and now, to make matters worse, scurvy and dysentery
had made their appearance. Yet, only on the *Adventure*, where,
at one time, a third of the crew were ill, was the situation
serious. Cook's few scurvy cases were put on a special diet and
the disease was checked. Nothing could more clearly vindicate
Cook's rigid stance on food and hygiene. It also demonstrates
one of the problems of a two-ship expedition. However
dedicated a second-in-command might be (and Tobias
Furneaux of the *Adventure* was a conscientious captain who
never questioned Cook's orders) he was to a large extent independent when aboard his own ship and thus unresponsive to
the finer points of direction by his superior.

At the beginning of August they came upon the Tuamotus
and threaded their way through them to westward. Cook had
his officers check carefully the positions of every island and
atoll against those recorded on the charts. Because of the plight
of the *Adventure* he found himself trapped into that very
dilemma which had affected so many other Pacific voyagers: his
suffering men urgently needed the rest and fresh food that a
friendly landfall could offer; yet he dared not hurry through
this dangerous region of reefs and shallows. Just how
dangerous it was became clear at dawn on 16 August. During
the night the ships had drifted to within two miles of a reef and
the tide was carrying them steadily closer. Cook ordered the
boats out and all morning *Resolution* and *Adventure* were
towed towards deeper water. They came parallel with a break
in the reef which caused a strong inward current. Within
minutes the two ships were almost upon the coral and so close
to each other that collision seemed inevitable. Hastily they
dropped anchor and swung head on to the surf with
Resolution's stern actually scraping the bottom as each wave
ebbed. Cook shouted for more anchors to be taken off by the
boats and dropped at some distance. Then everyone – sailors,
officers and civilians – strained at the capstans, easing the ship
away from the jagged reef. But all their efforts gained them only

a few yards. Not until dusk, when an evening breeze sprang up from the land, were *Resolution* and *Adventure* able to break free. It had been a strenuous day and one not made easier by the islanders. For in the midst of all the frenzy of shrieked orders, running feet, muttered curses and straining muscles the decks were littered with smiling Polynesians proffering goods for barter.

The voyagers spent a month in Tahiti, staying briefly in a variety of anchorages in order to establish friendly relations with several of the chiefs. On this second visit Cook learned more about the political rivalries and social customs of the people. He came to the conclusion that the Tahitians had a different set of moral values from Europeans and that one should not, therefore, condemn them for stealing or for indulging in casual sexual relationships. However, this did not prevent him dealing summarily with young men caught thieving on board. They were tied to the mainmast, flogged and flung into the sea. Such punishment seemed to be accepted by the islanders, not as just retribution for wrongdoing, but as the penalty for being caught. When the ships departed on 17 September, laden with meat, fruit and vegetables, Cook was satisfied that a rough and ready understanding had been established between the Tahitians and the subjects of His Britannic Majesty.

Now that the charts of the area to the north-east of the Great Barrier Reef were well filled with islands, more or less accurately located, a navigator could plot his course with more confidence than would have been possible a few decades before. Cook decided that he had time to visit the beautiful Tonga Islands before returning to New Zealand. It was a decision he had cause to regret. When his ships reached New Zealand waters in late October they ran into ferocious gales that prevented them reaching a sheltered harbour. It was 3 November before *Resolution* limped into Queen Charlotte Sound with tattered sails and a splintered fore topgallant mast. There was no sign of the *Adventure* and she did not reappear.

Cook waited as long as he could but with the spring well advanced and the Antarctic beckoning he would not delay more than a few days after his ship had been thoroughly overhauled. Leaving a message for the *Adventure*'s captain in a buried bottle beneath a marked tree, he put to sea on 25 November. Five days later the consort reached the rendezvous, badly battered by the storms. Cook's instructions were read and the captain swiftly set in hand repairs and revictualling, with every intention of following *Resolution* as soon as possible. Before he could complete his preparations the local people turned hostile. They attacked one of the ship's boats, killed the occupants and made a feast of them on the beach. The effect on their shipmates' morale was devastating. Though *Adventure* put to sea soon afterwards and set off in the wake of the *Resolution,* her crew had no stomach for further wanderings in the high latitudes. Early in the new year she set course for the Cape – and home.

Cook, meanwhile, spent the summer looking for continents. Twice he penetrated above the Antarctic Circle. In between he returned to 45° midway between New Zealand and South America. He found nothing but ice, fog and discomfort. In the midst of all this, he fell seriously ill. For weeks his strength ebbed but he drove himself on. Then he collapsed with violent intestinal pains and seemed close to death. All the skills of the ship's surgeon were needed to see the crisis through. It was well into March 1774 before the captain was restored to anything approaching full vigour but, at least, the cold latitudes now lay behind. *Resolution* had once more entered the tropics and was running north-west before the trade winds.

Cook had now crossed the southern Pacific from east to west and south to north. He had made the first accurate observations of the Antarctic pack ice. He had made several substantial corrections to the charts – better readings of longitude; a more comprehensive survey of Polynesia. It was, in all conscience, a mammoth achievement for one voyage. His subordinates may well have thought that enough was enough. They had endured great hardships and made important discoveries. They had now lost their consort and even their captain's health had broken under the strain. Surely it was time to pick up the normal homeward route via Batavia. No. Cook still had other plans. He visited the Marquesas, returned to Tahiti, visited Tonga again, then Fiji and New Hebrides. But instead of continuing westwards, he made for New Zealand yet again by way of New Caledonia and Norfolk Island. Scores more names were added to the charts; page after page of Cook's journal was filled with navigational information and observations about the lands and peoples visited, before *Resolution* returned to Queen Charlotte Sound in the spring.

On 10 November 1774 Cook once more sailed out of the now-familiar anchorage on the last leg of his eastabout circumnavigation. He crossed the South Pacific around the 56° parallel and *Resolution* made good time running before the westerlies. By this passage he confirmed his conviction that no major land mass lay in this segment of the ocean.

Most other captains would have given Cape Horn a wide berth and stood well to the south until they reached the Atlantic. Not so James Cook. There were interesting facts to be learned about this notorious and unvisited region. He coasted the bleak, jagged jumble of islands and channels at a few miles' distance. The wind was at his back and gentle. So gentle that he was able to find a safe anchorage on the south-west coast and remain there seven days to explore the inhospitable hinterland on foot. Here the ship's company kept Christmas (and the location went down on the chart as Christmas Sound) in some style, thanks largely to the abundance of wild geese in the locality. There, in that lonely anchorage, where grey rock fell sheer into grey sea, Cook reckoned 'our friends in England did not, perhaps, celebrate Christmas more cheerfully than we did'.[22]

Quitting the Horn, Cook continued in its latitude, his ship borne along by westerlies which now freshened to gale force. There was still one more area of sea to be explored before he would allow himself to regard his task as completed. Earlier voyagers had reported sightings of land in the far South

Atlantic and Cook had to satisfy himself whether these were accurate and, if so, whether they were the edges of a polar continent. And, on 14 January 1775, in 54°15′S, the lookout sighted the white peaks of what might have been an iceberg but turned out to be something stationary and more solid. Could this craggy terrain of bare rock and glaciers be the outermost cape of Antarctica? No. Cook travelled the length of its coast and realised that it was but an isolated island. He gave it the name of South Georgia and set course south-eastward, back into the ice floes. No more land was to be seen and before steering for the Cape, at last, Cook allowed himself a rare moment of boastfulness: if he had not found the Antarctic continent, no one could:

> . . . the greatest part of this Southern Continent (supposing there is one) must lay within the Polar Circle, where the sea is so pestered with ice, that the land is thereby inaccessible. The risk one runs in exploring a coast in these unknown and icy seas, is so very great, that I can be bold to say, that no man will ever venture farther than I have done and that the lands which may lie to the South will never be explored. Thick fogs, snow storms, intense cold and every other thing that can render navigation dangerous one has to encounter and these difficulties are greatly heightened by the inexpressibly horrid aspect of the country, a country doomed by Nature never once to feel the warmth of the sun's rays, but to lie for ever buried under everlasting snow and ice. The ports which may be on the coast are in a manner wholly filled up with frozen snow of a vast thickness, but if any should so far be open as to admit a ship in, it is even dangerous to go in, for she runs a risk of being fixed there for ever, or coming out in an ice island. The islands and floats of ice on the coast, the great falls from the ice cliffs in the port, or a heavy snow storm attended with a sharp frost, would prove equally fatal.[23]

'The lands which may lie to the South will never be explored'? Cook failed to make allowance for the existence of men as adventurous and determined as himself.

On 22 March *Resolution* entered Table Bay and, after a five week stay, sailed for England, which she reached on the penultimate day of July. The incredible journey was over. It was the greatest voyage of discovery ever made and one of the greatest circumnavigations. What it did for later sailors was to free them from the land. It established that going eastabout in the Roaring Forties was the best way of circuiting the globe. This meant longer periods at sea than earlier captains had cared to embark upon but Cook had now shown that it could be done. With no more medical knowledge than that available to all other naval officers, he had kept his crew fit and healthy in the most trying conditions that any group of sailors had ever encountered. In addition to all this, he had taken up the challenge of the Antarctic. It was inevitable that others would follow him. For, like every great pioneer, he both opened up the way and inspired others to follow it.

8

A COUNTRY DOOMED BY NATURE

Once the mystery of the southern continent had been solved, attention focused once more on the northern Pacific and, in particular, on the old quest for a north-west passage. This was what Cook was seeking when he set out in *Resolution* and *Discovery* once again on 12 July 1776. He reached the coast of Alaska in about 60°N before being forced to turn back and seek a warmer location for the winter months. While the ship was anchored at Kealakekua Bay, Hawaii, a dispute arose with the local people. It was the old misunderstanding about stealing metal equipment. But this time it had a tragic outcome. A dispute over a pair of armourer's tongs ended with Cook being hacked to death at the water's edge, on St Valentine's Day, 1779.

Cook's discoveries and his death at the height of his fame spurred others on to complete the work of Pacific exploration. They also kept Anglo-French rivalry alive. The two countries were once more at war between 1778 and 1783 but, as soon as the hostilities were over and ships could be released, the French Government:

. . . with a view of occupying usefully the leisure of peace, and of procuring for the officers of our navy great means of instruction, intended to give orders for the equipment of two frigates, which, in sailing round the world, should be employed in examining such portions of the earth as navigators had not yet visited; in completing various discoveries made in the Great Ocean by the French; and in improving, by astronomical observations and by researches into the different branches of physics and natural history, the general and particular description of the globe which we inhabit.[1]

The man entrusted with this expedition was Jean François de Galaup La Perouse, a seasoned and experienced captain. He sailed from Brest on 1 August 1785 in command of *La Boussole* and *L'Astrolabe*. Since his major objective was the North Pacific, he ignored Cook's route and reverted to the old westabout circumnavigation. By the following June he had reached roughly the same point on the American coast that Cook had reached before he, too, was forced to turn south. He explored the coastline and islands right down to Monterey in California, crossed to Macao and, in the summer of 1787, worked his way up the Asiatic coast of the Pacific. He reached the region of 62°N. Realising that contrary winds would again force him to abandon his search for the Straits of Anian, he decided to send a report back to Paris overland. From Petropavlovsk-Kamchatskiy, the extreme outpost of the Russian empire, he despatched Jean, Baron de Lesseps, on the 8,000 mile trans-Siberian journey to France.

De Lesseps was the only member of the expedition to complete the circumnavigation. La Perouse sailed away before the harbour iced over for the winter. In Samoa the captain of the *Astrolabe* was murdered with ten of his men. The ships sailed on, calling at Tonga, Norfolk Island and then at Port Jackson, the newly-established British penal settlement on the coast of New South Wales. La Perouse and his companions left there in February 1788 and were never seen again. Several expeditions were despatched to look for the missing men but it was thirty-eight years before evidence was found that *La Boussole* and *Astrolabe* had both come to grief on the vicious reefs of Vanikoro, an atoll in the New Hebrides.

Businessmen, like Nature, abhor a vacuum. As Europe passed from the age of Enlightenment into the era of unbridled commercial expansion, merchants sought ways of exploiting the newly-discovered regions on the surface of their planet. The Australian settlements grew, not just as penal colonies, but as places where massive land grants and cheap convict labour enabled rough pioneers to become estate owners of substance. Western entrepreneurs fixed their eyes on the virtually closed economies of China and Japan: surely some way could be found to force these haughty orientals to trade with Europe and the USA. The western seaboard of America also had commercial potential. The local people were experienced trappers eager to exchange the skins of bears, beavers and sea-otters for cheap manufactured goods. As more and more ships travelled to the Pacific coasts and islands, circumnavigation ceased to be the preserve of explorers and adventurers. More and more merchant captains braved the Horn, the Roaring Forties and the empty Pacific.

But national pride was still a major factor. The heirs of La Pe-rouse were just as eager as the heirs of Cook to claim their share of the commercial results of exploration:

The English have too long taken advantage of our silence; too long have they had the honour of those discoveries in which we have anticipated them: what! because unfortunate circumstances, too well known to the whole world for me not to spare myself the mortification of repeating them, and the reader that of reading them, have presented insurmountable obstacles to the publication of the voyage of our countryman, at the time that it ought to have appeared, must we suffer, without complaining, that this unfortunate navigator should not, after his death, enjoy his immortal labours? Ah! if his destiny has not allowed us to engrave them on his tomb; at least, in claiming this inheritance, let the feeling and just nation, for which he sacrificed his life, for ever consecrate in the annals of history, his services, his death, and its gratitude![2]

So wrote Monsieur Charles Fleurieu in his exceedingly pompous account of Etienne Marchand's circumnavigation of 1790–1792.

Marchand was a man on whom fortune did not smile. He emerged from obscurity to lead a pioneering commercial expedition. It failed and he returned to obscurity. The failure was not due to any flaw in the project. Only the timing was wrong. Unfortunately, in business bad timing is even more disastrous than a bad product. The main objective of the voyage was to trade skins from North America with Cantonese merchants and return laden with Chinese wares for the home market. Marchand was also anxious to stake out colonial claims for France. All this had been planned under the *ancien régime* but, by the time Marchand sailed, at the end of 1790, that regime had been swept away. No one at that stage realised how far the French Revolution would go. Days before Marchand's return in August 1792, the royal family were thrown into prison. Within weeks the slaughter of aristocrats and officials had begun. A government that was violently over-throwing society at home and fighting enemies on its borders had little time or enthusiasm to spare for overseas adventures. Thus, when Marchand's journal was turned into a highly-coloured, nationalistic report it was completely ignored. Its author could not even find a French publisher prepared to have it printed.

Marchand set off westabout in the 300-ton *Solide* and rounded the Horn during the month of April. His first halt for watering was in the Marquesas. While there, he explored the islands thoroughly and was able to add another cluster to the group shown on his chart. He called his discovery Revolution

Isles and claimed them for France. But such imperialistic behaviour agreed ill with the new philosophy reigning in Paris, and M. Fleurieu found it necessary to explain away the good captain's behaviour:

> Since navigation has made known to Europeans parts of the terrestrial globe of which the ancients did not suspect the existence, they have persuaded themselves that the whole world belongs to them and that the lands which they happen to discover are portions of their universal domain . . . Captain Marchand, following the example of his numerous predecessors, thought it incumbent on him to take possession, in the name of the French nation. . This ceremony which would be only ridiculous from its inutility, if it were not contrary to the law of nature and of nations, was performed by fastening with four nails, against the trunk of a large tree, an inscription containing the name of the ship and of the captain and the act of taking possession of the island by the French.[3]

Fleurieu was less critical, though excessively arch, about another aspect of the *Solide's* visit to the Marquesas:

> Among the islanders brought by the canoes from Santa Christina and La Dominica, was a pretty considerable number of women and young girls: the greater part were remarkable for their youth and beauty. Their looks, their gestures, and repeated allurements, left no doubt of the motive of their visit; and the men who accompanied them, vied with each other in their eagerness to serve them as interpreters, and to make a tender of them to their entertainers. The ladies were admitted on board, and were welcomed by some young seamen of the southern provinces of France, whose senses six months of fatigues had not been able to deaden. At first sight, negotiations were begun; and the contracting parties not opposing to each other any dilatory

or evasive clauses, they presently flew down between decks to conclude the treaty . . . Let us throw a thick veil over what is passing. I shall only say that, on the approach of night, the young Mendoca belles were seen to re-appear on deck, loaded with nails, small looking-glasses, little knives, coloured glass-beads, ribbands, bits of cloth, and other productions of our arts, which they had bartered for the only commercial article that they had at their disposal. Often, in the sequel, they introduced less mystery into their traffic; they have been seen, without any other clothing than that of nature, to climb to the masthead by the ratlings, with an agility which the young sailors, who hastened to follow them, could scarcely equal; and, more than once, the tarry top was transformed into a temple of Gnidus.[4]

Marchand reached the coast of North America in August and in the region of Queen Charlotte Islands he found a group of Amerindians willing to trade in furs. Uncouth these fellow human beings may have seemed to sophisticated eyes – and noses: 'on approaching them the olfactory organs experience a most unpleasant sensation, which apprises the stranger to go no farther'[5] – but they proved to be shrewd businessmen. They were used to dealing with white men, mainly Spaniards, and were quite clear about what they wanted in exchange for their skins. Pots, pans and tools were welcomed, as were any utilitarian metal goods. Trinkets, beads and decorative items did not interest them at all. They were vaguely aware that the Europeans had come a long way to obtain furs and could not afford to return empty-handed. They were in a sellers' market, and they knew it. The 'civilised' Frenchmen discovered that there was nothing they could teach the 'primitives' about business. For example, when one of the Indians struck a particularly good bargain, his neighbours immediately put him in charge of negotiating on their behalf. However, patience and persistence brought their reward: after a couple of months, Marchand had a hold well loaded with otter, seal, bear, beaver, racoon and marmot skins.

He set sail across the Pacific and, via the Sandwich Isles and the Marianas, he came to Canton. There he had a double shock. The Chinese, having recently concluded a commercial treaty with the Russians, had put an embargo on trade in furs with all other foreign nationals. The other unwelcome news came from Captain James Ingraham of the United States brig *Hope*. Ingraham had been on a similar voyage. He, too, had called at the Marquesas and he had discovered the 'Revolution Isles' just a few weeks before Marchand arrived.

These were cruel blows but Marchand was resilient. As soon as possible, he made sail for Île de France. He had arranged for money to be deposited there for further mercantile ventures. But all he found waiting for him when he arrived on 30 January 1792 was news of the confused state of affairs in France. There was no money and, therefore, no possibility of returning to the Orient to salvage something from the commercial ruins of the voyage. There was nothing to be done but to return to France. The *Solide* reached Toulon on 14 August.

But there were, of course, the furs. They should fetch a good price in European markets. Alas, Marchand's precious cargo was the final victim of his genius for bad timing. The skins were sent to Lyons. Now Lyons was a royalist centre and not a safe place to be. Within months the city was besieged by government forces. When it fell, in October 1793, it was decided to make an example of the place. Many of its buildings were razed and 2,000 citizens were executed. As for the furs, they were confiscated, thrown into a warehouse and forgotten. After a long struggle with the revolutionary bureaucracy, the owners eventually established title to their property. It was too late. The cargo that Etienne Marchand had brought two-thirds of the way round the world had been almost completely destroyed by worms.

War and ideological ferment preoccupied the nations of Europe for many years. The political climate was not congenial to adventurous ocean voyages. Yet, paradoxically, one of the oddest circumnavigations sprang directly from the clash of ideas which so much engaged men's minds in the dying years of the eighteenth century.

Thomas Muir was a young Scottish lawyer and an advocate of parliamentary reform. In the revolutionary 1790s the views he expressed could only be alarming to the government. In 1793 he survived a charge of sedition and fled across the Channel where he spent some months being fêted by kindred spirits among the new ruling élite in Paris. The moment he set foot once more upon his native soil he was arrested and subjected to a mockery of a trial. He was found guilty on a number of ridiculously vague counts and sentenced to be transported for fourteen years. The members of the jury were appalled and would have made a plea for commutation of sentence had not the government made their will plain by means of a threatening letter to one of the jurymen. Thus, in March 1794, Muir set off in a convict ship on the first leg of his circumnavigation.

At Botany Bay he decided on making the best of his captivity. He bought some land and settled down to become a farmer. But not everyone was prepared to let him disappear into obscurity. He was widely regarded as a martyr for political freedom, nowhere more so than in the USA. A group of Americans decided to rescue him and, a little more than a year after his arrival in Australia, he was brought away in the US sloop *Otter*. But his adventures were only just beginning. He was taken across the Pacific. Then his ship was wrecked in Nootka Sound. He and the other survivors were captured by Amerindians, made their escape, and travelled in an open boat right down the coast to Mexico. They were well treated there and, making their way across the country, were able to find a ship bound for Cuba. There, Muir's luck changed yet again. England was now at war with Spain and Muir was arrested by the authorities and shipped back to Cadiz. He thus returned to Europe as he had left it – as a prisoner. Just off the Spanish coast the frigate in which he was travelling fell in with two English ships. There was a fierce exchange of fire and the

Spanish captain sustained heavy losses before he was able to get his vessel into harbour. Among those given up for dead was Thomas Muir. A cannon ball had taken away half his face. Amazingly, he survived. The French government intervened and he was welcomed back to Paris as a hero, in February 1798. There his strange journey ended. But he was not destined to be able to recollect adversity in tranquillity. His terrible wound eventually got the better of him. He died seven months later, at the age of thirty-three. Perhaps it was as well. He was spared the prospect of seeing the egalitarian revolution collapse and be replaced by the tyranny of Napoleon Bonaparte.

That tyranny rose and fell. It left in its wake a dynamic and turbulent Europe: a continent of rapid commercial expansion, changing social aspirations and sporadic political upheaval. Much that was true of the old world was also true of the new. Certainly, on both sides of the Atlantic scientists and scientifically-minded captains vied with each other in taking up the interrupted task of exploration. Scarcely had the Napoleonic Wars ceased before expeditions were being fitted out to the Pacific and the North-West Passage. But, within a few years, mariners turned their attention to that territory which Cook had declared unexplorable – Antarctica.

The impetus for this area of enterprise was, as usual, commercial. It was the quest for whale oil and seal skins which drew men to the inhospitable seas on the edge of the pack ice. At the same time that Marchand was making his unsuccessful voyage (1790–1792), an American captain, Daniel Greene, completed a circumnavigation during which he visited South Georgia to hunt seals and did a lucrative trade in them at Canton. Over the next thirty years US, British and Australian captains were increasingly active in pillaging the natural resources of this remote region.

But it was not trade which drew Baron Thaddeus von Bellingshausen to the Antarctic, to stake a small but significant claim for Russia in the process of polar exploration. Not until 1803 did the empire of the tsars take an interest in long-distance navigation. By that time their colonisation of the northern landmass had extended to Kamchatka, on the Pacific coast. Overland communication was difficult and the only satisfactory way of supplying the new settlements was by ship, which, whether eastabout or westabout, involved a journey more than half-way round the globe. The pioneering voyage was made between 1803 and 1806 by Baron A. J. von Kruzenstern, who reached Kamchatka via the Horn and continued westwards, returning to the Baltic without having lost a single crew member from his two ships. The young fifth lieutenant in the *Nadezhda* was Thaddeus Bellingshausen. Thirteen years later he was given the command of his own expedition.

By this time Russia had rapidly emerged as one of the leading European powers and national prestige demanded that she demonstrate her capability in all fields of human endeavour. But that was not the only reason for Bellingshausen's voyage. It was obvious in St Petersburg that any further colonial and commercial expansion would depend on an efficient navy. To help achieve this the government decided to commission a voyage which would test men and ships to the uttermost. Bellingshausen's own prime motivation came from his intensely high regard for Captain Cook. He wanted to complete the great pioneer's work in the Antarctic by circumnavigating as far as possible within the circle.

After a personal send-off by Tsar Alexander I, Bellingshausen quitted the port of Kronstadt with two ships, the *Vostok* and the *Mirnyi*, on 23 June 1819. He sailed for the South Atlantic where he completed the survey of South Georgia begun by Cook. He followed his hero's eastward path but aimed to strike farther south. He crossed the Antarctic Circle at the beginning of 1820 and travelled south-eastwards through the steadily thickening ice-fields. Three weeks later, in about 69°S, Bellingshausen made the following entry in his immaculately-kept journal:

The ice towards the south-south-west adjoined the high icebergs which were stationary. Its edge was perpendicular and formed into little coves, whilst the surface sloped upwards towards the south to a distance so far that its end was out of sight even from the masthead.[6]

Without realising it, Bellingshausen had become the first explorer to see the edge of the Antarctic continent. (The terrain he failed to identify lies due south of the Cape of Good Hope. It was not charted until 1931, when it was named Princess Ragnhild Land.)

Leaving the polar region for the winter, Bellingshausen now undertook a thorough survey of the treacherous Tuamotu group of islands and reefs. Then he made a refreshment stop at Tahiti. The place had changed. The Society Islanders were still very friendly. But now they were clothed in dresses, shirts and jackets of European manufacture. A number of white men (mostly sailors) who had deserted had settled among them. Missionaries had arrived. The people had pulled down their shrines. And on their first Sunday, when the officers went ashore,

. . . we saw only children about the houses, all the grown-up natives having gone to the service. When we arrived at the Church, it was already quite full . . . All the islanders were dressed very neatly in their best white and yellow holiday robes; almost all wore the umbrella-shaped head-dress and the women had fastened white or red flowers above their ears. All were very attentive to the Christian teaching of Mr Nott, who spoke with great feeling. Coming out of church the natives greeted us and then scattered to go home, whilst we returned to the cutter. After dinner the officers of both ships went ashore again, where they were received in the usual friendly way and were entertained with cocoa-nut milk. Some of the natives would not accept any presents on Sunday.

This strict observance of the religious law enjoining disin-
terestedness in a people whose former savage instincts cannot
have completely faded from memory, must really be regarded
as exemplary.[7]

The preacher was Henry Nott, one of the missionaries who,
with the active help of King Pomare II had brought Christianity
to the islands. (There was a considerable relapse into paganism
after the king's death in 1824.)

As soon as the weather became warmer, Bellingshausen
pointed *Vostok's* bow once more to the southern Pacific and
the Antarctic. In January 1821 he discovered the first land
located within the circle: two islands which he named Peter
Island and Alexander Island. When he eventually left the
Antarctic Circle for the South Shetlands and the warmer seas
beyond, Bellingshausen had added to the charts another 42° of
explored ocean above the line. It was a considerable achievement. (All the captains who steered their vulnerable little ships
through that maze of towering, fragmenting ice command our
admiration.) Yet it attracted little public attention. Nor did the
voyage of English whaler John Biscoe, ten years later
(1830–32). He followed a similar route to Bellingshausen's but
reached farther south at several points and identified at a
distance the coast of Enderby Land, the first part of the
continent to be discovered within the circle.

Perhaps the reason for the public's apathy was its preoccupa-
tion with the brave voyages of Parry and Franklin in their search
for the North-West Passage. Another decade was to elapse before
any more scientific expeditions were launched towards the
Antarctic. But then everything happened with a rush. Within the
space of two years, no fewer than three national projects were
mounted – one French, one British and one American. Jules
Sébastien César Dumont D'Urville was a scholar-captain in the
tradition of Bougainville. In addition to his native tongue, he had
mastered four European languages, as well as Greek and
Hebrew, and was a keen student of botany and entomology.

Early in his career he established a unique place in history. During the course of a Mediterranean hydrographic survey he called at the Greek island of Melos. There a local peasant showed him an old statue he had recently dug up. To most naval captains one piece of Greek marble looked much the same as another but D'Urville recognised the quality of this item and rushed to Constantinople to make an excited report to the French consul. The result was that the world's most famous statue, the Venus de Milo, was obtained for France. In the 1820s he took part in two important voyages of exploration: a circumnavigation (1822–5) and an extensive Pacific expedition (1826–9) during which he discovered more evidence concerning the fate of La Perouse. (D'Urville had an immense admiration for the unfortunate explorer, and even renamed his ship, *Coquille*, as *L'Astrolabe* in La Pérouse's honour.) Soon after his return, the 1830 revolution deposed Charles X and D'Urville was chosen by the ex-monarch to convey him into exile in England.

But the new regime of Louis-Philippe, the 'citizen king', had important work for the captain to do. In 1836 news reached Europe that the United States was planning an Antarctic survey. D'Urville, not wanting France to be left behind in the work of exploration offered to lead an expedition. He was, however, still under something of a cloud with the new regime and the idea met firm opposition. But Louis-Philippe liked the scheme and, therefore, D'Urville sailed in September 1837, with *L'Astrolabe* and *La Zélée*. He took the, now little-used, Magellan's Strait and made a careful survey of it before striking south-eastwards. He reached impenetrable pack ice in 63°29′, followed it eastwards for three hundred miles but failed to find a way through. D'Urville turned round to see whether there might not be a channel to westward. His search was rewarded, not with an opening in the ice, but a landfall. He touched on a part of the polar continent and shrewdly gave it the name Louis-Philippe Land. Unfortunately, his crews were now suffering so much from disease and cold that he was compelled to head for warmer climes.

In Chile D'Urville refitted the ships while his sick men recuperated. The rest of 1838 and the whole of 1839 were spent on a Pacific cruise. He visited Fiji, the Pulau Islands and Borneo, then headed south once more. In December *Astrolabe* and *Zélée* arrived in Hobart, Tasmania, ready for another assault on the Antarctic at a point almost 1800 from the coast D'Urville had already discovered. On 1 January 1840 the expedition set sail towards 'the country doomed by nature'. This time D'Urville was able to reach farther south. On 19 January he was, once more, confronted by a land barrier in 66°30′. Two days later he landed a boatload of men who returned with samples of earth and rock. This time he was able to explore the territory he called Adélie Coast (after his wife) for about two hundred miles. Then, just at the point where the ice cliffs turned sharply southwards, D'Urville was again obliged by the state of his crews to abandon his attempt to get closer to the pole than any predecessor (James Weddell had reached 74°15′ in 1823). He returned home via Hobart and the Cape, a disappointed man. Yet his had been a brave and important foray into earth's most inhospitable environment and he had marked two stretches of coast on the virtually empty charts of the Antarctic.

In January 1840, while the French were exploring far to the south of Australia, an American convoy was working in the same area. The Great United States Exploring Expedition was one of the most ill-managed scientific ventures that ever set sail. For twenty years scholars and patriots had been urging the government in Washington to bestir themselves to stop their nation falling further and further behind in the march of scientific research. It took persistent argument and lobbying to get a circumnavigation project off the ground and right up to the moment the ships sailed preparations were bedevilled by political and naval opposition. As a result, the scientists were ill-equipped for their work and their relationship with the officers had not been adequately defined. All this would not, perhaps, have mattered greatly if a competent, wise and sensitive leader had been selected for the expedition. Unfortunately, the man chosen was Lieutenant Charles Wilkes.

The word 'chosen' is not strictly accurate. The post had been offered to several experienced captains, each of whom, in turn, had declined it. Wilkes had been considered because his name was put forward by friends in high places and because the organisers of the expedition were becoming desperate. Giving the command of a six-ship squadron to such a junior officer was quite unprecedented in the annals of the US Navy. Of forty lieutenants currently on the active list only two had less sea experience than Wilkes. It was true that the thirty-eight-year-old New Yorker was unique among his colleagues in having a genuine interest in science but the appointment of someone so apparently ill-suited could only foster jealousy and mistrust among the other officers of the expedition.

But it was the effect upon Wilkes himself of shouldering a too-great responsibility which proved most damaging to the whole venture. Charles was the son of a successful, east-coast businessman and had grown accustomed as a child to getting his own way. Early obsessed with dreams of travel and discovery, he had refused to enter the family business, choosing instead the merchant marine and transferring later to the US Navy. He mastered the sciences of geography and hydrography and, in 1830, was given the superintendency of the department of instruments and charts. Wilkes was thrusting and ambitious. He took every opportunity to commend himself to superiors and to wield his family contacts to good effect. In 1838, having gained the prize he had so long sought, the young officer was at pains to impress his authority on the expedition and to reap from it the maximum personal glory. Wilkes liked to compare himself with Cook. In reality he was closer in spirit to Bligh and Queeg.

Wilkes drove himself hard – too hard. He never seemed to take more than five hours' sleep and was always around checking, finding fault, giving orders, countermanding orders. He was authoritarian to the point of barbarity and suspicious to the point of paranoia. He was indecisive in crisis and often wrong in matters of routine ship management. Yet, in the way of men whose shoes are too big, he could not take advice. Any contradiction smacked to him of insubordination and incipient mutiny. Officers constantly felt the lash of his tongue and men the cut of the cat. Incidents like the following were commonplace: one night Wilkes, shouting from the deck of the *Vincennes,* ordered the schooner *Flying Fish* to heave-to. The captain, Robert Pinkney, could not hear the command above the howl of the wind and came in closer to clarify his instructions:

Wilkes repeated the order and Pinkney, knowing that to heave-to in this position would result in collision, waited for the opportunity to comply. Wilkes shouted a third time, 'Why don't you heave-to Sir, heave-to immediately.' Pinkney did so and the schooner shot up into the wind across the *Vincennes'* bows, just clearing the latter's flying jib boom, and clearing it, not through the prompt action of Wilkes, who did not act at all, it was noted, but of Lieutenant Underwood in stopping the way of the *Vincennes.* Bustling forward and stamping the deck, Wilkes sang out through the trumpet,

'What do you mean, what do you mean by such conduct as this. I never saw the like of it in my life.'

'I hove to in obedience to your orders,' replied Pinkney.

'God damn it Sir,' the commander shouted, fairly dancing in his fury, 'I never ordered you to heave-to under my bows.'[8]

Little wonder that the only common bond between officers, civilians and crewmen was their dislike of their skipper. During the cruise one hundred and twenty-four sailors deserted, a fact which obliged Wilkes to fill the gaps with a motley collection of harbour riff-raff – yet another cause of friction.

The uncomfortable voyage began in August 1838 and lasted three years and ten months. The arguments and recriminations to which it gave rise were to go on much longer. Antarctic survey was only one aspect of the expedition's work but it loomed large in Wilkes's mind. He was determined to cap any achievement of his French and English rivals. For another of this turbulent man's attributes was acute xenophobia.

Like D'Urville, he sailed to the south of the Horn and reached the pack ice surrounding the northernmost spur of the Antarctic continent, known as Graham Land. But he was able to achieve little and retreated for the time being to concentrate on other aspects of the expedition's work. There were courtesy calls to be made in various South American ports and scientific investigation in the Tuamotu and Samoan islands. By the end of 1839 the convoy had reached Sydney and Wilkes was ready for a fresh onslaught on the Antarctic. His questionable activities over the next few weeks put his name firmly upon the polar map and stirred up unpleasant controversy.

Wilkes went with four ships – the *Vincennes, Porpoise, Peacock* and *Flying Fish* – and took much the same course as D'Urville (though without sighting his rival). He tried to keep his southbound convoy together, a stratagem which only resulted in all the ships travelling at the speed of the slowest, while the brief polar sailing season slipped agonisingly by. Day after day, Wilkes fretted and fumed if one of the vessels was lost sight of. He distributed a code of signals to be used in foggy conditions. An officer on the *Flying Fish* noted cynically in his journal, 'as we have neither bells, gong, or horn they had as well been left out'.[9] Throughout the squadron opinion was united on the reason for the commander's solicitousness: Wilkes did not want the credit for such discoveries as might be made to go to any of his subordinates. The other captains were, therefore, far from dismayed when the convoy was scattered by a combination of wind and fog.

The vessels all reached the ice barrier in about 65°S on what D'Urville had named Adélie Coast and each travelled along it hoping to find a way through into clear water. Wilkes, in the *Vincennes,* surveyed some 1,600 miles of the permanent ice limit between 150°E and 97°E. Yet 'surveyed' is not a wholly appropriate word. Sighting conditions changed from day to day, sometimes from hour to hour. Calm weather and clear visibility could give way with little warning to fog or storms which forced the *Vincennes* away from the ice-edge. There were times when the lookouts saw what was unmistakably land. These stretches of coast were marked on the chart. But so were others. Wilkes later confessed that the procedure he and his officers followed was that of 'laying down the land, not only where we had actually determined it to exist, but in those places also in which every appearance denoted its existence'.[10] He had come to believe (correctly as it transpired) that the 'icy barrier' marked the edge of a great polar continent. Intent on claiming this great discovery for the USA, he allowed himself to be deceived by the mirage-like effects of clouds and ice-formations. He even deduced the proximity of land from discoloration of water or the presence of basking seals or walruses. He thus marred an important piece of geographical detection by producing a chart showing several stretches of coastline, some of which were simply wrong. Moreover, he omitted from his map some of the discoveries of earlier explorers who were not American.

Wilkes was under orders from his government to keep the results of his expedition secret until he had made his official report. However, he could not resist the temptation to put one over on his rivals. On his return to New Zealand in April 1840, he left a letter and a tracing of his Antarctic chart which was relayed to Hobart for Captain Ross, the commander of the British expedition due to explore the polar region the following season. It was, as Wilkes insisted, a gesture of friendship and assistance from one explorer to another. But it was also designed to confirm the American claim to the discoveries made. As we shall see, this gesture was to have serious repercussions. For the moment, we must record that Wilkes next visited Fiji and Hawaii and made an accurate survey of the western coast of North America. He paid particular attention to the Oregon territory, sovereignty of which was currently in dispute between Britain and the USA. Wilkes then re-crossed the Pacific, returning to New York via the Philippines, Sulu and the Cape. He completed his circumnavigation in June 1842.

When Wilkes arrived home the British expedition still had over a year to complete what was the most thorough Antarctic survey so far attempted. Its leader, Captain James Clark Ross, was a seasoned polar explorer, having been on several expeditions within the Arctic Circle. He had, in fact, established the position of the north magnetic pole in 1831. Therefore, when the Admiralty determined, in 1839, to send two ships in search of the south magnetic pole, Ross was the obvious choice as commander. He had at his disposal two stout vessels, especially strengthened for work in icy seas: the *Erebus* (370 tons) and the *Terror* (340 tons).

Ross set sail on 30 September 1839 and took the now-established 'British' route, via St Helena and Cape Town. He called in at the remote Crozet and Kerguelen islands and remained some time at the latter to carry out a survey of its coastline. After leaving their anchorage the ships were subjected to the full force of the Roaring Forties. They were separated by gales. Then, on 30 July, disaster struck the *Erebus*.

Mr Roberts, the boatswain, whilst engaged about the rigging, fell overboard and was drowned. The life-buoy was instantly let go, and two boats lowered down; they reached the spot where we saw him sink only a few seconds too late! The gloom which the loss of one of our small party, at the outset of our voyage, occasioned, was for a time merged in feelings of painful anxiety, and afterwards of heartfelt gratitude, for the merciful preservation of the whole crew of one of the boats, who, in their humane endeavours to save the life of our unfortunate shipmate, very nearly sacrificed their own. Mr Oakley, mate, and Mr Abernethy, the gunner, had returned to the ship with one boat, when the other, still at a considerable distance from us, was struck by a sea, which washed four of the crew out of her. Mr Abernethy immediately again pushed off from the ship, and succeeded in saving them from their perilous situation, completely benumbed and stupefied with the cold. The boats were, with much difficulty, owing to the sea that was running, hoisted up, and not until after one of them had been again swamped alongside.[11]

The two ships were reunited in Tasmania and it was at Hobart that Ross received news of the French and American expeditions. The information was both disturbing and comforting. Ross was piqued that his rivals had both chosen the route that he had proposed. On the other hand, by following it D'Urville and Wilkes had met an impenetrable barrier around 66°S. Ross, therefore, decided to travel further east before making his ascent towards the pole. It was his best decision of the entire voyage. He sailed towards New Zealand, then turned south along the 170°E line of longitude. On 10 January he broke through the pack ice into open water and found himself able to proceed unhindered until he crossed the 78° parallel. But reaching a more southerly point on the globe than any other human beings had yet attained was not the only excitement Ross and his colleagues experienced. For day after day, except when it was obscured by bad weather, they had a clear view of a coastline to the west, running almost due south. They observed mountains and a smouldering volcano (named Mount Erebus). They called the whole stretch of coast Victoria Land. The expanse of water, which was to become the main access for later polar explorers, was appropriately called (though not by its discoverer) Ross Sea. At last they came upon the frozen bastion which guards the pole against any waterborne assault: a continuous ice cliff two to three hundred feet high.

Ross gazed day after day at that formidable bastion and wondered, as sixty years later his fellow countryman, Ernest Shackleton, was to wonder, what lay beyond.

We have sailed from your farthest
   West, that is bounded by fire* and snow
We have pierced to your farthest East,
   till stopped by the hard-set floe.
We have steamed by your wave-worn caverns;
   dim, blue, mysterious halls.
We have risen above your surface,
   we have sounded along your walls.
And above that rolling surface
   we have strained our eyes to see
But league upon league of whiteness
   was all that there seemed to be.
Ah, what is the secret you're keeping
   to the southward beyond our ken?
This year shall your icy fastness
   resound with the voices of men?
Shall we learn that you come from the mountains?
   Shall we call you a frozen sea?
Shall we sail to the North and leave you,
   still a Secret, forever to be?[12]

Ross now looked for a safe place to spend the winter. He hoped that by establishing a base close to the magnetic pole he could lead an overland expedition to it and thus achieve the unique distinction 'of being permitted to plant the flag of my country on both the magnetic poles of our globe'.[13] However, the thickening pack ice demonstrated that this would be an extremely hazardous enterprise. The ships, therefore, retraced their route, keeping as close as possible to Victoria Land to fill in gaps in the chart they had made on their outward journey. It was now late February and the brief polar summer was fading. Snow storms were frequent. The temperature fell steadily. The ice-floes were solidifying. Several times *Erebus* and *Terror* came close to being trapped. And there was another apparent hazard:

*i.e. Mount Erebus

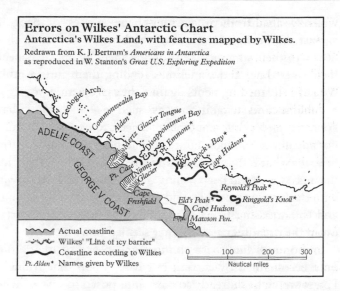

Errors on Wilkes' Antarctic Chart
Antarctica's Wilkes Land, with features mapped by Wilkes.

Redrawn from K. J. Bertram's *Americans in Antarctica*
as reproduced in W. Stanton's *Great U.S. Exploring Expedition*

... we made all sail to the N.E., on account of the wind having increased to a gale from E.S.E., placing our ships in a very critical situation; for on the chart which Lieutenant Wilkes was so good as to send me ... is laid down a range of mountainous land extending about sixty miles in a S.W. and N.E. direction; its centre being in lat. 65° 40′, and long. 165°E., with the eastern extreme of the barrier in 167½°E., and thus presenting a formidable lee shore in our present position. We were therefore in a state of considerable anxiety and uncertainty for some hours as to whether the ships could weather the land and barrier.[14]

But there was no mountainous land. It was clear to the British explorers that Wilkes had erred by several miles in the location of the north eastern extent of the landmass he claimed to have discovered.

If the coast was illusory, the icebergs were not:

We found we were fast closing this chain of bergs, so closely packed together that we could distinguish no opening through which the ships could pass, the waves breaking violently against them, dashing huge masses of pack ice against the precipitous faces of the bergs; now lifting them nearly to their summit, then forcing them again far beneath their water-line, and sometimes rending them into a multitude of brilliant fragments against their projecting points.

Sublime and magnificent as such a scene must have appeared under different circumstances, to us it was awful, if not appalling. For eight hours we had been gradually drifting towards what to human eyes appeared inevitable destruction: the high waves and deep rolling of our ships rendered towing with the boats impossible, and our situation the more painful and embarrassing from our inability to make any effort to avoid the dreadful calamity that seemed to await us.

In moments like these comfort and peace of mind could only be obtained by casting our cares upon that Almighty Power which had already so often interposed to save us when human skill was wholly unavailing. Convinced that he is under the protection and guidance of a merciful God, the Christian awaits the issue of events firm and undismayed, and with calm resignation prepares for whatever He may order. His serenity of mind surprises and strengthens, but never forsakes him; and thus, possessing his soul in peace, he can with the greater advantage watch every change of circumstance that may present itself as a means of escape.

We were now within half a mile of the range of bergs. The roar of the surf, which extended each way as far as we could see, and the crashing of the ice, fell upon the ear with fearful distinctness, whilst the frequently averted eye as immediately returned to contemplate the awful destruction that threatened in one short hour to close the world and all its hopes and joys and sorrows upon us for ever. In this our deep distress 'we called upon the Lord, and He heard our voices out of His temple, and our cry came before Him.'

A gentle air of wind filled our sails; hope again revived, and the greatest activity prevailed to make the best use of the feeble breeze: as it gradually freshened, our heavy ships began to feel its influence, slowly at first, but more rapidly afterwards; and before dark we found ourselves far removed from every danger. 'O Lord our God, how great are the wondrous works Thou hast done; like as be also Thy thoughts, which are to us-ward! If I should declare them and speak of them, they should be more than I am able to express.'[15]

The expedition regained Hobart safely and spent the cooler months in Australia and New Zealand. While his ships and men were recouping, Ross assessed the work of the previous season. Inevitably, this meant comparing his claims with Wilkes's. And, inevitably, news of Ross's complaints against him reached the American. Wilkes was, of course, furious that the British expedition had capped his own achievements and that Ross was questioning the accuracy of his information. He put the Englishman's reaction down to jealousy and pique and never forgave him. Even before the American returned home news of this disagreement was creating doubts about Wilkes's achievement within the scientific establishment. But it was not only the English with whom the aggressive patriot was at odds. He disputed with the French the primacy of discovery. D'Urville claimed to have sighted Adélie Coast on 19 January 1840. Wilkes put no dates on his chart but later claimed to have made his first land sighting on 16 January. Clearly a storm was brewing which would rumble on for years.

Ross, meanwhile, was very impressed with most of what he saw in Australia but the introduction of a degree of democracy in New South Wales he regarded 'a measure of very doubtful benefit to the colony, and considered by many to be the first great step towards its separation from the mother country'.[16] At the end of November 1841 he set off to return to the scene of his former discoveries, hoping to find another edge to the barrier past which he could slip in order to sail farther south. He did not accept the theory, espoused by Wilkes among others, that all the sightings of land within the circle would prove to be parts of one continuous coastline embracing a single continent. To him it seemed more reasonable to suppose that, like the Arctic, this ice cap covered only sea and islands. If that were so, it should prove possible to get closer to the pole. Ironically, it was Ross, the thorough, conscientious explorer, who was wrong on this matter and Wilkes, the less scrupulous chart-maker, whose hunch was correct. Ross reached six miles farther south than he had the previous year but was unable to add significantly to his discoveries. He, therefore, resolved to try his luck in a different quarter.

Sailing close to the sixtieth parallel, he set course for Cape Horn, wintered in the Falklands, then made for Graham Land. But he was able to add little to what predecessors had observed and, eventually, steered for home via the Cape. He reached England on 4 September 1843, having completed the most southerly circumnavigation yet achieved (almost all close to or above the fiftieth parallel).

Thus ended a remarkable burst of 'Antarctic mania'. It was rendered all the more extraordinary by the fact that scientific interest in the southern polar region now lapsed once more until the very end of the century.

The subsequent careers of these three Antarctic pioneers were as diverse as their respective characters. Dumont D'Urville's was brief and tragic. On his return, his achievements were recognised by the Geographical Society, who awarded him their Grand Gold Medal. He did not long enjoy the honour. On 8 May 1842, he was returning to Paris from Versailles with his wife and son on the recently-constructed railway when his train was involved in an appalling crash. All three of them were killed along with scores of other travellers. D'Urville's body was among the many incapable of recognition. The news reached James Ross during the course of his expedition and he took the first opportunity to honour the Frenchman. On Louis-Philippe land he sighted a great tower of rock and named it D'Urville's Monument 'in memory of that enterprising navigator, whose loss not only France, but every civilised nation must deplore'.[17]

No hero's return awaited Charles Wilkes. The scientific establishment was dubious about the utility of his expedition. The general public was totally indifferent. Enemies in high places were

not slow to exploit the conflict generated by his claimed discoveries. And several of the men who had been forced to endure
his tantrums for nearly four years were thirsting for revenge. The
chagrin Wilkes experienced at receiving no popular acclaim, no
immediate scholarly recognition (not until 1847 was he awarded
the Royal Geographical Society's Founder's Medal) and no naval
promotion was balm to the bodies and egos which the
commander had so often bruised. But Wilkes's disappointment
alone could not assuage their wrath. Some of his officers lodged
official complaints and these resulted in Wilkes being court-
martialled on an array of charges grouped under seven heads:
oppression, cruelty, illegal punishment, disobedience of orders,
scandalous conduct, conduct tending to the destruction of good
morals, and conduct unbecoming an officer. Several of the
charges failed on technicalities. Perhaps they would not have done
had the naval authorities not found themselves caught between
the demands of justice and expediency. On the one hand they
could not permit Wilkes's blatantly bad leadership to go unpun-
ished. On the other, they could not allow a major US enterprise
involving the national honour to be sullied in the eyes of the
world. There was an inevitable compromise: Wilkes was found
guilty on seventeen counts of illegal punishment and was
sentenced to the mild punishment of a public reprimand.

He was little chastened by his experience. Wilkes and controversy remained frequent bedfellows. In 1861 he almost started
single-handed a war between Britain and the USA. The incident
occurred during the American Civil War and is known to
history as the *Trent* affair. Wilkes stopped and boarded the
British mail packet *Trent* in order to arrest two Confederate
envoys travelling from New Orleans to Paris. The British
government were furious at this flagrant violation of their
neutrality and President Lincoln was obliged to apologise and
release the two Southern representatives. Wilkes was no
respecter of diplomatic niceties nor did he find it easy to submit
to authority. Another incident in 1864 led to his being court-
martialled again – for disobedience, disrespect, insubordination

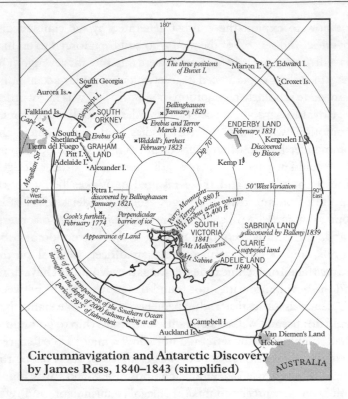

Circumnavigation and Antarctic Discovery by James Ross, 1840–1843 (simplified)

and conduct unbecoming an officer. He was publicly reprimanded and suspended from active duty.

James Ross ended his days, by contrast, full of honours and high in public esteem. His 1839–43 expedition won him a knighthood and the Gold Medals of the Geographical Societies of London and Paris. The University of Oxford conferred an honorary doctorate on him and he was widely acknowledged as the leading expert on polar geography. This venerated sailor finally came home from the sea in 1849 and enjoyed several years of quiet, distinguished retirement before being gathered to his fathers in 1862.

D'Urville, Wilkes, Ross – three great circumnavigators; three very different men; three explorers whose names, deservedly, are permanently recorded on the map of Antarctica.

9

PROFIT AND PLEASURE

Those splendid ships, each with her grace, her glory,
Her memory of old song or comrade's story,
Still in my mind the image of life's need,
Beauty in hardest action, beauty indeed.
'They built great ships and sailed them' sounds most brave,
Whatever arts we have or fail to have;
I touch my country's mind, I come to grips
With half her purpose thinking of these ships.

That art untouched by softness, all that line
Drawn ringing hard to stand the test of brine;
That nobleness and grandeur, all that beauty
Born of a manly life and bitter duty;
That splendour of fine bows which yet could stand
The shock of rollers never checked by land.
That art of masts, sail-crowded, fit to break,
Yet stayed to strength, and back-stayed into rake,
The life demanded by that art, the keen
Eye-puckered, hard-case seamen, silent, lean,
They are grander things than all the art of towns,

Their tests are tempests, and the sea that drowns.
They are my country's line, her great art done
By strong brains labouring on the thought unwon,
They mark our passage as a race of men
Earth will not see such ships as those again.

JOHN MASEFIELD

Who built the first clipper ship is still a matter of dispute. What is beyond doubt is that in the 1840s and 1850s the merchant sailing ship reached the apogee of its development. Sleek of build and carrying thousands of square yards of canvas, these vessels were capable of amazing speed. The 436 miles run in one day by *Lightning* in 1854 is just one of the records set up by the clippers which will never be broken. They were, of course, made for speed, in obedience to the age-old commercial dictum that 'time is money'. They were made for profit-hungry owners, who exerted pressure on flamboyant and often brutal captains, who drove their ships and men with a ruthless disregard for anything except making port in the shortest possible time.

Why all this frantic activity? The rapidly expanding international markets of the mid-Victorian era provided countless opportunities for clever shipowners to make fortunes: taking emigrants to the colonies, bringing tea back from China, gold and wool from Australia, conveying meat, and exotic fruit to the markets of London, Paris and New York. Speed was of the essence for a variety of reasons. Perishable cargoes had to be brought home in the shortest possible time. Tea and wool merchants wanted to be first of the season in the auction houses, to obtain the best prices. Owners tendering for the Royal Mail concession had to guarantee delivery in Melbourne in 68 days and pay a penalty of £100 for every day over that limit. So keen was competition for this contract that in 1854 the owner of the *James Baines* offered to deliver the mails within 65 days – and did so. But, as the years passed, the fact that the clippers had steamships breathing down their necks became the main incentive to maintain their reputation for speed and reliability. The titanic struggle between the old and the new continued until the end of the century and, despite the rapid improvements in steamship construction and efficiency, the square riggers saw off the challenge for fifty years.

The rivalry between shipping lines and individual captains in the heyday of the clippers was intense. Record runs were proudly announced in the newspapers and on company hand-bills in the hope of attracting more business. Merchants were not slow to exploit this competition, which could, at times, be literally suicidal. Many a captain with a reputation at stake or a bonus to earn took one risk too many, sending ship, cargo, passengers and crew to the bottom.

The extraordinary career of James Forbes indicates the pressures merchant captains were under or placed themselves under. Forbes was a tough Scot who arrived on the Liverpool waterfront at the age of eighteen with little sailing experience, and in thirteen years worked his way up to command of the *Marco Polo*, the pride of the Black Ball Line's fleet. He achieved this meteoric rise by being a 'harder' man than most of his contemporaries. He drove his ships and men to the limit and took incredible risks. He soon earned the nickname 'Bully' and, though this sobriquet was carried by other shipmasters, no man better deserved it. His fiery temper was legendary and many were the stories told about him in ports round the world. It was said that he stomped about the quarterdeck in the fashion of a seventeenth century buccaneer with a brace of pistols in his belt, and that when his ship was carrying full canvas he had the lines padlocked to prevent any fainthearted subordinate short-ening sail. Once a group of terrified passengers appealed to him to reduce sail. Gruffly he dismissed them, adding that it was his intention 'to get to hell or Melbourne'.

The maiden voyage of the *Marco Polo* in 1852 was Forbes's greatest triumph. He made Melbourne in 68 days and beat the steamer *Australia* by a clear week. Before leaving Liverpool he had made the boast that he would bring his ship back to the

Mersey inside six months. One potential obstacle to the achievement of this target was the likelihood of losing men ashore. Once they had escaped his clutches some of his crew were likely to disappear in the town or sign on with other captains desperate for experienced sailors. Forbes obviated this threat by the simple expedient of arresting his entire crew for 'insubordination' and handing them over to the police. *Marco Polo* was loaded and ready to sail in good time. Forbes then dropped the charges against his men, brought them back aboard and weighed anchor. He had an excellent return passage via the Horn of 76 days and regained Liverpool on Boxing Day. When the news of her return went round the town, amazed crowds gathered on the quayside. There, sure enough, was the *Marco Polo* with a painted slogan hung from her rigging: 'THE FASTEST SHIP IN THE WORLD'. Forbes had comfortably made good his boast: he had circumnavigated the globe in 175 days, of which 144 had been spent at sea.

It was an amazing record but Forbes intended to beat it. At the start of his next trip he announced to the passengers, 'Ladies and gentlemen, last trip I astonished the world with the sailing of this ship. This trip I intend to astonish God Almighty.' *Marco Polo* had a good outward voyage of 75 days. At Melbourne she turned round in less than a fortnight. Forbes now wore as far to the south as possible in the hope of finding the westerlies at their most ferocious. He crossed the sixtieth parallel, and took his ship well within the drift-ice limit, in the middle of the southern winter. And he paid the price. *Marco Polo* found herself among the ice and had part of her copper sheathing ripped away. The captain's gamble had not paid off this time but he still completed the round trip in exactly six calendar months.

In 1854 the Black Ball Line took delivery of their latest ship, the American-built *Lightning*. On her journey across the Atlantic she established the remarkable record of 436 miles in 24 hours. Great things were, therefore, expected of her on the Australia run. There was only one man who could be relied upon to get the best out of her. 'Bully' Forbes, now commodore of the fleet, took *Lightning* out of Liverpool on 14 May. Much to his anger and frustration this excellent ship was delayed in the Doldrums and arrived at her destination in 77 days; not nearly good enough for the hero of the *Marco Polo*. Forbes was determined to make up for lost time on the return run. He kept maximum canvas up on the crossing to the Horn. As the ship bounded along at eighteen and nineteen knots with her lee rail dipping below the water, Forbes prowled the deck, swearing at his men and threatening to shoot the first one who let go the royal or topgallant halliards. Once again, he pushed his ship too hard. A violent gust of wind snapped the foretopmast clean off and the fore royal, topgallant and topsail followed it overboard. Forbes was forced to reduce sail for four days while the repairs were carried out but, amazingly, he still established a new record for the Melbourne to Cape Horn leg. But the best was yet to come: *Lightning* accomplished the whole homeward voyage in 64 days, 3 hours, 10 minutes, a feat which has never been surpassed by a vessel under sail. Forbes had knocked spots off his own circumnavigation record. He was back on the quayside at Liverpool 162 days after going aboard.

To shipowners and merchants alike this wiry, ferocious little Scot seemed to have the Midas touch. He was a mercantile genius who could do no wrong. When the Black Ball Line's latest ship, the *Schomberg*, came into commission the following year Forbes was given command of her. He set sail on 6 October, making even more flamboyant promises than usual. A flag signal, hoisted as he left port, declared '60 days to Melbourne'. He soon discovered that the *Schomberg* was a much poorer sailer than his previous commands, and the discovery made him angry and sullen. After 82 days the ship was near Cape Otway, still about 150 miles short of Melbourne and battling with head winds. Forbes was so disgusted with his 'sluggish' craft that he spent hours below playing cards with some of the first-class passengers and left his officers in command. At 10.30 p.m. the mate went down and reported that the ship was drifting onto a lee shore. Forbes was in no hurry to come on deck and when he did appear it was too late to avert the danger. *Schomberg* grounded on a sandbank. At this point the captain washed his hands of her. 'Let her go to hell!' he bellowed and returned below. It was left to the mate to give the order to abandon ship. Passengers and crew were all saved but the *Schomberg* was pounded to pieces.

If Forbes trusted to his reputation to save him, he miscalculated. The gratitude and generosity of his employers had very narrow limits. At the age of thirty-four this remarkable captain's career came to an end. Sacked by the Black Ball Line, he drifted round the world, picking up whatever commands he could. But he was a broken man with little of the old braggadocio left. He died in Liverpool in 1874, at the age of fifty-two. It was a sad end for one of the most remarkable circumnavigators of all time, a man who had made, not one, but three spectacular voyages round the world.

Not all the majestic clipper ships, of course, made regular circuits of the globe. They plied a variety of long-distance routes. Those engaged in commerce with the Orient, for example, travelled out and back across the Indian Ocean, making use of the trades. Yet, they were all designed to withstand the world's heaviest seas and to seek out the wild winds earlier vessels had shunned. It was the colonisation and economic development of Australia and New Zealand which created the demand for ships built to follow the eastward route pioneered by Cook.

First there were the emigrant ships on which thousands of hopeful or desperate men and women fled from the squalor of industrial slums and the threat of the debtors' prison to seek a better life as pioneers in a new land. Not all shipowners exploited human misery by cramming poor passengers on board like cattle but many certainly deserved the reputation for callousness which has traditionally attached itself to this trade. The offer of cheap fares enabled captains to pack their steerage-class accommodation with men, women and children prepared to accept overcrowding, lack of privacy and poor diet. The three months or so that such passengers spent on board were months of sheer misery, compounded of sea-sickness, disease, airless, ill-ventilated accommodation, the constant crying of unhappy infants and the contempt expressed by captain, crew and first- and second-class passengers. Men travelling steerage could be pressed into service as extra deck hands and some captains deliberately kept their crews to a minimum in order to exploit this source of free labour. Many passenger journals have survived describing these dreadful voyages. An emigrant on the *Stag* in 1850 noted:

10 o'clock, the sun is now beating out with increased power and we shall have another sweating day. A canvas sheet is now spread over the part of the deck occupied by the females . . . men, however, not so favoured . . . Many will sleep on deck during the remainder of the hot weather . . . No restriction now as regards the bed hour of the single men. They are allowed on deck as late as they think proper. All the scuttles on windows in single men's departments recommended by surgeon to be kept open during the night.[1]

Passengers were given a daily allowance of food and had to cook their own meals:

Scale Showing the Daily Issue of Provisions[2]

	Biscuits	Flour	Oatmeal	Pork	Preserved Meat	Potatoes	Rice	Raisins	Suet	Peas	Cocoa	Sugar	Butter	Beef	Water
	oz	oz	oz	oz	oz	oz	oz	oz	oz	oz	oz	oz	oz	oz	oz
Monday	8	6	3	6	–	–	–	–	–	¼	½	4	2	–	3
Tuesday	8	6	3	–	6	–	4	2	1½	–	–	–	–	–	3
Wednesday	8	6	3	6	–	–	–	–	–	¼	½	4	–	–	3
Thursday	8	6	3	–	6	4	–	2	1½	–	–	–	–	–	3
Friday	8	6	3	6	–	–	–	–	–	¼	–	4	2	–	3
Saturday	8	6	3	–	–	–	4	2	1½	–	–	–	–	–	3
Sunday	8	6	3	–	6	4	–	2	1½	–	–	–	–	6	3

There was little to stop the stronger or more unscrupulous passengers taking food away from the less robust. Those laid low by sea-sickness or other infirmity frequently grew weaker through lack of nourishment in the noisome tween-decks conditions described thus in a parliamentary committee report:

> It was scarcely possible to induce the passengers to sweep the decks after their meals or to be decent in respect to the common wants of nature; in many cases, in bad weather, they would not go on deck, their health suffered so much that their strength was gone, and they had not the power to help themselves. Hence the between decks were like a loathsome dungeon. When hatchways were opened, under which the people were stowed, the steam rose and the stench was like that from a pen of pigs. The few beds they had were in a dreadful state, for the straw, once wet with sea water, soon rotted, besides which they used the between decks for all sorts of filthy purposes.[3]

It is scarcely surprising that incidents such as this were recorded by emigrants:

> The child I mentioned yesterday evening expired during the night. The body lies upon the poop of the vessel awaiting the last few words to be read over it ere it be cast into the ocean beneath us . . . 10 o'clock all is over. The poor, perishable body is no more but the soul of this infant, we hope, is for ever happy. The grief of the parents is very great as it was their only child . . .[4]

With the discovery of gold in 1850 the flow of hopeful settlers dramatically increased. The following years were a bonanza for the shipping lines. The new colonies created an ever-increasing demand for manufactured goods for the clippers to take out. The homeward voyages brought nuggets and gold dust for the bullion-hungry financial markets of Europe and America. They also brought wool. The great sailing ships raced each other to get the fleece back to the auctions held between January and March. For merchants supplying the busy Yorkshire mills it was a highly profitable trade. But of all cargoes wool was the one sailors hated most.

You can dunnage casks o' tallow; you can handle hides an' horn;
You can carry frozen mutton; you can lumber sacks o' corn;
But the queerest kind o' cargo that you've got to haul and pull
Is Australia's 'staple product' – is her God-abandoned wool.
For it's greasy an' it's stinkin', an' them awkward, ugly bales
Must be jammed as close as herrings in a ship afore she sails.
    For it's twist the screw and turn it,
    And the bit you get you earn it;
You can take the tip from me, sir, that it's anything but play
    When you're layin' on the screw,
    When you're draggin' on the screw,
In the summer, under hatches, in the middle o' the day.
                                                   G. J. Brady

The wool was 'screwed' into the hold; that is the bales, compressed by hydraulic presses, were packed in as tight as possible. It was a hot, smelly cargo – and dangerous. Bales could expand, break their lashings and put enormous pressure on a ship's timbers. Worse still, they could overheat and catch fire because of water trapped within them. Several ships were lost because of such spontaneous combustion. The most famous was the *Lightning*.

In 1869 she was loading at Geelong when fire broke out in the forward hold. The flames spread so rapidly that the crew could not steer her away from the jetty and she swung round her anchor across the harbour. The fire was quite uncontrollable so it was decided to sink the ship. The result was not encouraging. Cannon shot, fired at a range of three hundred yards, either missed or made holes which allowed in fresh currents of air to fan the flames. The stricken *Lightning* burned all day before slipping beneath the water in a great cloud of steam and smoke.

By then other fine clippers had joined her in the record books. But the achievement of fast passages to and from the Antipodes is not only attributable to demanding shipowners and reckless captains. Behind every magnificent ship was a yard where a thousand skills were concentrated in the hands of craftsmen. The best vessels, such as *Lightning*, *Red Jacket* and *Sovereign of the Seas* came out of Nova Scotia and New England. They were narrow in the beam yet balanced. Their masts were strong and well braced to carry maximum canvas without springing. So superbly designed were these craft that captains and passengers alike testified that they could run up to eighteen and nineteen knots before a following wind without burying their noses in the waves.

The New World made another important contribution to the reputation of the great square-riggers. This was Matthew Fontaine Maury. Maury spent fourteen years in the navy (during which time he made a circumnavigation, 1826–1830) before being invalided out, in 1839, and placed in charge of the depot of charts and instruments. He devoted himself, henceforth, to the study of oceanic winds and currents. In order to gather as much information as possible he had special log books distributed to naval captains and he persuaded his counterparts in other countries to pool information. One result was an international conference at Brussels in 1853, the first such gathering to discuss maritime meteorology. It was Maury who advocated the Atlantic and southern ocean routes which were followed by all sailing masters looking for a fast passage. Previously, captains had avoided the potential lee shore of Brazil, coasted the Cape of Good Hope close to and then steered north-east until they were clear of the Roaring Forties. Maury told them to steer for Cape San Roque, on the north-east coast of Brazil, then swing in an eastward arc through the southern Atlantic in order to pick up the westerlies as soon as possible, passing as much as ten degrees to the south of the

Cape and remaining in the forties all the way to Australia.

When the White Star Line's *Red Jacket* followed this course on her maiden voyage in 1854 she went so far to the south that frozen spray made her bow heavy. But that did not prevent her notching up a remarkable record. She went out in 69 days and came back in 75. She did not overhaul *Lightning's* record, established a few weeks before but she did achieve the fastest actual circuit of the globe. On 2 September she 'tied the knot' – that is she crossed her own outward track – in a sailing time of 62 days 22 hours, a feat which has never been bettered.

The palm for the best ever round voyage went, the following year, to *Red Jacket's* rival, the Black Ball Line's *James Baines*. She reached Melbourne in 63 days 18 hours 15 minutes. Her return trip took 69 days 12 hours. She came literally within a stone's throw of not completing the voyage: her captain, knowing that a record was within his grasp, took some fearful risks tacking off Ireland. *James Baines* passed the Mizenhead rocks so close that some passengers claimed they could have hit them with a stone. But the ship came safe to harbour to throw down the gauntlet to her rivals. They all found her record of 133 days 6 hrs 15 mins under sail to be unassailable.

It goes without saying that the men who manned such ships were 'hard-core seamen', among the toughest mariners who ever put to sea. Drunken brawls, murders and attempted mutinies were almost commonplace for the polyglot crews who sailed the clippers. Thomas Fraser, who went to sea in 1865, and whose career spanned both the heyday and the decline of the clippers, recorded many of the incidents that made up the rough-and-ready life of these men. He recalled how the mate of the *Corea* got involved in a fight in Adelaide during a circumnavigation in 1872–3. He found himself against an assailant with a knife and had his face cut from mouth to eyebrow. He lost no time in taking his revenge:

After the Captain had stitched up his dreadful wound [many captains were, of necessity, practitioners of minor surgery], the Mate was so enraged that he went to the place the man who had defaced him was confined, knocked him down, turned him over, and with the knife that had so cruelly cut him, made a deep cross on each of the man's buttocks, then took a handful of coaldust from a bunker there and rubbed it in the deep cuts, making an indelible mark.[5]

The men, like the ships they sailed, were larger than life. Many of them became legends whose exploits were passed on from generation to generation in dockside bars or became the subject of ribald songs. They were mariners for whom sailing round the world and racing round the world had become a commonplace. Captain John Wyrill who commanded clippers for forty-four years made thirty-six circumnavigations. That may or may not be a record but it is some measure of the accomplishments of a remarkable breed of men.

But they had now been joined on the world's oceans by sailors of a quite different kind.

On the evening of Wednesday, 2 October 1872 four members of the Reform Club sat, in the large drawing room, playing whist and discussing the latest *cause célèbre,* a robbery at the Bank of England:

'I maintain,' said Andrew Stuart, 'that the chances are in favour of the thief, who is sure to be no fool.' 'Nonsense!' replied Ralph, 'there is not a country left in which he can take refuge. What an idea! Where do you want him to go?' 'I can't say,' replied Andrew Stuart, 'but after all, the world is large enough.' 'It was so . . .' said Phileas Fogg in an undertone . . .

The discussion was interrupted during the rubber. But Andrew Stuart soon took it up again, saying: 'What do you mean by *was?* Has the world got smaller, eh?' 'Of course it has,' rejoined Gauthier Ralph; 'I agree with Mr. Fogg. The world has got smaller, since one can travel over it ten times more rapidly than a hundred years ago.'[6]

The scene from *Around the World in Eighty Days* is fictional but the subject of discussion was one which fascinated many of Jules Verne's contemporaries. The Frenchman, himself a keen traveller and yachtsman, published his story three years after the opening of the Suez Canal in 1869 (it was translated into English in 1874). It was an era in which continent after continent was being crossed by steam locomotives, and ocean after ocean was being traversed by the faster, more reliable steamships. The world was, indeed, getting smaller. More people travelled to distant lands to satisfy their curiosity. And if to distant lands, why not right round the world?

As the sea lanes filled rapidly with the burgeoning commerce of the industrial nations, a new kind of vessel was beginning to appear amidst the clippers and the tramps – the pleasure yacht. Sailing, long the pursuit of princes, was in the second half of the nineteenth century a smart hobby taken up with enthusiasm by the *nouveaux riches* of Europe and America. Boatyards from Hamburg to Marseilles, Clydeside to Falmouth, Boston to Charleston vied with each other in building trim, luxurious craft for their wealthy clients, craft which would be crewed by professionals and were designed as much for showing off the affluence of their owners as for seaworthiness.

One of these floating palaces was the *Sunbeam,* laid down in Bowdler and Chaffer's yard, Liverpool, about 1870. She was a 157-foot, three-masted, topsail schooner, carrying a mass of sail but also driven, when necessary, by a steam-powered screw propeller. She was designed by St Clare Byrne for Thomas Brassey, Liberal MP for Hastings. This keen amateur yachtsman was the heir of railway pioneer Thomas Brassey senior, who amassed a large fortune from constructing lines in four continents and eventually worked himself to death in 1870.

The younger Thomas was thirty-six when he came into his inheritance and had already decided to devote himself to matters maritime. The sea was his passion. In parliament he specialised in legislation concerning the royal and merchant navies, currently undergoing such immense changes. He had inherited his father's passion for hard work; his biographers described him as 'a rich man of no outstanding ability but with great powers of industry'.[7] Reports, pamphlets and articles poured from his pen, culminating in the five volume *British Navy*, published 1882–3. He became first civil lord of the Admiralty in 1880. He attracted honours and titles and at the time of his death in 1918 he was first Earl Brassey of Bulkeley and Viscount Hythe.

He exemplified the Victorian 'work hard, play hard' ideal, for he followed his hobby of yachting with as much enthusiasm as he devoted to his chosen profession. As soon as he had graduated at Oxford he was elected to the Royal Yacht Squadron, the sailing world's élite corps. He later became the first private yachtsman to sit the Board of Trade examination and be granted a master's ticket. And in 1876–7 he notched up another first when he completed a voyage round the world in *Sunbeam*.

Just how and when the idea occurred we do not know. Was *Sunbeam* designed with a round the world voyage in mind? Or did Brassey suddenly decide that she was an ideal craft for the first ever circumnavigation for pleasure? The owner himself insisted that his wife was the prime mover in the venture: 'The voyage would not have been undertaken, and assuredly it would never have been completed, without the impulse derived from her perseverance and determination'.[8]

In 1876 Annie Brassey was in her thirties, a mother of four children and a woman of that English *memsahib* breed who, whether at home or abroad, was accustomed to having all her whims carried into effect with the aid of a disciplined contingent of servants. From the account of the voyage which she wrote it is clear that her enthusiasm for it was without reserve. If the thought ever occurred to her that running a household at sea and in foreign ports was different from presiding over her establishments in Park Lane and Chapelwood Manor, Sussex, she dismissed it instantly. The project, once resolved upon, would be accomplished. Thus, we see her, in her long skirt and wide-brimmed sun hat, buying food in native markets for dinner parties of up to forty guests aboard the *Sunbeam;* coping with frequent bouts of seasickness and even one case of smallpox; learning Spanish; giving daily lessons to the children; caring for the shipwrecked crew of a merchant vessel; and never failing to spend an hour a day at her desk writing up her journal.

That journal is quite unlike any other first-hand circumnavigation account. It is essentially a tourist's chronicle, very short on nautical detail but bubbling over with enthusiastic observation of strange sights and sounds. Annie and her family visited twenty countries at a time when holiday travel seldom took wealthy Britons beyond the Continent. Annie's comments on unfamiliar peoples and customs fascinated her countrymen when they were first published but their interest to us is in what they reveal about Victorian attitudes towards other cultures at a time when Britannia ruled the waves.

When *Sunbeam* left Cowes on 6 July 1876 she carried a complement of 43 persons, two dogs, three birds and a kitten. As well as the Brassey family and four friends there were a doctor, a nurse, a lady's maid, four stewards, a stewardess, three cooks and a crew of 22. The schooner's voyage was west about by way of the Guinea coast, Rio, Magellan's Strait, Valparaiso, Tahiti, Hawaii, Japan, Singapore, Colombo, the Suez Canal (in which Disraeli had just secured a controlling British interest) and Lisbon. She accomplished 15,000 miles under sail and 12,800 miles propelled by her auxiliary engines. Brassey took down the removable funnel and used canvas whenever possible because, 'it is pleasant to be free from the thud of engines, the smell of oil, and the horrors of the inevitable coaling', but, as an expert on ships and shipbuilding, he valued the convenience of steam power and he seldom hung about waiting for a breeze. For this reason, and also because he encountered little in the way of really bad weather, he completed the journey in 324 days.

On the second day out the voyage came close to a tragic, premature end. *Sunbeam* was crossing the unpredictable Bay of Biscay and making ten knots under canvas before a north-easterly. The Brasseys were hugely enjoying their new adventure:

. . . the sea came popping in and out at the most unexpected places; much to the delight of the children, who, with bare feet and legs, and armed with mops and sponges, waged mimic war against the intruder and each other, singing and dancing to their heart's content . . . After our five o'clock dinner . . . we were all sitting or standing about the stern of the vessel, admiring the magnificent dark blue billows following us, with their curling white crests, mountains high . . . Tom was looking at the stern compass with Allnutt [their thirteen-year-old son). Mr Bingham and Mr Freer were smoking, half-way between the quarter-deck and the after companion, where Captain Brown, Dr Potter, Muriel, and I, were standing. Captain Lecky [Brown and Lecky were naval friends of Brassey's], seated on a large coil of rope, placed on the box of the rudder, was spinning Mabelle a yarn. A new hand was steering, and just at the moment when an unusually big wave overtook us, he unfortunately allowed the vessel to broach-to a little. In a second the sea came pouring over the stern above Allnutt's head. The boy was nearly washed overboard, but he managed to catch hold of the rail, and, with great presence of mind stuck his knees into the bulwarks . . . The coil of rope, on which Captain Lecky and Mabelle were seated, was completely floated by the sea. Providentially, however, he had taken a double turn round his wrist with a reefing point, and throwing his other arm round Mabelle, held on like grim death; otherwise nothing could have saved them. She was perfectly self-possessed, and only said quietly, 'Hold on, Captain Lecky, hold on!' . . . Captain Lecky, being accustomed to very large ships, had not in the least realised how near we were to the water in our little vessel, and was proportionately taken by surprise. All the rest of the party were drenched, with the exception of Muriel, whom Captain Brown held high above the water in his arms, and who lost no time in remarking, in the midst of the general confusion, 'I'm not at all wet, I'm not'. Happily, the children don't know what fear is. The maids, however, were very frightened, as some of the sea had got down into the nursery, and the skylights had to be screwed down. Our studding-sail boom, too, broke with a loud crack when the ship broached-to and the jaws of the foreboom gave way. Soon after this adventure we all went to bed . . .'[9]

Having learned a much-needed lesson in respect for the sea.

Sunbeam entered the tropics. Annie suffered from sea sickness whenever the weather was rough and from mild heat exhaustion when the air was still. She never, of course, divested herself of her enveloping garments even when the temperature rose into the nineties Fahrenheit; the Victorians abhorred direct sunshine on the skin. Yet, the moment the schooner dropped anchor, she was ready for a shore excursion. She scrambled up the side of a volcano in Tenerife, went deer hunting in Patagonia and tramped into the Brazilian rain forest. Her descriptions are colourful and detailed – at times almost too much so. Everything was 'interesting', whether flora, fauna or human behaviour and was noted down in the journal with emotionless, clinical detachment:

> We have all been so much interested in the advertisements we read in the daily papers of slaves to be sold or hired, that arrangements were made with a Brazilian gentleman for some of our party to have an opportunity of seeing the way in which these transactions are carried on.

Because slave dealing was illegal for British subjects, Tom Brassey and his companions had to pose as American plantation owners in order to be allowed in the sale room:

They were taken to a small shop in the city, and, after some delay, were conducted to a room upstairs, where they waited a quarter of an hour. Twenty-two men and eleven women and children were then brought in for inspection. They declared themselves suitable for a variety of occupations, indoor and out, and all appeared to look anxiously at their possible purchaser, with a view to ascertain what they had to hope for in the future. One couple, in particular, a brother and sister, about fourteen and fifteen years old respectively, were most anxious not to be separated, but to be sold together; and the tiny children seemed quite frightened at being spoken to or touched by the white men. Eight men and five women having been specially selected as fit subjects for further consideration, the visit terminated.[10]

British contemporaries penetrating the 'Dark Continent' in the 1870s, such as Livingstone and Stanley, wrote angry, heart-rending prose in denunciation of the traffic in human lives. The Brasseys observed the slave market in Rio, recorded what they saw – and went on to visit the botanical gardens.

Off the Plate estuary the voyagers came upon a trading barque in distress. The *Monkshaven* was out of Swansea bound for Valparaiso with smelting coal. Her cargo had ignited and for days a slow, smouldering fire had been raging in the hold, forcing the crew to batten down all hatches to deny oxygen to the inferno, and live on deck. The captain was reluctant to abandon ship but, by the time the *Sunbeam* appeared on the scene, the *Monkshaven*'s situation was hopeless and he allowed himself and his men to be taken aboard the schooner. For a week the fifteen crewmen of mixed nationality were the Brasseys' guests. Then they were transferred to a homeward-bound mail-boat. Annie was rather apprehensive about taking the stranded mariners to her bosom: 'an incursion of fifteen rough lawless spirits on board our little vessel would have been rather a serious matter'. However, her anxiety proved ill-founded, as the *Monkshaven*'s crew turned out to be 'quiet, respectable men'.[11]

When the time came for the temporary guests to leave, Annie noted, they were very distressed, some even breaking into tears. Well might those rough seamen be reluctant to depart the yacht. Not only had they cause to be grateful to their deliverers, they had also enjoyed seven days of unprecedented luxury. The Brasseys kept a table which was little short of sumptuous. Fresh meat, fish, fruit and vegetables were brought aboard at every opportunity. The *Sunbeam*'s 'cellar' was well-stocked. (After a particularly exhausting day ashore at Tenerife Annie casually recorded that they went back aboard with only enough energy to gulp down a little 'supper and champagne' before falling into their beds.) And it was a black day, indeed, when they ran out of ice. As for the accommodation, that resembled, in miniature, the splendid houses in which the Brasseys normally resided. The principal cabins boasted ornate fireplaces (and more than once during the voyage an open fire set off a minor conflagration) and were decorated with all the fussiness of a normal Victorian middle or upper class home – tasselled velvet drapes, rosewood and mahogany furniture, fringed table cloths, and overmantels heavy with ornaments and photographs in silver frames (which presumably had to be stowed away whenever heavy seas threatened). Little wonder, then, that the *Monkshaven* men had little enthusiasm for transferring to an ordinary merchant vessel nor that they were envious of Arthur Turner, one of their number, who was hired as a member of *Sunbeam*'s crew.

Annie had prepared herself for the voyage by reading the works of Cook, Dampier, Darwin and other travellers and had noted some of the sights she was particularly anxious to see. These included the fierce natives of Tierra del Fuego. Accordingly she had herself rowed ashore at Sandy Point, 'the only civilised place in the Straits', to observe three women recently 'rescued' by the local medical officer from some intercommunity war:

They appeared cheerful and happy, but we are told they are

not likely to live long. After the free life and the exposure to which they have been accustomed, civilisation – in the shape of clothing and hot houses – almost always kills them. Their lungs become diseased, and they die miserably.[12]

The *Sunbeam* had a fine, clear passage of the Straits and was through in five days. Tom Brassey and the crew then took her round to Santiago while Annie went on a sightseeing tour of inland Chile. As her coach or railway carriage rattled through the landscape she noted in considerable detail the trees, shrubs and flowers to be seen from the window. Mrs Brassey was an expert gardener who knew her plants. On the cool Chilean uplands, as on tropical islands and temperate coasts, she could name most of the native flora. What she could not recognise she could usually discover by using her smattering of self-taught Spanish:

Just now the whole country wears a golden tint from the bloom of the espinosa, which seems to grow everywhere . . . The branches of this shrub are so completely covered with little yellow balls of flowers, which come before the leaves, and which have no separate stalk, but grow along the shiny, horny branches that they look as if they were made of gold . . . If I bore you by saying too much about the flowers, forgive me. I want to make you all realise, if possible, what a lovely flowery land Chili [sic] is.[13]

But if every Chilean prospect pleased the fastidious traveller it was also true that only man was vile. Annie Brassey complained bitterly of swindling hoteliers, importunate street salesmen and dishonest natives generally. The coming of the railways had led to the rapid development of commerce and tourism. Every major town had its resident European population, its exclusive clubs and at least one hotel of a tolerable standard. In Santiago the boom years had, apparently, already come and gone:

The Grand Hotel, which used to be considered the best in South America, is now shut up, the company who owned it having recently failed; so all the smaller hotels, none of which are very good, are crowded to overflowing. The Hotel Ingles is considered the best, though I cannot say much in its favour. The rooms are good, but the situation is noisy, being at the corner of two streets; the servants are attentive, but the cuisine and arrangements are bad.[14]

Such a distinguished traveller as Mrs Brassey was, of course, seldom at the mercy of the locals in South America or elsewhere. Her main points of call were European settlements where she was looked after by friends and business acquaintances of her husband, or British consuls, or by other expatriates to whom she had letters of introduction.

On 30 October the *Sunbeam* left Valparaiso for her long haul across the Pacific. At this point husband and wife quarrelled. Tom was determined to make the crossing entirely under sail. Annie, worried about losing time and, perhaps, not a hundred per cent convinced of her spouse's navigating skills, thought they should at least make a start under steam power. She faced the prospect of several weeks at sea, suffering bouts of *mal de mer*, having to keep the children amused and deprived of the more refined comforts of civilised living. Not unnaturally, she wanted to reduce this phase of the journey as much as possible. Her arguments did not prevail. *Sunbeam* left port under canvas and carrying a minimum amount of coal.

Despite its romantic associations, the Brasseys decided to give Juan Fernandez a miss – 'There is nothing particular to be seen . . . and the scenery of the island is not remarkable.'[15] Tom set course north-westwards in search of the trade winds – and did not find them. After a week of wallowing in calms and sidling to catch light, sail-flapping breezes, *Sunbeam* had covered a mere seven hundred of the four thousand, three hundred miles that lay between Valparaiso and the next landfall. Faced with diminishing provisions and, probably, the 'I told you so' glances of his wife, Tom Brassey gave way and ordered the boilers stoked. Annie could not resist a self-satisfied comment in her journal: 'The alacrity with which the order to stow sails and raise the funnel was obeyed – every one lending a hand – and the delight expressed on every countenance, must have assured him at least of the popularity of his decision.'[16] A few days later the crew's rations were found to be severely depleted and the matriarch of the *Sunbeam* once more confided to her journal her conviction that men are quite lost without female guidance:

> Sailors are more like children than grown-up men, and require as much looking after. While there is water in the tanks, for instance, they will use it in the most extravagant manner, without thought for the morrow; and they are quite as reckless with their other stores.[17]

The voyagers sighted land after twenty-eight days and on 2 December went ashore in Tahiti. A few days previously Annie had had herself rowed over to a small island to meet the local people but Tom had been very anxious and insisted on her taking a posse of armed men with her (he did not accompany her himself). However, Tahiti was a French protectorate with a sizeable expatriate population and, therefore, both safe and respectable.

In fact, the Brasseys fell in love with Tahiti. It had just that mixture of ideal climate, colour, native charm and European civilisation to appeal to them. Even when they made a safari to the interior they found their sophisticated tastes well catered for. They passed the night at the tiny Hôtel de l'Isthme, run by two retired French sailors:

> The dinner itself really deserved a detailed description, if only to show that one may make the tour of Tahiti without necessarily having to rough it in the matter of food. We had crayfish and salad as a preliminary, and next, an excellent

soup followed by delicious little oysters, that cling to the boughs and roots of the guava and mangrove trees over-hanging the sea. Then came a large fish, name unknown, the inevitable *bouilli* and cabbage, *cotelettes aux pommes, biftek aux champignons,* succeeded by crabs and other shellfish, including *wurrali,* a delicate-flavoured kind of lobster, an *omelette aux abricots,* and dessert of tropical fruits. We were also supplied with good wine, both red and white, and bottled beer.

Unfortunately, 'bed' did not reach the same standard as 'board':

The heat in the night was suffocating, and soon after twelve o'clock we both woke up, feeling half-stifled . . . In the moonlight I could see columns of nasty, brown cockroaches ascending the bedposts, crawling along the top of the curtains, dropping with a thud onto the bed, and then descending over the side to the ground. At last I could stand it no longer, and, opening the curtains cautiously, I seized my slippers, knocked half a dozen brown beasts out of each, wrapped myself in a poncho – previously well shaken – gathered my garments around me, surmounted a barricade I had constructed to keep the pigs and chickens out of our doorless room, and fled to the garden.[18]

Christmas and New Year were spent at Honolulu and on 4 January 1877 *Sunbeam* headed for Japan – and sailed into the worst weather of the voyage. Days of tall seas and shrieking winds threw the yacht around. One wave tore away the fore gig. Another snapped off the jib-boom. Several times *Sunbeam* bottomed out with a juddering thud which convinced the crew that she had struck rock. She lost the top of her foremast with the topgallant spars and yards. The crew, some of whom were weakened with influenza, coped expertly with the crises. Annie was seasick:

Nothing annoys me more than to find that, after having sailed tens and tens of thousands of miles, I cannot cure myself of sea-sickness . . . many are the days when nothing but the firmest determination not to think about it, but to find something to do, and to do it with all my might keeps me on my feet at all. Fewer, happily, are the days when struggling is of no avail, when I am utterly and hopelessly incapacitated . . . and when no effort of will can enable me to do what I most wish to accomplish.'[19]

Mrs Brassey was certainly a tough lady, as adventurous and emancipated as Victorian convention permitted. She was determined that her sex would deny her no experience throughout the voyage. She hitched up her skirt to tramp mountains, daringly divested herself of outer garments to swim from tropical beaches, had herself hauled to the masthead to admire the view and braved the fierceness of the elements although she knew she had no stomach for it. She was a woman of spirit and we should not be too hard on her if her cultural vision was blinkered by a Victorian detachment and an assumption of superiority.

Japan, where the Brasseys spent a month in enthralled sight-seeing, was in the grip of winter. Snow and frost gave way to steady rain. But nothing dampened the visitors' ardour for exploration. They made a frenzied tour of palaces, temples, ornamental gardens, castles and markets. Tom was even presented to the Mikado. And, of course, they had to buy souvenirs. It is surprising that there was any space left below decks for more curios. At every port of call hours had been spent bartering with the natives for basketwear, needlework, horse harness, jewellery and other examples of local crafts. Now they added to the collection toys, clothes, fans, embroidered silks and brocades, lacquerwork, vases – and birds. The quantity of livestock on board was by now prodigious:

I bought some fine bantams at Yokohama, and a whole cageful of rice-birds. They are the dearest little things, and spend most of the day bathing and twittering, occasionally getting all together into one nest, with their twenty-five heads peeping out . . . I hope I shall take them home alive, as they have borne the cold very well so far. We have also some mandarin ducks on board, and some gold and silver fish with two tails. Our sailors have over a hundred birds of their own . . . don't know where they can keep them.[20]

This was obviously in the days before quarantine restrictions and health regulations governing the import of livestock.

If Japan was to Annie's liking, China or, at least, Canton, the only city she visited, was not. Why, the people actually ate the flesh of cats and puppy dogs – 'you could see the poor creatures hanging, skinned, in the butchers' shops.' As for Canton, itself, it was 'a filthy city, full of a seething, dirty population, where smells and sights of the most disgusting descriptions meet you at every turn.'[21]

At Johore the Brasseys were the guests of the maharaja, who gave a state banquet in their honour and, when they left, showered them with expensive presents – tropical plants, silk sarongs, elephant tusks and a pet lizard. It was at this point that one of the crew was discovered to be suffering from smallpox. Tom Brassey changed course for Malacca, where a British doctor was found who came to the *Sunbeam* with vaccine for everyone aboard. But some of the crewmen were reluctant to submit to being treated and, after long argument, two stubbornly held out, one insisting that he had made a promise to his grandfather that he would never be vaccinated. The Brasseys could not go ashore in Malacca but this did not prevent them buying more souvenirs from the throng of sampans that came alongside. Thus were added to the cargo seven monkeys, about fifty birds and bundles of malacca canes. (Later in the journal Annie casually referred to several birds and animals dying in their stuffy, cramped quarters.)

A run in sultry heat across the northern Indian Ocean brought the party to Ceylon (Sri Lanka) where the Brasseys spent several days in Kandy and the central uplands, visiting friends and seeing the sights. Ceylon is one of the most beautiful islands in the world and as such has always attracted discernmg expatriates who have settled to grow tea or rubber or simply to live in peace and harmony with nature (the most celebrated in recent times being Arthur C. Clarke). In 1877 it had the double attraction for the Brasseys of being beautiful and ruled by the British. The high point of their stay was a visit to an army friend at Neuera-ellia who took them to see the regimental sports, followed by a full-dress ball. The gardens at that altitude (7,000 ft) were aglow with roses and other English flowers. Gentlemen played cricket on immaculate, rolled lawns. Even the venomous snakes that abound in the island, Annie was assured, had a proper respect for their imperial masters – they never attacked Europeans. Her importunate host urged her and her husband to stay for some hunting with the two packs of hounds kept in the area. But by now the Brasseys were 'homeward bound and must hurry on'. Annie does not tell us why their return to England was so urgent but she does lament the fact that their stay could not be prolonged from a week to a month.

It was 5 April when the Brasseys left Colombo and they wasted no time making for the Mediterranean by the new canal. They made a very brief stop at Aden and reached Suez on the 25th. Here, like many passengers, Tom and Annie disembarked and travelled overland to Alexandria, via Cairo. They had both been in Egypt in 1869 for the elaborate cere-monies inaugurating Khedive Ismail's engineering miracle. Now they were interested to see the changes brought about by Egypt's over-ambitious ruler. They noted the fresh fields of corn near the capital on land recovered from the desert, the new canal linking Cairo to the sea at Ismailia, the skilfully laid-out gardens and parks, and the much-improved Shepherd's Hotel. But not everything met with Annie's approval; she did not like the western areas of the city, laid out by Ismail in imitation of Second Empire Paris:

> . . . alas! Cairo is being rapidly Haussmanised*. For the capitalist or resident Cairo may be improved, but for the traveller, the artist, the lover of the picturesque, the quaint, and the beautiful, the place is ruined. Cairo as a beautiful and ancient oriental city has ceased to exist and is being rapidly transformed into a bad imitation of modern Paris . . . Only a few narrow streets and old houses are still left, with carved wooden lattices, where you can yet dream that the *Arabian Nights* are true.[22]

The Brasseys left Alexandria on 2 May and reached Cowes on the 26th, having stopped very briefly at Valletta, Gibraltar and Lisbon.

Thus ended the first circumnavigation-for-pleasure. By the end of the century scores of other yachtsmen had repeated the Brasseys' exploits but they could not reproduce their unique accomplishment. Not only was the voyage of the *Sunbeam* a pioneer voyage it was an expression of British imperial and commercial confidence. Everywhere the Brasseys went they found their fellow countrymen. Even where the Union Jack was not flying, British merchants and planters were well ensconced. The world was open to Victoria's subjects. Annie was occasionally conscious of growing foreign competition and even confided a slight misgiving to her journal: 'It will be a bad day when the confidence in England's honesty as a nation throughout the world, and consequently her well-earned supremacy in commerce, have passed away.'[23] But it was a passing shadow. The more substantial reality was theatrically represented in the spontaneous tableau created to celebrate Muriel Brassey's fifth birthday:

---

*Georges-Eugène, Baron Haussmann (1809–91), the minister largely responsible for turning Paris into a city of wide boulevards and spacious squares, had, according to his critics, a finer eye for security than taste.

Mabelle and the Doctor and the men have been arranging a surprise for her all day, and none of us were allowed to go on the port side of the deck, but after dinner we were taken to a hastily fitted-up theatre, very prettily decorated with flags and Japanese lanterns. On a throne covered with the Union Jack, Muriel was seated, the two pugs being on footstools on either side of her to represent lions *couchant*. Some of the men had blackened their faces, and gave us a really very excellent Christy Minstrel entertainment.[24]

10

THE ANCIENT MARINER

To face the elements is, to be sure, no light matter when the
sea is in its grandest mood. You must then know the sea, and
know that you know it, and not forget that it was made to
be sailed over.[1]

If ever a man had a love affair with the ocean that man was
Captain Joshua Slocum who, at the age of fifty-four, became
the first man to sail around the world single-handed. He had
learned his craft in four decades on the clippers, and had
become one of the finest mariners afloat. Yet he also possessed
another talent, rare among nautical men: he could translate
experience into rugged but tender prose. His two published
works, *The Voyage of the Liberdade* and *Sailing Alone Around
the World,* are like extended love sonnets but crammed with
keen observation and fine detail about the handling of small
sailing craft. They are the sort of books that Coleridge's ancient
mariner might have written if the poet had left him to his own
devices. *Sailing Alone* is both a practical and a moving account
of circumnavigation; it is not surprising that it has become the
deep-sea yachtsman's bible.

In true romantic fashion, Joshua Slocum ran away to sea at the age of twelve. That was in 1856 when, because 'the wonderful sea charmed me from the first',[2] he could no longer endure life on his father's Nova Scotia farm. Over the next thirty years he worked his way up from cabin boy to owner-master, achieving promotion to command, as he put it 'over the bows and not in through the cabin windows'.[3]

Slocum's career thus coincided with the last, glorious days of commercial sail. He served on several of the magnificent tall ships plying to China and Australia out of London and San Francisco. By 1890 the triumph of steam was established but Slocum stuck defiantly to the life that he knew. He was by this time sailing his own vessel, the *Aquidneck,* 'a little bark which of all man's handiwork seemed to me the nearest to perfection of beauty, and which in speed, when the wind blew, asked no favours of steamers.'[4] Sadly, his pride and joy was wrecked on the coast of Brazil. Immediately, he set to, with such local materials as lay to hand, to build himself a replacement. The result was a unique twenty-five-foot, sampan-rigged craft which he referred to as a 'canoe' and christened the *Liberdade.* (The appropriate name was compounded from two words 'liber' meaning free and an archaic verb 'dade' which the dictionary defines as 'to move slowly, totteringly'.)

Sailing the *Liberdade* back to Boston (Slocum had become a naturalised American) with his family was a remarkable achievement and one which attracted considerable publicity. The middle-aged mariner was not slow to cash in on this. He wrote an account of the building and the voyage of his little vessel. The book was well received and Slocum's earnings from it went some way towards compensating him for the loss of the *Aquidneck.*

Now followed two years of frustration and hardship. Sailing-ship masters looking for a command were ten a penny on the New England coast and even a celebrated mariner like Slocum could not get a ship and earn his keep. It was not just his own plight that depressed him; he pined for the passing of an age.

'Nearly all our tall vessels had been cut down for coal-barges, and were being ignominiously towed by the nose from port to port.'[5] Slocum, 'cast up from old ocean', felt as helpless as the fine ships humiliatingly downgraded or rotting away in their muddy berths.

It was when he was offered one of these old craft that life took on a new meaning and purpose. A certain Captain Eben Pierce gave him a decrepit old sloop called the *Spray* which he had acquired seven years before and which had, ever since, lain on her side in a field, becoming something of a local joke. Pierce's comment that 'she wants some repairs' was a historic understatement. If she was ever to see salt water again the *Spray* needed to be completely rebuilt. Slocum looked at the sad old ship and made an incredible decision: not only would he restore her to her former glory; he would sail her round the world.

What motives lay behind the formulating of this remarkable vision? On this Slocum was strangely reticent. He passed off his intention to rescue a decaying vessel and attempt to achieve in her something that had never been done before as though it were the most unremarkable thing in the world: 'the voyage . . . was a natural outcome not only of my love of adventure, but of my life-long experience.'[6] Is it fanciful, I wonder, to see the voyage of the *Spray* as a gigantic gesture of defiance? Was Slocum, on the very threshold of a new century, with its throbbing steam engines and turbines, making a statement in vindication of old ships, old shipmen, old ways, and the old understanding between mariner and ocean? Once, in mid-Atlantic, *Spray* was hailed by the liner *Olympia*. Slocum noted, with scant approval, that her captain was young, and he expressed the hope that man and ship were a match for the sea. 'There were no porpoises skipping along with the *Olympia*,' he observed. 'Porpoises always prefer sailing ships.'[7]

Slocum rebuilt his sloop from the keel up. It took him thirteen months and cost $553.62, some of which money he earned doing occasional work in a whaleship fitting yard. As the result of his labours the owner-shipwright-captain had a vessel thirty-six feet nine inches overall and fourteen feet, two inches in the beam. She carried a yawl-rigged mainsail, a jib and flying jib, in addition to which an aft sail could be hoisted on a removable jigger mast. She was designed for solidity and ease of handling rather than for grace; for reliability rather than speed. She bore more resemblance to a North Sea trawler than to any of the fashionable yachts of the day, and she caused many raised eyebrows among the smart pleasure-boat fraternity in the various harbours where she berthed. Slocum was no yachtsman, as he freely admitted, and his ship bore all the hallmarks of a vessel designed by a practical, no-nonsense professional sailor, who had experienced the ocean's every whim. Seventy years later Francis Chichester, a true yachtsman, paid this tribute to the *Spray*'s design:

> Joshua Slocum's *Spray* in the 1890s could attain a speed of 8 or 9 knots, though her hull shape would give modern yacht-designers the horrors. Her stem and stern were nearly up and down, so that her waterline length and overall length were nearly the same. Whatever the modern designer's views on *Spray*, the fact remains that she not only made fast passages – the 1,200 miles Slocum sailed in eight days in 1897 stood as a single-handed record for seventy years . . . – but she was also a splendid, seaworthy boat.[8]

After the building of *Spray* Slocum spent more than a year in trials, fitting and adjustments. On 7 May 1895 he put out of Gloucester, Massachusetts and made a leisurely progress back up the familiar coastline to Nova Scotia. It was on 2 July that he said goodbye to the American mainland and put out into the Atlantic – alone.

No man knows, until the experience is embraced or thrust upon him, how he will react to complete solitude. You can do little to prepare for it. You can do nothing to stave it off. When the mind is alert and there is plenty to occupy it you are scarcely aware of the problem. It is in moments of boredom and fatigue that it makes itself felt, sometimes in the most bizarre ways. If Slocum had wondered how he would respond he soon found out. Three days out he ran into fog:

. . . in the dismal fog I felt myself drifting into loneliness, an insect on a straw in the midst of the elements . .

During these days a feeling of awe crept over me. My memory worked with startling power. The ominous, the insignificant, the great, the small, the wonderful, the commonplace – all appeared before my mental vision in magical succession. Pages of my history were recalled which had been so long forgotten that they seemed to belong to a previous existence. I heard all the voices of the past laughing, crying, telling what I had heard them tell in many corners of the earth.

The loneliness of my state wore off when the gale was high and I found much work to do. When fine weather returned, then came the sense of solitude, which I could not shake off. I used my voice often, at first giving some order about the affairs of a ship, for I had been told that from disuse I should lose my speech. At the meridian altitude of the sun I called aloud, 'Eight bells,' after the custom on a ship at sea. Again from my cabin I cried to an imaginary man at the helm, 'How does she head, there?' and again, 'Is she on her course?' But getting no reply, I was reminded the more palpably of my condition. My voice sounded hollow on the empty air, and I dropped the practice. However, it was not long before the thought came to me that when I was a lad I used to sing; why not try that now, where it would disturb no one?. . . You should have seen the porpoises leap when I pitched my voice for the waves and the sea and all that was in it. Old turtles, with large eyes, poked their heads up out of the sea as I sang 'Johnny Boker', and 'We'll Pay Darby Doyl for his Boots', and the like. But the porpoises were, on the whole, vastly more appreciative than the turtles.[9]

A few days later Slocum was suffering from hallucinations – or was he? He had partaken rather too freely of plums and cheese and, as a result, was smitten with the most violent indigestion. Then, just when he was at his lowest ebb with exhaustion and pain, the *Spray* ran into a storm. Slocum should have taken in sail and laid to but he was too weary. Instead, he went below and collapsed on the cabin floor. The sloop was left to run wild before the wind, out of control:

How long I lay there I could not tell, for I became delirious. When I came to, as I thought, from my swoon, I realized that the sloop was plunging into a heavy sea, and looking out of the companionway, to my amazement I saw a tall man at the helm. His rigid hand, grasping the spokes of the wheel, held them as in a vise . . . His rig was that of a foreign sailor, and the large red cap he wore was cockbilled over his left ear, and all was set off with shaggy black whiskers . . . While I gazed upon his threatening aspect I forgot the storm, and wondered if he had come to cut my throat. This he seemed to divine. 'Señor,' said he, doffing his cap, 'I have come to do you no harm.' And a smile, the faintest in the world, but still a smile, played on his face, which seemed not unkind when he spoke . . . 'I am one of Columbus's crew,' he continued. 'I am the pilot of the *Pinta* come to aid you. Lie quiet, señor captain,' he added, 'and I will guide your ship tonight . . .' I was still in agony. Great seas were boarding the *Spray,* but in my fevered brain I thought they were boats falling on deck, that careless draymen were throwing from wagons on the pier to which I imagined the *Spray* was now moored, and without fenders to breast her off. 'You'll smash your boats!' I called out again and again, as the seas crashed on the cabin over my head. 'You'll smash your boats, but you can't hurt the *Spray*. She is strong!' I cried.

I found, when my pains and calentura had gone, that the deck, now as white as a shark's tooth from seas washing over it, had been swept of everything movable. To my astonishment, I saw now at broad day that the *Spray* was still heading as I had left her, and was going like a race-horse. Columbus himself could not have held her more exactly on her course. The sloop had made ninety miles in the night through a rough sea.

The gale eased off and Slocum slept. In his dreams the old pilot reappeared:

'You did well last night to take my advice,' said he, 'and if you would, I should like to be with you often on the voyage, for the love of adventure alone.' Finishing what he had to say, he again doffed his cap and disappeared as mysteriously as he came, returning, I suppose, to the phantom *Pinta*. I awoke much refreshed, and with the feeling that I had been in the presence of a friend and a seaman of vast experience. I gathered up my clothes, which by this time were dry, then, by inspiration, I threw overboard all the plums in the vessel.'[10]

A sceptic might be disposed to dismiss all this talk of a phantom helmsman as a sailor's yarn. Only in works of imagination do dead crewmen work ships:

I woke, and we were sailing on
As in a gentle weather:
'Twas night, calm night, the moon was high;
The dead men stood together.

All stood together on the deck,
For a charnel-dungeon fitter:
All fixed on me their stony eyes,
That in the Moon did glitter.

The pang, the curse, with which they died,
Had never passed away:
I could not draw my eyes from theirs,
Nor turn them up to pray.

And now this spell was snapt: once more
I viewed the ocean green,
And looked far forth, yet little saw
Of what had else been seen –

Like one, that on a lonesome road
Doth walk in fear and dread,
And having once turned round walks on,
And turns no more his head;
Because he knows, a frightful fiend
Doth close behind him tread.[11]

But there are many yachtsmen, mountaineers and explorers who would not dismiss Slocum's story so readily. The strong sense of another presence is one of the most familiar experiences of people who undergo long periods of loneliness and hardship. Ann Davison, solo yachtswoman, tells how, exhausted at the end of a transatlantic crossing, she met with such a phenomenon off Gibraltar:

Life now simply resolved itself into one of imperative urges, and the most imperative urge of all was sleep. I wanted oblivion with every fibre of my being. And here we were right at the entrance to the Straits where ships were crowding through like sheep at a gate. One might as well pull up in the middle of Broadway for a quiet nap.

Extreme fatigue does strange things. As in a dream I became aware of two other people aboard, and as in a dream it seemed perfectly natural that they should be there. One of them sat on the coachroof and the other came aft holding on to the boom, quiescent in its gallows. 'O.K.,' he said, 'You kip down. We'll keep watch.' Obediently I went below and slept till morning.

Stretching and yawning and still weary, I climbed into the cockpit in the light of day. 'Thank you,' I said. 'That was good . . .' but they had gone. Never had the cockpit looked so empty.[12]

Slocum, too, made for Gibraltar, intending to go by way of the Suez Canal. But he was cautioned about Barbary pirates and, indeed, had a brush with a Moroccan felucca as soon as he left the Rock. Thus warned, Slocum changed his plans. In fact, he completely reversed them and decided to go west about. The man's nonchalance is breathtaking. Only a mariner fully conversant with the world's tides, winds and currents could have calmly made such a radical change to well-laid plans. The course he now followed was to be very similar to that taken by the first circumnavigator of all, 370 years before.

Recrossing the Atlantic, *Spray* came to Brazil on 5 October, where her owner had many nautical friends and business contacts, thanks to the years spent trading in and out of South American ports. Indeed, it seems that Slocum was a stranger in very few of the places he called at. Everywhere he went he was received hospitably and usually found some sea captain, consul or factor to smooth his path through local formalities. In Pernambuco it was Dr Perera, proprietor of El *Commerciojornal*, who entertained the wayfarer in his waterfront mansion and insisted on feeding him up for the voyage. Slocum, like all brave men and women who attempt the 'impossible', was heavily dependent on those who gave him encouragement and support. It was not just the practical assistance he valued. Even more important were the assurances of goodwill that met him in every port of call and the morale- boosting encomiums of those who told him 'you can do it'. There were Jeremiahs in plenty who had told him before he set out that he was crazy. Indeed, when he came to write his account of the voyage, Slocum dedicated it, 'To the *one** who said: "The *Spray* will come back".' Was there really only one? Something armchair critics never realise is the effect their words have on adventurers like Slocum. Perhaps it is because they look upon such bold spirits as belonging to a different order of being, impervious to such common afflictions as self-doubt and hesitancy. Slocum would have agreed with Chichester: 'negative wishings and

*Author italics.

willings on the part of different people use up valuable strength
in resisting them, just as prayer and positive wellwishing give
strength, and lend support.'[13]

Slocum made his way steadily southwards, planning to reach
the Straits of Magellan at the height of the southern summer.
He made frequent stops to take on food and pay social calls. By
now the lone yachtsman's fame was going before him. At
Montevideo he:

> was greeted by steam-whistles till I felt embarrassed and
> wished that I had arrived unobserved. The voyage so far
> along may have seemed to the Uruguayans a feat worthy of
> some recognition; but there was so much of it yet ahead, and
> of such an arduous nature, that any demonstration at this
> point seemed, somehow, like boasting prematurely.[14]

However, fame had its compensations. A local shipping agency
insisted on paying for any repairs *Spray* needed and on giving
Slocum twenty pounds towards his expenses. At Buenos Aires,
where he arrived on New Year's Day 1896, the *Spray* was given
free berthing and her captain was entertained at the home of
Mr Mulhall, 'the warmest heart, I think, outside of Ireland'.

But the elements were not so hospitable. The seas off the
Plate estuary are notorious. Thomas Chaloner, three hundred
years earlier, had encountered there 'the fury of storms which,
indeed, I think to be such as worser might not be endured'.[15]
Slocum's departure from Buenos Aires on 26 January was
deceptively peaceful. He had to be towed out of harbour in a
flat calm, the water's surface looking 'like a silver disk'. But the
mood rapidly changed:

> a gale came up soon after, and caused an ugly sea, and
> instead of being all silver, as before, the river was now all
> mud. . . . I cast anchor before dark in the best lee I could find
> near the land, but was tossed miserably all night, heartsore of
> choppy seas.[16]

Soon he was off the desolate coast of Patagonia, which those who have seen it know to be the bleakest and most cheerless stretch of coastline on the face of the earth. Even Slocum, the seasoned mariner, was depressed by it and 'resolved then that I would anchor no more north of the Strait of Magellan'.[17] He stood well out to sea to avoid the treacherous currents swirling around the craggy shore, only to find that he had exchanged one potential danger for another:

> . . . while the sloop was reaching under short sail, a tremendous wave, the culmination, it seemed, of many waves, rolled down upon her in a storm, roaring as it came. I had only a moment to get all sail down and myself upon the peak halliards, out of danger, when I saw the mighty crest towering masthead-high above me. The mountain of water submerged my vessel. She shook in every timber and reeled under the weight of the sea, but rose quickly out of it, and rode grandly over the rollers that followed. It may have been a minute that from my hold in the rigging I could see no part of the *Spray*'s hull . . . However, the incident, which filled me with fear, was only one more test of the *Spray*'s seaworthiness. It reassured me against rude Cape Horn.[18]

Generally speaking, Slocum had timed his arrival well. After the incident with the freak wave he had a good run as far as Cape Virgins, and slipped easily inside Magellan's Strait.

But this hostile region was not going to let him off scot free. A storm sprang up that night as he lay at anchor and pummelled *Spray* for thirty hours. But she withstood it and thereafter Slocum enjoyed a trouble-free passage through the Straits. On 3 March he passed Cape Pilar, believing that 'the blind Horn's hate' was behind him. He was wrong. Ahead of him lay what he would later call his greatest adventure.

Spray sailed out of the shelter of the land straight into a north-westerly tempest. There was nothing for it but to take in all sail and run before the wind under bare poles. Day after day

the little boat was driven back towards Cape Horn. Slocum
again changed his plans: he would make for the Falklands, refit
there and cross the southern Atlantic, going east about after all
– if he survived the screeching fury of wind and waves:

> No ship in the world could have stood up against so violent
> a gale . . . And so she drove southeast, as though about to
> round the Horn, while the waves rose and fell and bellowed
> their never-ending story of the sea . . . She was running now
> with a reefed forestaysail, the sheets flat amidship. I paid out
> two long ropes to steady her course and to break combing
> seas astern, and I lashed the helm amidship. In this trim she
> ran before it, shipping never a sea. Even while the storm
> raged at its worst, my ship was wholesome and noble. My
> mind as to her seaworthiness was put at ease for aye . . . The
> first day of the storm gave the *Spray* her actual test in the
> worst sea that Cape Horn or its wild regions could afford,
> and in no part of the world could a rougher sea be found
> than at this particular point, namely, off Cape Pillar, the grim
> sentinel of the Horn . . . the *Spray* rode, now like a bird on
> the crest of a wave, and now like a waif deep down in the
> hollow between seas; and so she drove on. Whole days
> passed, counted as other days, but with always a thrill – yes,
> of delight.[19]

There speaks the true adventurer, the man who could put
himself and his lovingly-built ship at risk of instant destruction
– just for the hell of it. For him the voyage was a contest.
Sometimes he had to give his opponent best, such as now, when
he was obliged to steer an easterly course round the Horn, but
if he did so it was only to stay in the game. The voyage was a
contest – and only a contest. No other motives diluted the thrill
of facing and overcoming challenges. For the first time in
history a man sailed round the world with no commercial or
imperialist objectives. No national pride was at stake. No
scientific discoveries beckoned. He did not even travel to see

other lands, for there were few he had not already visited. Every adventurer has something of the gambler in him. Beneath the calculation, the careful preparation, the determination to succeed, lies a love of the game for its own sake.

On the fourth day of the storm Slocum saw and grasped a chance to escape from the tempest and rescue his plan of a westward crossing of the Pacific. Through cloud, rain and driving spray he caught a glimpse of a mountain thrusting out of the sea. He reckoned that it marked an alternative entrance to Magellan's Strait. He hoisted a tiny sail (his mainsail had been torn to shreds in the first moments of the storm) put the tiller over and made for land:

. . . on the outside coast of Tierra del Fuego. It was indeed a mountainous sea. When the sloop was in the fiercest squalls, with only the reefed forestaysail set, even that small sail shook her from keelson to truck when it shivered by the leech . . . Under pressure of the smallest sail I could set she made for the land like a race-horse, and steering her over the crests of the waves so that she might not trip was nice work. I stood at the helm now and made the most of it.

Night closed in before the sloop reached the land, leaving her feeling the way in pitchy darkness. I saw breakers ahead before long. At this I wore ship and stood offshore, but was immediately startled by the tremendous roaring of breakers again ahead and on the lee bow. This puzzled me, for there should have been no broken water where I supposed myself to be. I kept off a good bit, then wore round, but finding broken water also there, threw her head again offshore. In this way, among dangers, I spent the rest of the night. Hail and sleet in the fierce squalls cut my flesh till the blood trickled over my face; but what of that? It was daylight, and the sloop was in the midst of the Milky Way of the sea, which is northwest of Cape Horn, and it was the white breakers of a huge sea over sunken rocks which had threatened to engulf her through the night. It was Fury Island I had

sighted and steered for, and what a panorama was before me
now and all around! It was not the time to complain of a
broken skin. What could I do but fill away among the
breakers and find a channel between them, now that it was
day? Since she had escaped the rocks through the night,
surely she would find her way by daylight. This was the
greatest sea adventure of my life. God knows how my vessel
escaped.

The sloop at last reached inside of small islands that
sheltered her in smooth water. Then I climbed the mast to
survey the wild scene astern. The great naturalist Darwin
looked over this seascape from the deck of the *Beagle,* and
wrote in his journal, 'Any landsman seeing the Milky Way
would have nightmares for a week'. He might have added,
'or seaman' as well.[20]

Spray was now in the Cockburn Channel which leads *back*
into the main strait. She was able to make her way back to
Cape Froward and pick up again her westward course. The
next problem Slocum had to contend with was a night attack
by Fuegian Indians. Fortunately he had anticipated this emergency by sprinkling the deck with carpet tacks. The screams,
shouts and howls which woke him at midnight were gratifying
proof of the success of this stratagem. For three more wearying
days and nights *Spray* was tossed around by the unpredictable
winds and tidal races which swirl round Tierra de Fuego.

In Fortescue Bay Slocum had his first sight of civilisation in
several weeks. It took the shape of the SS *Columbia* out of New
York bound for San Francisco. Those were the days when the
Panama Canal was still a distant and dubious prospect. De
Lesseps' company having gone bankrupt in an attempt to cross
the isthmus, other men were not anxious to take up the challenge, so that many big ships were still obliged to use the
hazardous Straits of Magellan. The first mate of the *Columbia*
turned out to be an old colleague of Slocum's and he gave his
friend a generous gift of miscellaneous provisions. As he

enjoyed a delicious late supper and gazed across the harbour to where the steamer's rows of electric lights were reflected in the black water Slocum mused on the difference between the two vessels. Ironically, it was the frail little *Spray* that proved the more durable. SS *Columbia* was wrecked off California the following year.

Slocum had much work to do repairing sails and damaged gear before braving the open sea again and took his time along the channel. One day he came upon the wreckage of a vessel that had been less fortunate than *Spray* in the great gale and salvaged several casks of tallow which he planned to trade during the next leg of the journey. He reached Port Angosto, close to the exit from the strait, at the end of March. Six times he tried to reach the Pacific and six times he was driven back by contrary winds. At last, on 13 April, *Spray* broke free of the land and Slocum raised his voice in relief and exultation. "'Hurrah for the Spray!" I shouted to seals, sea-gulls and penguins; for there were no other living creatures about.'[21]

He bore away for Juan Fernandez, an island intermittently occupied since Dampier's visit and now ruled on behalf of the Chilean government by a governor of Swedish extraction. Slocum stayed eight days among the hospitable islanders, who much to his surprise, had read of his exploits in newspapers brought out from Valparaiso. He climbed to the mountain lookout to gaze upon the memorial to Alexander Selkirk placed there twenty-eight years before by the officers of HMS *Topaze*. And he wondered why the castaway had ever left what seemed to be an idyllic location:

The hills are well-wooded, the valleys fertile, and pouring down through many ravines are streams of pure water. There are no serpents on the island, and no wild beasts other than pigs and goats . . . The people lived without the use of rum or beer of any sort. There was not a police officer or a lawyer among them. The domestic economy of the island was simplicity itself. The fashions of Paris did not affect the inhabitants; each dressed according to his own taste. Although there was no doctor, the people were all healthy, and the children were all beautiful. There were about forty-five souls on the island all told . . . Blessed island of Juan Fernandez![22]

The Pacific crossing, according to Slocum, was the most relaxed period of the whole voyage. The *Spray,* well provisioned and recovered from her ordeal, scudded along before the trade winds for seventy-two days. As if to make up for the recent chastening she had administered, the sea now spoiled Slocum:

> I sat and read my books, mended my clothes, or cooked my meals and ate them in peace. I had already found that it was not good to be alone, and so I made companionship with what there was around me, sometimes with the universe and sometimes with my own insignificant self; but my books were always my friends, let fail all else. Nothing could be easier or more restful than my voyage in the trade-winds.[23]

Slocum steered by the sun and the stars. He set a course for Samoa, ignoring the Marquesas and the Society Islands, where he could easily have made a landfall, and brought *Spray* to rest in the port of Apia on 16 July.

This chain of islands is one of the most beautiful in the world and, for Europeans, perhaps, the most pleasant. Slocum arrived in the middle of the cool season, when the temperature seldom rises above 27°C. The heavy rain which keeps the inland ridges perpetually covered with an aura of cool, hazy green falls mostly at night and in the morning. Samoa today looks much as it did ninety years ago. Sadly, the unaffected life style of the people, which so impressed Slocum has changed with constant exposure to the customs and attitudes of supposedly more sophisticated cultures. When the *Spray*'s captain visited a village chief he found him cheerfully contemptuous of western materialism: "'Dollar, dollar,'" said he; "white man know only dollar. Never mind dollar. The *tapo* [village hostess] has prepared *ava;* let us drink and rejoice".'[24]

The Samoan islands were at that time under a rather uneasy tripartite protectorate administered by Britain, Germany and the USA. Slocum was welcomed and entertained by the American consul-general and his wife but an invitation from another resident was much more exciting to the visitor. Mrs Fanny V. de G. Stevenson came down to the *Spray* in person to ask Captain Slocum to come to her home.

Robert Louis Stevenson, after several years of wandering, had settled in Samoa with his American wife, his mother and his stepchildren in 1890. Here he wrote some of his finest works: *Catriona*, several short stories and the fragmentary *Weir of Hermiston*. And here he died suddenly, in December 1894, at the age of forty-four. It was his widow who now warmly greeted Slocum as a traveller and adventurer after her husband's heart. For Joshua Slocum, a devotee of Stevenson's books, it was an unbelievable experience to be entertained in his hero's own home, Vailima, and even to be invited to sit and write letters at Stevenson's own desk. The most emotional moment of the entire voyage came when Mrs Stevenson, whom Slocum describes as a creature with sparkling eyes and an irrepressible spirit, presented him with a set of books from the author's library bearing the inscription:

TO CAPTAIN SLOCUM. These volumes have been read and re-read many times by my husband, and I am very sure that he would be pleased that they should be passed on to the sort of seafaring man that he liked above all others.

Fanny G. de V. Stevenson[25]

It is not surprising that, when he left Samoa on 20 August 'a sense of loneliness seized upon me as the islands faded astern'. Slocum crammed on sail for Sydney 'but for long days in my dreams Vailima stood before the prow'.[26] Samoa had also been kind to Slocum in another way: he had sold the last of his salvaged tallow to a German trader there and was, as a result, well in funds.

After close on two months in Sydney, largely spent in social engagements with old friends and smart members of the yacht club who made a great fuss of the visiting celebrity, Slocum moved on to Melbourne. Here he found, to his indignation, that the harbour authorities charged him tonnage dues, something that had happened in no other port except Pernambuco. The captain found himself out of pocket to the tune of six shillings and sixpence. He lost no time in recouping this sum from the citizens of Melbourne:

> I squared the matter by charging people sixpence each for coming on board, and when this business got dull I caught a shark and charged them sixpence each to look at that. The shark was twelve feet six inches in length, and carried a progeny of twenty-six, not one of them less than two feet in length. A slit of a knife let them out in a canoe full of water, which, changed constantly, kept them alive one whole day. In less than an hour from the time I heard of the ugly brute it was on deck and on exhibition, with rather more than the amount of the *Spray's* tonnage dues already collected.[27]

However, the traveller did not find all Australians mean. An anonymous lady sent him five pounds 'as a token of her appreciation of his bravery in crossing the wide seas on so small a boat and all alone without human sympathy to help when danger threatened'.[28]

Once again Slocum found himself having to give the 'wide seas' best. He had planned to travel south round Australia but foul weather and ice drifting up from the Antarctic obliged him to go the other way about the continent. He spent the rest of the summer on a pleasant cruise round Tasmania and, on 9 May 1897, set sail once more from Sydney.

Anyone who loves travel and thrills to nature in her more

grandly beautiful moods, should sail, at least once, the long lagoon between the rugged coast of Queensland and the Great Barrier Reef. Even now, when the tourist industry has filled every port with entrepreneurs offering fishing trips and scuba diving expeditions, this stretch of water provides unparalleled vistas both above and below the waves. For Slocum, sailing single-handed and non-stop from Great Sandy Cape to Cooktown it was a voyage of wary delight. He exulted in 'the waters of many colours studded all about with enchanted islands' but always kept a sharp lookout for outcrops of jagged coral and trusted to 'the mercies of the Maker of all reefs'.[29] He stopped at Port Denison (modern Bowen) then made for Cooktown, the settlement recently sprung up on the Endeavour River to serve the nearby goldmines. For Slocum this was a pilgrimage, for Cooktown was built around the harbour where Captain Cook had brought his ship for repair in 1770 after brilliantly negotiating the hazards of the Barrier Reef. From there the *Endeavour* had made her way through uncharted Torres Strait between Queensland and New Guinea and thither the *Spray* followed. But not before her captain had witnessed a tragedy: 'I saw coming into port the physical wrecks of miners from New Guinea, destitute and dying. Many had died on the way and been buried at sea.'[30] In 1877 New Guinea had experienced its own 'gold rush'. Hopeful prospectors from Australia and farther afield had flocked to the Mai-Kusa river in pursuit of exaggerated rumours of mineral wealth. The failure of the pioneers had not dampened the optimism of others, and successive contingents of adventurers crossed to the island (divided up and annexed by Holland, Germany and Britain in 1884–5). The results were almost always dismal scenes such as Slocum witnessed. He was sufficiently moved to deliver a lecture to the local people at which a subscription was taken up for the miners.

The 22 June 1897 found Joshua Slocum on tiny Thursday Island, off the northern tip of Queensland. And in that remote and insignificant outpost of empire he represented the United

States of America in the celebrations marking the diamond jubilee of Queen Victoria. The main attraction was a corroboree, a dance festival performed by four hundred aborigines specially brought over from the mainland by the resident magistrate. The frenzied dancing went on, by the light of fires, late into the night. It was, in Slocum's words, 'a show at once amusing, spectacular, and hideous'.[31] Two days later he quitted Australian waters and twenty-three days later, after a magnificent run before the trade winds, he reached Cocos Keeling Islands, 2,700 miles away. It was during this run that he notched up the single-handed speed record of 1,200 miles in eight days.

As we have already observed, the 'South Sea Islands' were no sooner discovered than various adventurers – misfits, social outcasts, younger sons of the nobility, and the like – began settling them in the hope of discovering or creating their own tropical paradise. One of the most successful escapists was undoubtedly Captain John Clunies Ross RN who, on retiring from active service, in 1827, took his family to live on the Cocos Keeling Islands. The only occupants were fellow adventurer Alexander Hare and forty concubines and slaves he had recently brought from Malaysia. Ross swiftly established his ascendancy and when Slocum arrived, seventy years later, he found a well-ordered community under the leadership of Sidney Clunies Ross, the founder's grandson.*

Slocum found the islands swarming with Malay and Eurasian children. At first they feared the solitary seaman, believing him to be a spirit from the deep. But, largely with bribes of ship's biscuit thick-spread with blackberry jam, he won them over. For days on end they sat on the beach and watched wide-eyed as Slocum re-tarred and caulked his vessel.

One of the unique features of Cocos Keeling is the giant clams (the largest in the world) which are found in its waters. It was while on an expedition to collect some of these that

*Although the islands were brought under British protection in 1857, the Ross family received a grant of them in perpetuity from Queen Victoria in 1886.

Slocum came closer to death than he had been when alone in mid-ocean or battling with breakers off treacherous shores:

> I found myself with a thoughtless African negro in a rickety bateau that was fitted with a rotten sail, and this blew away in mid-channel, in a squall that sent us drifting helplessly to sea.

The dinghy had no oars and, while there was an anchor there was 'not enough rope to tie a cat':

> With Africa the nearest coast to leeward, three thousand miles away, with not so much as a drop of water in the boat, and a lean and hungry negro – well, cast the lot as one might, the crew of the *Spray* in a little while would have been hard to find.[32]

Slocum could not escape the crisis by leaping overboard and striking out for the shore, because, like many ancient mariners, he could not swim. Fortunately, he discovered a pole in the bottom of the boat. Plying this as a makeshift paddle, he was able to work the craft into shallow water.

A trouble-free run before the trade winds from 22 August to 8 September brought him to the British island of Rodriguez, where the natives all fled in panic at his approach. It transpired that the local priest had recently warned his largely Roman Catholic flock of the imminent appearance of Antichrist. A lone figure emerging from the sea seemed to fit the bill perfectly. At Mauritius, which he reached on 19 September, Slocum decided to see out the rest of the winter so as to have good weather for rounding the Cape. Thus it was 17 November before he reached Durban.

We find little reference to major political events in Slocum's account of his travels. Like most adventurers, he considered himself an individualist above, or at least outside, the realm of international statesmanship. But now he was walking into the

world's number one trouble spot. President Kruger was fever-
ishly rearming the Boer republics and open war between them
and England was only months away. Slocum spent four months
in South Africa, where being by now a major celebrity, he met
several leading personalities, including Kruger, Sir Alfred
Milner, the British High Commissioner, and the explorer H. M.
Stanley, who was back in Africa to work on his latest book
(Through South Africa).

In both Natal and Cape Town Slocum found a tense atmosphere and one constantly exacerbated by the press of both sides.
Despite himself, he was caught up in this political tennis match.
On the occasion of his meeting with Paul Kruger, Slocum was
introduced as the captain who was sailing round the world. Like
most Boers, the president was a biblical fundamentalist who
stubbornly held to the view that the earth was flat. 'You don't
mean *round* the world,' he snapped, 'It is impossible. You mean
in the world.' And he walked away muttering 'Impossible!
Impossible!' A local journal, the Cape Town *Owl* picked up the
story and made it the subject of a wicked political cartoon.

This was not the first brush Slocum had had with the 'flat-
earthers' in the Cape. He had already crossed swords with
fanatics who had taunted him publicly and told him that whatever else he had been doing for the last thirty-two months he
had *not* been sailing round the world. Slocum did not allow this
to colour his impression of the Afrikaner race as a whole:

> While I feebly portray the ignorance of these learned men, I
> have great admiration for their physical manhood. Much
> that I saw first and last of the Transvaal and the Boers was
> admirable. It is well known that they are the hardest of
> fighters, and as generous to the fallen as they are brave before
> the foe. Real stubborn bigotry with them is only found
> among old fogies, and will die a natural death.[33]

Which suggests that Joshua Slocum was a better mariner than
a prophet.

On 26 March 1898, *Spray* put out from Cape Town on the last leg of her odyssey. As she whipped along under set sails her captain read books acquired in South Africa or watched the porpoises, dolphins and flying fish which cavorted all around his vessel. All seemed now, quite literally, plain sailing. But the sea kept one of its master strokes till last.

Having crossed the Atlantic by way of St Helena and Ascension, then put in at Grenada and Dominica, Slocum sailed from his last port of call on 5 June 1898 and set course for New York. On the tenth he was becalmed in the Sargasso Sea for eight days. Then, with a suddenness typical of this unpredictable quarter, windlessness gave way to a south-westerly gale. Suddenly, the tough little *Spray*, which had withstood so much, began to succumb to the battering of wind and waves: 'Under a sudden shock and strain her rigging began to give out. First the main-sheet strap was carried away, and then the peak halyard-block broke from the gaff.' Slocum did makeshift repairs but, two days later: 'Just as I was thinking about taking in sail the jibstay broke at the masthead, and fell, jib and all, into the sea.' Without its stay the mast wiggled about like a reed but Slocum managed to hold it with a block and tackle. For days and nights together he battled to hold his boat on course through intermittent storms, till he was 'tired, tired, tired of baffling squalls and fretful cobble-seas'.[34] But there was no respite. As *Spray* drew nearer to land she ran into cannonades of hail and a lurid electrical storm. Although he did not realise it until later, he was running into a celebrated hurricane that had just torn across New York, doing immense damage. At length it fell upon *Spray* in all its fury. Slocum lashed everything down, took in all sail, put out a sea anchor and wedged himself into his bunk. *Spray* lunged and bucked like a tethered colt. The wind shrieked. Thunderbolts hurtled into the sea. When the storm had passed, the sloop was still there. Wearily Slocum changed course and made for the nearest anchorage on Long Island.

On 27 June 1898, at one o'clock in the morning, Joshua

Slocum brought his boat into Newport RI after a voyage of 46,000 miles. But the voyage was not quite over:

> I had myself a desire to return to the place of the very begin-ning . . . So on July 3, with a fair wind, [*Spray*] waltzed beautifully round the coast and up the Acushnet River to Fairhaven, where I secured her to the cedar spile driven in the bank to hold her when she was launched. I could bring her no nearer home.[35]

What does a man do who has accomplished the ultimate in his chosen sphere of endeavour? The experience inevitably leaves him with empty horizons unless he can find some fresh chal-lenge. For Joshua Slocum there were months of acclaim and excitement. He received a rapturous welcome. He wrote and published his account of the voyage. He enjoyed the celebrity and the congratulations. He gave lecture after lecture, until he grew tired of his own anecdotes. Then, bit by bit, the excite-ment surrounding his great exploit died down and left him just another man facing the prospect of old age. That was a state of affairs he could not tolerate.

A modern psychiatrist, himself a yachtsman, has described the category of sailor into which Joshua Slocum most assuredly fits as one who has:

> . . . a relationship with the sea that has a dominating effect on his life . . . the relationship can be described in terms of a lifelong love affair with the sea. Sailors seek, and maybe occasionally find, in this relationship something which never seems accessible to them on land. It is hard to say precisely what it is they seek or experience out at sea, but clearly it is an attraction powerful enough to draw them time and again back to the apparently lonely expanses of the ocean. This fascination can make them restless on land, and many sailors lead unfulfilled lives ashore because they put little energy into anything not directed towards the next journey over the

horizon. It is almost as though there were an irresistibly alluring woman beckoning to them from somewhere beyond the reach of land.[36]

She beckoned Slocum again one day in 1909, when he and *Spray* once more slipped anchor. They headed south from Bristol, Rhode Island and disappeared from the world of the living.

It was a fitting end, a poetic end, for one who had overcome everything the sea could throw at him and won a unique place in the annals of maritime adventure.

11

THE OCEAN WITHIN

The first solo circumnavigation marked the end of the great epoch of round-the-world sailing but by no means did it put a stop to mariners sailing round the world. That apparent contradiction in terms is simply explained. Circumnavigation voyages after 1900 (or more accurately after 1918) had a different character from all of those that had gone before. To be sure, the dangers and the thrills were still there. The cruel sea had not become more benign. For all the advantages of twentieth-century technology, modern sailing vessels were still minute, vulnerable craft alone in an alien environment. What was different was the passing of the 'unknown'. The surface of the planet no longer included mystery zones. The oceans had been charted and, if there remained any tiny islands or atolls unvisited by voyagers, satellite mapping had pinpointed them before the century's end. There was nothing 'out there' to be discovered or claimed as a colonial prize or probed with a naive curiosity. Air travel enabled millions in the world's more affluent nations to take holidays in distant lands. Creeping globalisation ensured that what they discovered at their destinations would be, in many respects, what they had left behind them in their home towns and cities. Circumnavigation in the modern age is still an adventure but an adventure located on the ocean within.

The 'war to end wars' was a profound shock to the system of western society. It left many survivors with a malaise, a cynicism, an emotional void, a compulsion to go in search of meaning or perhaps just to escape from an environment that had none. 'After the war I could neither work in a city nor lead the dull life of a businessman. I wanted freedom, open air, adventure.'[1] So wrote one ex-World War I flying ace who turned to the sea for the thrills he now needed. Another restless young man, who refitted an old square-rigger for his venture explained that he and his companions 'looked upon our voyage as a gesture of defiance in a gloomy world'.[2]

The sense of adventure was strong among young men who had survived the war or had stayed at home while friends and brothers went to the front or had been too young to be sacrificed on the altar of human folly. New Englander Bill Robinson named his 32-foot ketch-rigged yacht *Svaap*, which is Sanscrit for 'Dream' before setting out to escape from humdrum reality. His meandering around the world certainly brought him life-enhancing experiences in plenty. They included a passionate affair with a Norwegian girl in the Galapagos, an extensive tour of the South Sea Islands, eating human flesh at a cannibal banquet, being nearly swamped by a waterspout and being abducted by Arab tribesmen on the Red Sea coast.

The advent of the popular press and the newsreel turned several of these long-distance sailors into celebrities. Some, like French military aviator Alain Gerbault, craved fame. After the war he did everything he could to stay in the limelight. He became a national tennis champion and also represented his country at the bridge table. When those pastimes palled he deliberately took up yachting as a means of staying in the headlines. His westabout meandering from Cannes to Le Havre between 1923 and 1929 was an extended publicity tour. He sent messages on ahead to ensure that cheering crowds and reporters would be at every quayside to greet him. He gave interviews, played demonstration tennis matches, delivered after dinner speeches and produced a steady stream of articles and books. Returning to a hero's welcome, he was decorated with the Légion d'honneur by a grateful nation for raising the profile of France with such panache. Ordinary people increasingly looked for, and perhaps needed, vicarious thrills and glamour, and circumnavigating free spirits took their place among film stars, cricketers and baseball players in the popular hall of fame. Not all sailors, however, thrived on such adulation. Stiff-upper-lip George Muhlhauser, a genuine naval hero of World War I, hated it. Wherever he and *Amaryllis* went he was mobbed and fêted. In Sydney he was made the subject of a newsreel film and in Alexandria the yacht club greeted him with a guard of honour formed from the local scout troupe. But his own country was more nonchalant. No medal ceremony awaited him when he slipped almost unobserved into Dartmouth at the end of his epic voyage.

A few of the new breed of deep ocean sailors managed their adventures on a shoestring or worked their way round the world, but yachting was essentially a rich man's hobby and the majority of circumnavigators between the wars were millionaire socialites, competing with each other to own the most luxurious vessels and travel in the greatest comfort. Their yachts were miniature versions of their Manhattan or Mayfair mansions. Their crews were treated in the same way as the below-stairs staff of their country estates. Ernest Guinness of the famous brewing dynasty took his family on a round the world cruise in *Fantome I*, the first of three boats of the same name which, with all mod cons including central heating and air conditioning, were among the most advanced craft afloat. Several stories are told about this genuine but eccentric yachtsman whose wealth was a barrier between him and the real world. Arriving at the ramshackle jetty of a tiny Caribbean island, Ernest landed with his companions and instructed his butler to locate suitable accommodation. The man prodded a slumbering waterside drifter into wakefulness with the words, 'Kindly conduct these gentlemen to the first class waiting room.'

Another motivation for long-distance voyaging, alongside restlessness, adventure and keeping ahead of the Joneses, was the romance of sail. The tall ships had not only been replaced by steamers, they also belonged to an age which seemed far away beyond the gulf of the unspeakable 1914–18 conflict. There grew up a profound nostalgia for that age, whose gracefulness and leisure, unbesmirched by the smoke and noise of steam propulsion, seemed to be typified by the sleek old clippers.

In 1923 the cult of the sailing ship, a purely archaeological interest, be it understood, was flourishing; and like many another devotee I was scouring second-hand bookshops in seaport towns for logs of the colonial passage. There was a good deal of sentiment in the impulse that sent me forth, as far as my circumstances permitted, in the wake of the *Lightning* or the *Oweenee*; together with a certain amount of curiosity as to what a really big sea looked like . . .[3]

That was how the Irish nationalist Conor O'Brien described the urge that sent a former gun-runner and blockade buster around the globe in the 1920s.

In a changed world the practicalities of oceanic voyaging were also changing. The demise of the commercial sailing vessel had diverted generations of design and construction expertise into the yacht-building industry. Pleasure boats were better made than ever before and anyone with the necessary capital and sense of adventure could buy a craft that would enable him to give substance to his dreams. For those whose courage or foolhardiness fell short of braving the terrors of the Horn one of the wonders of modern engineering had come to their aid. August 1914 went down in history for two great events: the opening of World War I and the opening of the Panama Canal.

Europeans and east coast Americans could now reach the Pacific islands without having to face the perils of the high south latitudes and most escapist circumnavigators took the Panama route.

Escapism was strong in the inter-war years and particularly the desire to visit the 'paradise' islands in which beautiful, smiling natives welcomed the white man to a land where palms and rippling waves exchanged sibilant whispers across swathes of white sand. It was a world away from the harsh realities of western so-called civilisation, where men stood on bread lines, went on strike for a living wage, took part in the mass hysteria of Nazi rallies or the mass-slaughter of the Spanish Civil War. Herman Melville was one of the most widely read authors. As well as his most famous book, *Moby Dick*, he offered the public in *Typee* and *Omoo* a romanticised picture of South Sea islands life, based on his own early experiences in Tahiti and the Marquesas. Some went in search of this idyll, the advance guard of the twentieth century's tourist migrations, like the two American young men who stopped off in the Society Islands:

> They had lost track of time and their upbringing faded away in Gauguinian euphoria. Others had done the cooking. The girls took care of their clothes and their sex life. A food surplus meant more pigs and more pigs meant more feasts.[4]

The world that emerged from the 1939–45 conflict was psychologically far removed from that which followed the earlier twentieth century demonstration of mass insanity. There was little evidence of nostalgic dreamers, footloose adventurers or gentlemen mariners attended by fawning servants. Men and, increasingly, women still encircled the globe in small craft but the new adventurers were of a different order. In the 1960s and 70s circumnavigation took on a new identity; it became a sport. That brought a new raison d'être to the business of sailing round the world. For all sportsmen and women the biggest questions demanding answers are those arising from their own physical, mental and spiritual limitations. Thus, it was no longer sufficient to battle against the realities of wind and wave and perilous shores. The mariner had to set himself new challenges – non-stop voyages, solo voyages, speed records.

One man provided the link between the heroes of the great era of circumnavigation and a younger generation of competitive racers. And a single moment focussed attention dramatically on that link. On 7 July 1967, at Greenwich, Queen Elizabeth II tapped a sword on the shoulders of a lean, elderly man kneeling before her and commanded, 'Rise, Sir Francis'. It was the reprise of a scene played out in the same place by another Queen Elizabeth and another Francis 386 years earlier. The twentieth century hero was Francis Chichester and he had, at the age of sixty-six just completed the fastest solo circumnavigation. By nature a loner, a rebel, a misfit, Chichester was a man who always needed a challenge. There had to be something new to attempt. 'If your try fails,' he wrote, 'what does that matter – all life is failure in the end. The thing is to get sport out of trying.' That spirit enabled him to become the second aviator to fly solo from England to Australia in 1930 and to conquer lung cancer in 1960.

Chichester set out eastabout on 27 August 1966 in his *Gipsy Moth IV* and reached Sydney after 107 gruelling days. He was exhausted and the boat needed substantial repair. The southern ocean had been a severe test of man and vessel and more than once the voyage had come close to ending in disaster. As soon as he stepped ashore the sailor faced a new hazard – the concerned advice of friends and wellwishers. Press photos of his arrival, telegraphed around the world, showed or seemed to show a weary, little (he had lost three stone in weight) old man close to breaking point. Urgent messages arrived begging him to give up. 'Experts', writing in the newspapers and pontificating on television, echoed this advice and millions of ordinary people shared their concern. All this emphasised the fact that a new age had begun in the history of adventure. Now, more than ever before, the bold pioneer was public property. Even for a naturally solitary man like Chichester there was no avoiding the communication age. He needed financial support and that meant acquiring media sponsorship. Throughout the voyage he had to make regular radio reports to the *Guardian* and the *Sunday Times*. On landing he was pledged to provide television interviews. That meant that, while part of him was all too conscious of his aches and pains and the battering *Gipsy Moth* had sustained, and quite ready to be satisfied with what was already a considerable achievement, his iron determination had to resist the temptation and the blandishments of hundreds of people, known and unknown, who had his best interests at heart.

He threw himself into the boat's refit. She had been the cause of much of his distress during the outward voyage. Anxious to be away from England, he had not left adequate time for sea trials and only discovered *Gipsy Moth*'s many defects when it was too late to do anything about them. Chichester spent five and a half weeks in Australia, doing everything that could be done to his floating home and then set out once more on a calm, sunny summer's morning escorted by a flotilla of Sydney harbour craft. Next day two things happened: Chichester was prostrated by food poisoning and *Gipsy Moth* was capsized by a cyclone. She righted herself but much of the laborious work of five and a half weeks had been wiped out. Several pieces of equipment had gone overboard. The self-steering gear was damaged, as was the electric pump. The cockpit was badly gashed. Below decks food, tools and clothes were sloshing about in salt water. Feeling like death, Chichester had to set to pumping out the cabin by hand and making running repairs. For many brave sailors this would have been the last straw. They could have put back into Sydney without dishonour. The world would still have applauded a gallant effort. But Francis Chichester was one of a special breed. He sailed on.

The next hazard he had to face was the Horn. It was the one part of the journey he had always dreaded but there was never any thought in his head of steering for the Panama Canal; that, to his mind, would not have qualified as part of a true circumnavigation. When it came to it, the rounding of the awesome southern cape passed off without serious incident. Indeed, the only remarkable thing that happened underscored the way that deep sea adventure had changed. While Chichester was enjoying his private view of the Horn, standing out of the sea, as he later described it, like a black ice cream cone, a light aircraft full of press photographers zoomed down from the clouds and circled the boat before heading back to land with a cheery waggle of its wings. It was a foretaste of things to come. The closer he got to home the more intrusive became the newshounds. Chichester was pestered by fatuous radioed questions, such as, 'What did you eat for your first meal after rounding the Horn?', and whenever he was near land boatloads of journalists and sightseers came to gawp and prevent him getting on with the necessary routines of running the boat.

Like many solo voyagers Chichester found it hard to make the adjustment to being with other people after months of isolation. In some ways the enthusiasm of the crowds was more difficult to deal with than the savagery of the waves. But he had to live with it because, of course, he returned to be acclaimed as the greatest Englishman of the age. Thousands thronged Plymouth Hoe on 28 May 1967, as *Gipsy Moth* slipped back into the harbour nine months and one day after her departure. More taxing celebrations were to come. The boat made a triumphant progress along the coast to the Thames estuary and thence to the Port of London, where she arrived to the wail of ships' sirens and the plumes of water cannon. Chichester was fêted at the Mansion House and the pageantry of his investiture at Greenwich was watched on television by almost as many people as had witnessed the queen's coronation.

It had been a magnificent achievement but, as the international yachting community fully realised, it pointed the way to something even more spectacular. Chichester's voyage had been in two stages. The ultimate challenge was a non-stop solo circumnavigation. The sportsmen were not the only ones to realise the potential of such an enterprise. Chichester's backers had profited handsomely from his headline-grabbing adventure. Books, newspapers, television films and various kinds of dedicated merchandise had made lots of money. A circumnavigation bandwagon had been set rolling and a host of marketeers were eager to keep it on the move. In less than a year the 'Golden Globe Race' was organised. It became one of the most dramatic maritime enterprises of all time – but not in the way the money men envisaged. In fact it was to demonstrate, tragically, that solo circumnavigation was only for the mentally strong and that big business and maritime adventure were not natural partners. The scores of entrants for the race, lured by prize money and fame, were whittled down to four. Of those four, two who failed to finish committed suicide, one during the race and one afterwards.

Of the remaining two, one deliberately cocked a snook at the race. Bernard Moitessier, having rounded the three southern capes in record time, calmly radioed the organisers that he had no intention of heading for the finishing line. In the 39-foot *Joshua*, named after his hero, Joshua Slocum, he sailed on – round Africa, round Australia, round New Zealand and fetched up, at last, in Tahiti, where the gods of commercial profit he so much despised had no power. He later tried to explain his decision in a book, the proceeds of which were donated to charity:

[*Joshua*] sailed round the world . . . but what does that mean, since the horizon is eternal? Round the world goes further than the ends of the earth, as far as life itself, perhaps further still . . .[5]

He was describing the boundless ocean within.

The winner of Golden Globe, Robin Knox-Johnson, completed his voyage in 313 days, a considerable achievement. However, it was destined to be overshadowed by the other events connected with the race. The celebratory dinner was postponed when news arrived of the death of competitor Donald Crowhurst, who had jumped overboard somewhere in the southern Atlantic and Knox-Johnson presented his prize money to the appeal fund which was set up for Crowhurst's family. Many of the yachting fraternity shared Moitessier's instinct that there was something tawdry about turning the supreme test of seamanship into a competition. It was comparable to organising a race up Everest.

But we live in a world in which marketing is king and, therefore, as long as there is profit to be made from promoting major sporting events, high profile competitions which capture the public imagination continue to be organised. The boat-building industry needs exciting exploits to ensure sales to new generations of sportsmen and pleasure yachtsmen. Money from big-business is vital to sustain research and development, for today's ocean-going craft are the products of high technology, equipped with sophisticated satellite navigation gear, computers and communication apparatus. Nor is it only the boats which attract investment. The courageous and skilled men and women who sail them are, like all sporting stars, highly bankable commodities. Publishers, newspaper editors and TV programme planners compete with each other to sign them up. The last quarter of the twentieth century, therefore, saw the establishment of regular circumnavigation races – the Whitbread (later Whitbread/Volvo) for fully manned yachts, single-handed contests such as the British Oxygen, BT Global Challenge and Vendée Globe events. Commercialism, with all the ambiguities it involves, has become an integral part of sailing, as of all sports.

That can create problems for competitors, who, unlike their backers, are not motivated by money. Those men and women who aspire to the highest accolades their chosen profession can bestow are still driven by the same demons that propelled so many of the mariners of the great age of circumnavigation. For them records exist for one reason and one only – to be broken. They long to pit themselves and their vessels against the worst conditions that nature can summon from its cauldron. They are impelled by the need to explore the ocean within; to discover how they will cope with weariness, pain, loneliness and fear. Yet what really drives them is, ultimately, beyond definition. A few years ago a teenage girl was studying for her A levels, the first hurdle on her chosen course to becoming a vet. Yet something inside tormented her with doubt.

> I was exhausted and felt pulled in opposite directions. I'd swing from happiness to misery with frightening speed. I would lie on the ground and sob . . . I wished I knew the solution. But I couldn't even figure the problem.[6]

It took a bout of glandular fever, during which she lay moodily watching television coverage of the Whitbread race, to pierce the fog of uncertainty.

> With a feeling of most intense energy and clarity, I suddenly realised that there was another way. In an instant my exam pressures evaporated. The world was out there, and there was not a shadow of doubt in my mind that I was ready to take it on . . . The sea was waiting.[7]

In 2001, that girl, Ellen MacArthur, now a young woman of twenty-four, came second in the Vendée Globe race and sailed into the record books as the fastest woman circumnavigator and the youngest competitor to complete the race.

It was a stunning achievement, in some sense worthy to be set alongside those of Elcano, Cavendish, Slocum and 'Bully' Forbes. For all the achievements of modern technology, mountainous seas are not a whit less frightening nor lee shores less perilous than they were a hundred, two hundred, five hundred years ago and the best equipped boat is still a matchstick on the shifting dynamic of ocean.

Yet, for the modern circumnavigator, the adventure *is* different. Everything that can be done is done to provide for the safety of skippers and crews. Race organisers were not slow to learn the lessons of the Golden Globe race. By the time of the 1985–6 Whitbread race regulations demanded that every boat be equipped with an Argos satellite tracking system and an elaborate radio checking routine was in place for purposes of both safety and news-gathering. As long as the equipment did not fail, every person aboard the seemingly-isolated boats was in touch with family, friends, sponsors and media personnel at home. In the event of disaster, rescue attempts could be rapidly launched to stricken vessels even hundreds of miles from land. And the race is not over when the crews return to port. They have to submit to demands for books, articles, interviews, talks and 'promo' tours. They belong to their sponsors, and very few modern heroes and heroines can afford the luxury of a purist approach to their adventures.

Every modern circumnavigator would acknowledge that he or she stands on the shoulders of giants. Those ancient mariners were a different race of men. They truly were *alone* on the high seas, seas whose boundaries were uncharted, and whose terrors were not fully understood. They sailed from horizon to horizon aware only that death or glory might embrace them in the tumult of the waves. They were the true heroes of what we justifiably look back on as the great age of circumnavigation.

SOURCE NOTES AND REFERENCES

Chapter 1

1. Antonio Pigafetta, *A Narrative Account of the First Circumnavigation,* translated and edited by R. A. Skelton, Yale, 1969, pp. 156–7.
2. Cf. C. R. Boxer, *The Portuguese Seaborne Empire 1415–1825,* 1969, pp. 36–7.
3. Cf. C. McK. Parc, *Ferdinand Magellan Circumnavigator,* 1964, pp. 23–7.
4. F. Chichester, *Gipsy Moth Circles the World,* 1967, p. 21.
5. J. and M. C. Ridgway, *Round the World with Ridgway,* 1978, pp. 273–4.
6. Joshua Slocum, *SailingAlone Around the World,* 1907, p. 84.
7. Pigafetta, *op. cit.*
8. *Ibid.,* p. 102.

Chapter 2

1. Cf. D. Wilson, *The World Encompassed: Drake's Great Voyage, 1577–1580,* 1977, p. 26.

2. W. S. W. Vaux (ed.), *The World Encompassed by Sir Francis Drake,* Hakluyt Society, 1854, p. 237.

3. E. G. R. Taylor, 'More Light on Drake', *Mariner's Mirror,* XVI, 1930, p. 150.

4. Vaux, *op. cit.*

5. *Ibid.,* pp. 143–4.

Chapter 3

1. R. *Hakluyt, Principal Navigations,* 1589, pp. 801ff.

2. F. Mulville, 'The Loneliness of the Long-Distance Sailor', *Yachting Monthly,* May, 1972.

3. Hakluyt, *op. cit.*

4. *Ibid.*

5. *Ibid.*

6. *Ibid.*

7. *Ibid.*

8. Antonio de Morga, *Succeros de las Islas Filipinas,* translated by J. S Cummins, Hakluyt Society, 2nd Series, No. 140, 1971.

9. J. and M. C. Ridgway, *Round the World with Ridgway,* 1978, p. 36.

10. John Hooker, Exeter City Record Office, Book No. 51. Cf. also Gwyneth Dyke, 'Finances of a Sixteenth Century Navigator, Thomas Cavendish of Trimley in Suffolk,' *The Mariner's Mirror,* 64, 1958, pp. 108–15.

11. D. B. Quinn (ed.), *The Last Voyage of Thomas Cavendish 1591–1592,* 1975, p. 56 (spellings modernised).

12. *Ibid.,* p. 62.

13. *Ibid.,* p. 63.

14. *Ibid.,* pp. 52, 53, 68, 70.

15. *Ibid.,* p. 110.

16. *Ibid.*

17. *Ibid.,* p. 112.

18. *Ibid.,* pp. 112, 114.

19. *Ibid.,* p. 122.

20. *Ibid.,* pp.126, 128.

Chapter 4

1. Cf. P. Geyl, *The Revolt of the Netherlands (1556–1609)*, 1932, p. 234.
2. H. R. Wagner, *Spanish Voyages to the North West Coast of America in the Sixteenth Century*, 1929, pp. 245–6.
3. *Journal du Voyage de Guillaume Schouten dans les Indes,* Paris, 1618, p. 127.
4. Christina Dodwell, *Travels with Fortune,* 1979; quoted in C. Bonington, *Quest for Adventure,* 1981, p. 308.
5. William Dampier,*A New Voyage Round the World,* 1937 edn, p. 55.
6. *Ibid.,* pp..56–7.
7. *Ibid.,* p. 63.
8. *Ibid.,* p. 62.
9. *Ibid.,* p. 70.
10. *Ibid.,* p. 68.
11. *Ibid.,* p. 81.
12. J. and M. C. Ridgway, *Round the World with Ridgway,* 1978, pp. 169–70.
13. Dampier, *op. cit.,* p. 200.
14. *Ibid.,* p. 205.
15. *Ibid.,* p. 243.
16. *Ibid.,* p. 229.
17. *Ibid.,* p. 233.
18. *Ibid.,* p. 232.
19. *Ibid.,* p. 277.
20. *Ibid.,* p. 325.
21. *Ibid.,* pp. 332–3.
22. *Ibid.,* pp. 336–7.
23. *Ibid.,* p. 346.
24. *Ibid.,* p. 357.
25. *Ibid.,* p. 356.
26. *Ibid.,* p. 359.
27. *Dictionary of National Biography.*
28. *The Diary of John Evelyn,* Vol. 2, Everyman edition 1937, pp. 351–2.

Chapter 5

1. Thomas Hobbes, *Leviathan,* Chapter 13.
2. W. G. Perrin (ed.), *A Voyage Round the World* by Captain George Shelvocke, 1928, pp. xx–xxii.
3. *Ibid.,* pp.40–41.
4. Samuel Taylor Coleridge, *The Rime of the Ancient Mariner.*
5. Leo Heaps, *Log of the Centurion Based on the Original Papers of Captain Philip Saumarez . . . ,* 1973, pp.45–7.
6. *Ibid.,* p. 84.
7. *Ibid.,* pp.76ff.
8. *Ibid.,* pp. 84–5.
9. *Ibid.,* p.112.
10. *Ibid.,* p.114.
11. *Ibid.,* p. 118.
12. *Ibid.,* p. 120.
13. *Ibid.,* p. 118.
14. G. Williams, *Documents Relating to Anson's Voyage Round the World 1740–44,* 1967, pp. 87–8.
15. *Ibid.,* p. 119.
16. Joshua Slocum, *Sailing Alone Round the World,* 1899, p. 140.
17. William Dampier, *A New Voyage Round the World,* 1937, p. 174.
18. 'A Voyage Round the World by Dr John Francis Gemelli Careri', in John Churchill, *A Collection of Voyages and Travels,* 1704, IV, p. 491.
19. Leo Heaps, *op. cit.,* p. 174.
20. *Ibid.,* p. 173.
21. *Ibid.,* p. 214.
22. *Ibid., p.* **223.**
23. *Ibid.,* p. 233.

Chapter 6

1. J. R. Forster, Preface to his translation of L. de Bougainville, *A Voyage Round the World . . . in the Years*

1766, 1767, 1768 and 1769 by Louis de Bougainville, pp. viii–xi.

2. Alexander Dalrymple, *A Historical Collection of Voyages . . . in the South Pacific Ocean,* I, pp. xxviii–xxix. Cf. also J. C. Beaglehole, *Life of Captain James Cook,* 1974, p. 121.

3. R. E. Gallagher (ed.), *Byron's Journal of his Circumnavigations,* Hakluyt Society, Second Series cxxii, 1964, p. 3.

4. *Ibid.,* p. 16.

5. *Ibid.,* p. 16.

6. *Ibid.,* p. 116.

7. *Ibid.,* p. 24.

8. *Ibid.*

9. *Ibid.,* p. 30.

10. *Ibid.,* p. 32.

11. *Ibid.,* pp. 46–7.

12. *Ibid.,* p. 186.

13. Cf. H. Wallis, *The Patagonian Giants,* cited in Gallagher, *op. cit.,* pp. 185ff.

14. Gallagher, *op. cit.,* p. 50.

15. *Ibid.,* p. 156.

16. *Ibid.,* p. 88.

17. *Ibid.,* p. 93.

18. *Ibid.,* p. 105.

19. *Ibid.,* p. 116.

20. *Ibid.,* p. 120.

21. H. Wallis (ed.), *Carteret's Voyage Round the World 1766–1769,* Hakluyt Society, 1965, I, p. 38.

22. *Ibid.,* pp.116–17.

23. J. Hawkesworth, *An Account of the Voyages . . . 1773,* Vol. I, p. 419.

24. *Ibid.,* p. 423.

25. *Ibid.,* pp. 467–8.

26. Wallis, *op. cit.,* p. 126.

27. *Ibid.,* p. 131.

28. *Ibid.*, p. 150.
29. *Ibid.*, pp.154–5.
30. *Ibid.*, p. 169.
31. *Ibid.* p. 184.
32. *Ibid.*, pp. 205–6.
33. *Ibid.*, p. 217.
34. *Ibid.*, p. 220.
35. *Ibid.*, p. 264.
36. *Ibid.*, p. 262.
37. *Ibid.*, p. 264.

Chapter 7

1. I. R. Forster, Preface to Bougainville's *A Voyage Round the World*, p. xxvii.
2. *Ibid.*, p. 124.
3. Gallagher, *Byron's Journal;* p. 83.
4. Bougainville, *op. cit.*, pp. 197–8.
5. *Ibid.*
6. *Ibid.*, p. 218.
7. *Ibid.*
8. *Ibid.*, pp. 306–7.
9. *Ibid.*, p. 364.
10. *Ibid.*, p. 368.
11. *Ibid.*, p. 469.
12. *Ibid.*, p. 300.
13. *Ibid.*, p. 30.
14. Cf. J. C. Beaglehole, *The Life of Captain James Cook*, Hakluyt Society, 1974, p. 148.
15. *Ibid.*, p. 166.
16. *Ibid.*, p. 197.
17. *Ibid.*, p. 243.
18. *Ibid.*, p. 294.
19. *Ibid.*
20. *Ibid.*
21. *Ibid.*, p. 438.

22. *Ibid.*, p. 426.
23. *Ibid.*, p. 431.

Chapter 8

1. C. P. C. Fleurieu, *A Voyage Round the World 1790–I 792 Performed by Etienne Marchand*, 2 vols, London, 1801, reprinted in Amsterdam 1969, I, p. lxix.
2. *Ibid.*, I, p. lxxviii.
3. *Ibid.*, I, pp. 155–6.
4. *Ibid.*, I, pp. 35–6.
5. *Ibid.*, I, p. 297.
6. Frank Debenham (ed.), *The Voyage of Captain Bellingshausen . . .*, Hakluyt Society, Second Series, xci, 1945, I, p. 128.
7. *Ibid.*, II, pp. 276–7.
8. W. Stanton, *The Great United States Exploring Expedition*, Los Angeles, 1975, pp. 139–40.
9. C. Wilkes, *Synopsis of the Cruise of the United States Exploring Expedition*, 1848, p.21.
10. *Ibid.*, p. 151.
11. J. C. Ross, *A Voyage of Discovery and Research . . . 1839–43*, 1847, I, pp. 100–101.
12. *Ibid.*
13. *Ibid.*, I. p. 247.
14. *Ibid.*, I, p. 276.
15. *Ibid.*, I, pp. 281–3.
16. *Ibid.*, II, p. 42.
17. *Ibid.*, II, p. 332.

Chapter 9

1. National Maritime Museum.
2. *Ibid.*
3. B. Lubbock, *The Colonial Clippers*, 1924, pp. 5–6.
4. National Maritime Museum.
5. M. Gee, *Captain Fraser's Voyages*, Stanford Maritime, 1979, p. 77.

6. Jules Verne, *Around the World in Eighty Days,* Everyman Edition, 1926, p. 215.
7. *Dictionary of National Biography,* Supplement 1900–1921.
8. Lady Brassey, *A Voyage in the Sunbeam,* 1878, Preface.
9. *Ibid.,* pp. 5–6.
10. *Ibid.,* pp. 55–6.
11. *Ibid.,* p. 113.
12. *Ibid.,* p. 125.
13. *Ibid.,* p. 179.
14. *Ibid.,* p. 169.
15. *Ibid.,* p. 185.
16. *Ibid.,* p. 191.
17. *Ibid.,* pp. 192–3.
18. *Ibid.,* pp. 234–5.
19. *Ibid.,* pp. 297–8.
20. *Ibid.,* p. 343.
21. *Ibid.,* p. 374.
22. *Ibid.,* pp. 459–460.
23. *Ibid.,* p. 453.
24. *Ibid.,* p. 449.

Chapter 10
1. Joshua Slocum, *Sailing Alone Around the World,* 1899, p. 292.
2. *Ibid.,* p. 2.
3. *Ibid.*
4. *Ibid.,* p. 3.
5. *Ibid.,* p. 4.
6. *Ibid.,* p. 4.
7. *Ibid.,* p. 31.
8. F. Chichester, *Gipsy Moth Circles the World,* 1967, p. 18.
9. Slocum, *op. cit.,* pp. 26–7.
10. *Ibid.,* pp. 39–42.
11. S. T. Coleridge, *Rime of the Ancient Mariner.*
12. A. Davison, *My Ship is so Small,* p. 81.

13. Chichester, *op. cit.*, p. 120.
14. Slocum, *op. cit.*, p. 73.
15. D. B. Quinn (ed.), *The Last Voyage of Thomas Cavendish 1591–1592*, 1975, p. 56.
16. Slocum, *op. cit.*, p. 79.
17. Ibid., p. 81.
18. *Ibid.*, pp. 81–2.
19. *Ibid.*, pp. 99–100.
20. *Ibid.*, pp. 100–101.
21. *Ibid.*, pp. 132–3.
22. *Ibid.*, pp. 139–40.
23. *Ibid.*, p. 145.
24. *Ibid.*, p. 157.
25. *Ibid.*, p. 155.
26. *Ibid.*, p. 167.
27. *Ibid.*, p. 174.
28. *Ibid.*, p. 180.
29. *Ibid.*, p. 193.
30. *Ibid.*, p. 198.
31. *Ibid.*, p. 204.
32. *Ibid.*, pp. 219–20.
33. *Ibid.*, p. 238.
34. *Ibid.*, pp. 274–5.
35. *Ibid.*, p. 278.
36. Glinn Bennet, *Beyond Endurance*, 1983, p. 96.

Chapter 11
1. A. Gerbault, *The Fight of the Firecrest*, 1926, p. 2.
2. A. Seligman, *The Voyage of the Cap Pilar*, 1939, p. 231.
3. C. O'Brien, *Across Three Oceans*, 1927, p. 18.
4. D. Holm, *The Circumnavigators, Small Boat Voyagers of Modern Times*, 1975, p. 125.
5. B. Moitessier, *The Long Way*, 1971, p. 151.
6. E. McAthur, *Taking on the World*, 2002, p. 37.
7. *Ibid.*, p. 36.

INDEX